Political Change, Democratic Transitions and Security in Southeast Asia

The fragility of democracy in Southeast Asia is a subject of increasing concern. While there has been significant movement in the direction of democratisation, the authoritarian tendencies of popularly elected leaders and the challenges posed by emerging security threats have given rise to a shared concern about the return of military rule in the region. This book examines the nature of political transitions in Southeast Asia and why political transitions towards political liberalisation and democracy have often failed to take off. It considers political systems in Southeast Asia that have gone through significant periods of transition but continue to face serious challenges toward democratic consolidation. Some key questions that the book focuses on are: Are emerging democracies in the region threatened by weak, failed or authoritarian leadership? Are political institutions that are supposed to support political changes toward democratisation weak or strong? How can democratic systems be made more resilient? and What are the prospects of democracy becoming the defining political landscape in Southeast Asia?

Mely Caballero-Anthony is an Associate Professor of Government and Politics in Southeast Asia at the Nanyang Technological University, Singapore. Some of her publications include *Regional Security in Southeast Asia: Beyond the ASEAN Way* (2005); *UN Peace Operations and Asian Security* (co-editor, London: Taylor and Francis Ltd, 2005); *Non-Traditional Security in Asia: Dilemmas in Securitisation* (co-editor, 2005).

Routledge Security in Asia Pacific Series
Series Editors
*Leszek Buszynski, International University of Japan,
and William Tow, Australian National University*

Security issues have become more prominent in the Asia-Pacific region because of the presence of global players, rising great powers, and confident middle powers, which intersect in complicated ways. This series puts forward important new work on key security issues in the region. It embraces the roles of the major actors, their defense policies and postures, and their security interaction over the key issues of the region. It includes coverage of the United States, China, Japan, Russia, the Koreas, as well as the middle powers of ASEAN and South Asia. It also covers issues relating to environmental and economic security as well as transnational actors and regional groupings.

Political Change, Democratic Transitions and Security in Southeast Asia

Edited by
Mely Caballero-Anthony

Routledge
Taylor & Francis Group

LONDON AND NEW YORK

First published 2010 by Routledge

2 Park Square, Milton Park, Abingdon, Oxon OX14 4RN
711 Third Avenue, New York, NY 10017, USA

Routledge is an imprint of the Taylor & Francis Group, an informa business

First issued in paperback 2016

Typeset in Times New Roman by Swales & Willis Ltd, Exeter, Devon

British Library Cataloguing in Publication Data
A catalogue record for this book is available from the British Library

Library of Congress Cataloging-in-Publication Data
Anthony, Mely Cabellero.
  Political change, democratic transitions, and security in Southeast Asia /
  [edited by] Mely Caballero-Anthony.
  p. cm.—(Routledge security in Asia Pacific series; 13)
  Includes bibliographical references and index.
  1. Southeast Asia—Politics and government—1945– 2. Social
  change—Political aspects—Southeast Asia. 3. Democratization—
  Southeast Asia. 4. National security—Southeast Asia. I. Caballero-
  Anthony, Mely. II. Title.
  DS526.7.A578 2009
  959.05'4—dc22
  2009016328

ISBN 978-1-138-99500-0 (pbk)
ISBN 978-0-415-49353-6 (hbk)
ISBN 978-0-203-86749-5 (ebk)

Contents

List of tables

Notes on contributors

Mely Caballero-Anthony is an Associate Professor at the S. Rajaratnam School of International Studies (RSIS), Singapore and Head of the RSIS Centre for Non-Traditional Security Studies. She is also the Secretary General of the newly established Consortium on Non-Traditional Security Studies in Asia (NTS-Asia). Her research interests include regionalism and regional security in Asia Pacific, multilateral security cooperation, politics and international relations in Association of Southeast Asian Nations (ASEAN), conflict prevention and management, as well as human security. At RSIS, she teaches courses on Non-Traditional Security, and Government and Politics in Southeast Asia.

Her current publications both single-authored and co-edited include *Non-Traditional Security in Asia: Dilemmas in Securitisation* (UK: Ashgate, 2006), *Studying Non-Traditional Security in Asia: Trends and Issues* (Singapore: Marshall Cavendish, 2006), *Regional Security in Southeast Asia: Beyond the ASEAN Way* (Singapore: ISEAS, 2005); *UN Peace Operations and Asian Security* (UK: Routledge, 2005). She has also published extensively on a broad range of security issues in Asia Pacific which appeared in peer-reviewed journals such as *Journal of International Affairs*, *Asian Survey, Asian Security*, *Asian Perspective*, *International Peacekeeping*, *Pacific Review*, *Southeast Asian Affairs* and *Contemporary Southeast Asia*. She has also contributed a number of book chapters on non-traditional security issues, human security, think-tanks and civil society.

Pavin Chachavalpongpun is a Visiting Research Fellow and Lead Researcher for Political and Strategic Affairs of the ASEAN Studies Centre at the Institute of Southeast Asian Studies (ISEAS), Singapore. Prior to this position, he served the Thai Foreign Ministry in many capacities, including most recently at the Royal Thai Embassy in Singapore. He received his PhD from the School of Oriental and African Studies (SOAS), University of London in 2002. Pavin is the author of *A Plastic Nation: The Curse of Thainess in Thai–Burmese Relations* (2005), and writes regularly for *The Nation, Bangkok Post, The Straits Times, South China Morning Post*, as well as web-based journals, *The Irrawaddy* and *Opinion Asia*.

Cherian George is Assistant Professor and Acting Division Head of the Division of Journalism and Publishing at the Wee Kim Wee School of Communication & Information, Nanyang Technological University (NTU). He received his PhD from Stanford University and his MSc from Columbia University. He was a journalist with *The Straits Times* for 10 years, where he wrote mainly on politics and media, and served as the paper's editor for art and photography. He joined NTU in 2004, after a postdoctoral fellowship at the National University of Singapore's Asia Research Institute. His PhD research focused on internet-based alternative journalism, and he continues to research the alternative press as well as state–media dynamics in Singapore and the Southeast Asian region. He maintains an active involvement in the industry and community service. He is engaged regularly as a trainer for newspaper journalists, and publishes a monthly current affairs newspaper for primary and secondary schools. His publications include *Singapore: The Air-Conditioned Nation* (2000) and *Contentious Journalism and the Internet: Democratising Discourse in Malaysia and Singapore* (2005).

Lee Hock Guan is a Senior Fellow at the ISEAS, Singapore. His research interests include religion and social change in Southeast Asia, ethnicity, nationality and citizenship in Malaysia, and Malaysia social stratification. He received his PhD in Sociology from Brandeis University and his MA in Demography from the University of Pennsylvania. His recent publications include 'Affirmative Action in Malaysia' (2005) in *Southeast Asian Affairs*; 'The First Post-Mahathir General Election' in *Regional Outlook Southeast Asia (2004–2005)*. Forthcoming publications include a co-edited book with Leo Suryadinata *Nation, Language and Development.*

Herman Joseph S. Kraft is Executive Director of the Institute of Strategic and Development Studies (ISDS), Philippines. He is also an Assistant Professor at the University of the Philippines where he teaches modules including introduction to international relations, and Society, Politics and Government. Dr Kraft's research interests include International Relations, Comparative Government and Politics. His recent publications include 'Building an East Asian Community: The Human Security Imperatives', *New Zealand Institute for International Affairs*, (2007) vol. 32, no. 5; *The Principle of Non-intervention and ASEAN: Evolution and Emerging Challenges* (2000), Centre for Strategic and Defence Studies, Australian National University; *Human Rights in Southeast Asia: The Search for Regional Norms* (East-West Center, Washington 2005); 'Track three diplomacy and human rights in Southeast Asia: the Asia Pacific Coalition for East Timor', *Global Network* (2002) vol. 2, no. 1; and *Unofficial Diplomacy in Southeast Asia: The Role of ASEAN-ISIS* (Canadian Consortium on Asia Pacific Security, 2000).

Helen E. S. Nesadurai is Senior Lecturer in the School of Arts and Sciences, Monash University, Malaysia. She has held previous appointments as Assistant Professor at the Institute of Defence and Strategic Studies, Nanyang

Technological University, Singapore, and as Senior Analyst at the Institute of Strategic and International Studies, Kuala Lumpur, Malaysia. Her research explores the link between globalisation and regionalism, focusing in particular on how this relationship plays out in the broad Asia-Pacific region through regional groupings such as ASEAN, APEC and ASEAN Plus Three. She is currently researching 'bottom-up', transnational articulations of economic governance proposed by the region's civil society and labour groups and the prospects that such processes could lead to a more just and inclusive form of regional economic governance in Southeast Asia. She is the author of *Globalisation, Domestic Politics and Regionalism: The ASEAN Free Trade Area* (Routledge, 2003) and the editor of *Globalisation and Economic Security in East Asia: Governance and Institutions* (Routledge, 2006). She holds degrees in Biochemistry (BSc & MSc, Universiti Malaya), Development Economics (MSc, University of Oxford) and Politics and International Studies (PhD, University of Warwick).

Sorpong Peou is Professor of Political Science at Sophia University in Japan, where he teaches courses in the field of security and democracy studies, including Contemporary Security Studies, International Relations Theory, Human Security, International Organization and Law, International Relations in Pacific Asia and Comparative Politics of East Asia. Dr Peou has also been a member of several organisations including the Centre for International and Security Studies, York University, Canada, The Academic Council on the United Nations System, USA, Cambodian Institute for Peace and Cooperation, Phnom Penh, Cambodia and Board of Directors, Cambodian Development Research Institute, Phnom Penh, Cambodia. His recent publications include *International Democracy Assistance for Peacebuilding: Cambodia and Beyond* (Palgrave Macmillan, 2007), *Intervention and Change in Cambodia: Towards Democracy?* (St. Martin Press & Institute of Southeast Asian Studies and Silkworm, 2000), and 'Merit in Security Community Studies', in *International Relations of the Asia-Pacific* (2005).

Rizal Sukma is currently Deputy Executive at the Centre for Strategic and International Studies (CSIS), Jakarta, Indonesia. He is also the Chairman of International Relations Division, Central Executive Board of Muhammadiyah (second largest Islamic organisation in Indonesia with approximately 25 million members); member of the board at Syafii Maarif Institute for Culture and Humanity; a visiting lecturer at Department of International Relations at Muhammadiyah University, Malang; and a member of the National Committee on Strategic Defence Review, Indonesia's Ministry of Defence. He received his PhD degree in international relations from the London School of Economics and Political Science (LSE), United Kingdom in 1997. His research interests include Southeast Asian security issues, ASEAN, Indonesian defence and foreign policy, domestic political change in Indonesia. Dr Sukma is the author of numerous papers and reports, and has published in several journals and other internationally circulated publications. His recent publications include 'Indonesia and the

Tsunami: Responses and Foreign Policy Implications' (*Australian Journal of International Affairs*, 2006); 'Ethnic Conflict in Indonesia: Causes and the Quest for Solution' in *Ethnic Conflicts in Southeast Asia* (Institute of Southeast Asian Studies, 2005); *Security Operations in Aceh: Goals, Consequences and Lessons* (East-West Center, 2004) and *Islam in Indonesian Foreign Policy* (Routledge, 2003).

Acknowledgements

The idea of this study grew from a series of conversations among my Southeast Asian colleagues and friends in late 2004. It was during that period when the region witnessed a number of highs and lows. Southeast Asia was coming out of a major crisis caused by the outbreak of the highly virulent pathogen SARS that almost paralysed a number of affected countries in Asia. There were also growing concerns about the new face of terrorism coming up in parts of the region. These and many other emerging non-traditional security issues more than highlighted the interconnectedness of the countries in the region and how closely intertwined their futures were with one another.

Yet despite the gloom cast by new security concerns, something exciting was happening in Southeast Asia. A number of general elections were held which witnessed significant political transitions taking place. In 2004, Indonesia had its first ever direct presidential elections since the New Order of 1965. A year later, Thailand had its first directly elected prime minister whose party, Thai Rak Thai, won a landslide victory, winning 374 out of 500 seats in Parliament. It was the largest number of parliamentary seats ever gained by a single party in Thailand's history as a democratic country. Meanwhile, long-serving leaders in Malaysia and Singapore were also stepping down in favour of new ones. Following Abdullah Badawi's resounding endorsement as prime minister in the 2005 Malaysian general elections, which was likened to a breath of fresh air after the stifling authoritarian rule of the country's former prime minister, Mahathir Mohamed, there was much anticipation that Southeast Asia was at the cusp of a democratic transformation.

But behind the enthusiasm about these new developments shared by many of us was also puzzlement about things that did not quite go "right" in transitioning countries. The political turbulence that hit Thailand soon after the 2005 elections, the seemingly endless political travails in the Philippines and the fragility of democratic gains in Indonesia, prompted us to ask the question: what ails democratic transitions in Asia? After convening an informal discussion in 2005, we then decided to take our initial discussions forward and embark on a more systematic study of political transitions in Southeast Asia.

This volume therefore is the result of a three-year project jointly convened by the Rajaratnam School of International Studies (RSIS), Singapore, and the Centre for Security and International Studies (CSIS), Indonesia. Following the informal 2005 meeting in Singapore, the first workshop was held in 2006 to discuss the first draft of the country studies, and followed a year later by a dissemination meeting held in Jakarta where the authors had a chance to share their findings with a wider audience.

The project as it turns out is more than just a study of politics and security. It is also a rewarding experience, a journey that allowed a group of us regional analysts to compare notes and reflect on how our respective case studies of political transitions compared with each other. I am deeply indebted to Rizal Sukma and Hadi Soesastro of CSIS for their steadfast support throughout the duration of this project. Rizal Sukma, who is also a contributor to this volume, is joined by Herman Kraft, Sorpong Peou, Lee Hock Guan, Helen Nesadurai, Cherian George and Pavin Chachavalpongpun – all of whom I am truly grateful to for their valuable contributions. I deeply appreciate their patience and good humour in agreeing to change their drafts more than once, to include in their analyses the significant changes that had taken place in their respective case studies. I would also like to thank Thitinan Pongsudhirak for the support and valuable insights he shared with us throughout this project. In more ways than one, this collegial community has so much to offer to both the academic and policy communities in Southeast Asia and beyond.

With my co-authors are a number of people who had joined us at one point or another and had generously shared with us their ideas, advice and their friendship. To Barry Desker, Kwa Chong Guan, Jusuf Wanandi, Carolina Hernandez, Clara Joewono, Khoo Boo Teik, Bob Hadiwinata, Vedi Hafiz, Ho Kai Leong, Aik Tangsupvattana, William Case, Amitav Acharya, David Camroux, Leonard Sebastian, Tin Maung Maung Than, Baktiar Effendi, Aneis Baswedan, Kusnanto Anggoro and Shamsul Hadi – our sincere thanks. I am also very grateful to Denis Hew whose support has made this study truly worthwhile.

The successful publication of this book owes much to the valuable contribution of the many individuals who have helped bring this project to fruition. I am especially grateful to Colin Duerkop of the Konrad Adenauer Foundation for being very supportive in giving life to an idea by providing the core budget for this project. My sincere thanks to my colleagues at RSIS, Sofia Jamil whose organisational skills had spared me the headaches of administration and Roderick Chia for providing valuable editorial assistance. We deeply appreciate the help of Leszek Buszynski and the anonymous reviewers for their valuable comments and suggestions, and last but not least, to Peter Sowden and the editorial team of Routledge for their important role in the production of this book.

Abbreviations

ACA	Anti-Corruption Agency
ADHOC	Cambodian Human Rights and Development Association
APA	ASEAN People's Assembly
ASEAN	Association of Southeast Asian Nations
ASG	Abu Sayaff Group
BA	Barisan Alternatif
BN	Barisan National
CCHR	Cambodian Center for Human Rights
CEC	Commune Election Committee
CIHR	Cambodian Institute for Human Rights
COFFEL	Coalition for Free and Fair Elections
COMFREL	Committee for Free and Fair Elections
CPP	(Cambodia) Cambodian People's Party
CPP	(Philippines) Communist Party of the Philippines
DAP	Democratic Action Party
DK	Khmer Rouge / Democratic Kampuchea
DPD	Regional Representative Council
DPR	House of Representatives
EA	Election Administration
FUNCINPEC	Royalist political party in Cambodia – National United Front for an Independent, Neutral, Peaceful, and Cooperative Cambodia
GAM	Free Aceh Movement
IFC	Inter-Faith Commission
KID	Khmer Institute of Democracy
KPNLF	Khmer People's Liberation Front
KPU	General Election Commission
LICADHO	Cambodian League for the Promotion and Defense of Human Rights
MCA	Malaysian Chinese Association
MIC	Malaysian Indian Congress
MILF	Moro Islamic Liberation Front
NEC	National Election Committee
NICFEC	Neutral and Impartial Committee for Free Elections in Cambodia

NGO	Non-governmental organisation
NU	Nahdlatul Ulama
PAD	People's Alliance for Democracy
PAN	National Mandate Party
PAP	People's Action Party
PAS	Partai Islam Se-Malaysia
PBB	Moon and Star Party
PD	Democratic Party
PEC	Province Election Committee
PDI-P	Indonesian Democratic Party of Struggle
PK	Justice Party
PKB	National Awakening Party
PKI	Indonesian Communist Party
PKK	Communist Party of Kampuchea
PKS	Justice Prosperity Party
PKR	Parti Keadilan Rakyat
PPP	(Indonesia) United Development Party
PPP	(Thailand) People's Power Party
PR	Pakatan Rakyat
PRK	People's Republic of Kampuchea
PRM	Socialist Party
SCM	Supreme Council of Magistracy
SOC	State of Cambodia
SRP	Sam Rainsy Party
SWS	Social Weather Stations
TRT	Thai Rak Thai Party
UDD	United Front of Democracy against Dictatorship
UMNO	United Malays National Organisation
UN	United Nations
USAID	United States Agency for International Development
WEF	World Economic Forum

1 Introduction

Political change and political development in Southeast Asia – transitology revisited

Mely Caballero-Anthony

Introduction

Over the last ten years, Southeast Asia has seen significant shifts in the political landscape of a number of states in the region. Among the most significant ones have been the dramatic changes in the political order of what appeared to be enduring/ resilient authoritarian regimes in countries like Indonesia and Thailand. The fall of the 32-year Suharto regime in Indonesia in 1997, preceded by the retreat of the military in Thailand in 1993, seemed to signal a push for political liberalisation in a region once described as resistant to the rising wave of democratisation that occurred in many parts of the world.

Samuel Huntington's seminal work entitled *The Third Wave: Democratisation in the Late Twentieth Century* (1991) had argued that the 'People Power' revolution in the Philippines was to be the start of the Third Wave of the democratisation process in Asia. Looking back therefore over the last decade, it seemed the euphoria that had followed Southeast Asia's 'democratic moment' was justified given the collapse of the Suharto Government in Indonesia, and the number of political transitions that followed signalling the partial consolidation of democracy elsewhere in the region, especially in Thailand, the Philippines and Cambodia.

However, as events in recent history have borne out, the excitement about democratisation was soon replaced by creeping doubts and uncertainty over the ability of the transitioning states to steer the course of political change toward democratic consolidation. The turn of events in Thailand that saw the ouster of a democratically elected leader, Thaksin Shinawatra, by the military in 2006, followed by a series of changes in government characterised by short-lived regimes, have certainly raised questions about the nature and trajectory of political developments in the region. The recent political travails in Thailand – when stacked with the seemingly enduring political incoherence in the Philippines, the fragility of a young democracy in Indonesia and the increasing anti-democratic trends found in Cambodia – have raised questions among a number of political analysts regarding whether the push for democracy in the region could lose its momentum. This is despite the fact that new rounds of elections are scheduled to be held from 2009 in Indonesia and in 2010 in the Philippines. The nagging concern is that the elections in unconsolidated democracies could possibly bring about countervailing forces that could open the way for either the return of the military to power or the sliding back to authoritarianism by popularly elected leaders.

The different experiences of political transitions in the region have salient implications for the broader context of political development in Asia. Following his 1991 work on the Third Wave of democracy, Huntington has also argued that in non-Western societies, the introduction of democracy can create what is called the 'democracy paradox' – one that has facilitated the coming to power of groups that appeal to indigenous ethnic and religious loyalties and are very likely to be 'anti-western and anti-democratic'.[1] According to Huntington, the problem of the Third Wave of democracy is not the issue of overthrow of regimes but rather its potential for self-erosion – the intermittent or gradual weakening of a democracy by those elected to lead it. As one examines the turn of events in Thailand, one would therefore ask whether such a phenomenon is indeed happening in Southeast Asia.

It is against the chequered history of political development in Southeast Asia that this study was conceived. Its main objective is to examine the nature of political change and democratic transitions in Southeast Asia. It brings together selected case studies of political systems in the region that have gone through significant periods of political transitions from military-led authoritarian regimes to liberal, democratic systems but continue to face serious challenges in democratic consolidation. This volume, therefore, is not only about democratisation but also about what takes place during periods of political transitions in developing states in Asia.

In order for the study to take a more comprehensive and comparative approach in what could clearly be an unwieldy project, the authors were asked to examine some key questions at the commencement of the project. Among these are: how would you characterise the nature of political transition that has taken place? Do these developments lean more toward democratic or status quo regimes? Who are the drivers of change? To what extent do new political actors alter the dynamics of state–society relations within these states? Do these changes lead to more democratic regimes?

We considered these initial questions as critical at the very start, since we wanted to come up with some general observations about the nature of political transitions that have or are still taking place in the selected cases, and offer some propositions on the nature of political development in Southeast Asia. The questions were also prompted by the shared observation among the authors on the difficulties and the challenges faced by states and societies, as they work toward the establishment of democratic political systems and the kinds of struggles faced by people in their fight against authoritarian regimes.

Central to our study is revisiting the assumption that political transitions eventually lead to the establishment of democratic regimes, despite the notion that there are different paths to democratisation. Our challenge, therefore, was to analyse the extent to which this is borne out in the Southeast Asian experience. With these preliminary questions as a basis, the authors were then asked to reflect on the following set of related questions as they finalised the findings of their respective studies:

- Are emerging democracies in the region threatened by weak, failed or authoritarian leadership?
- Can democratising political systems be made more resilient?
- With the number of transitions taking place, will democracy become the defining political landscape in Southeast Asia?
- If not, will democratic political transitions engender regional instability rather than promote security in Southeast Asia?

As the convenor of this project, I believe that the last question on the impact of democratic transitions on regional security, though not the main thrust of this study, is nevertheless important in light of the significant institutional developments that are taking place in the region. These include, among others, the adoption of an ASEAN Charter in 2008 as well as the establishment of an ASEAN Security Community. While few doubt that contemporary Southeast Asia is undergoing change in those directions, it remains unclear whether these transitions would facilitate better management of inter-state relations in the region.

Hence, aside from examining what happens during democratic transitions, it is equally important to explore whether changes to the region's political systems would improve or deteriorate regional relations. Paying attention to how these countries accommodate and manage political change, particularly in their domestic polities, would be an interesting concern in the overall understanding of political development and security in Southeast Asia. This examination is also in response to the influential argument which presupposes that democratic change, though not without risk, would benefit the region in the long run insofar as Asia's institutional architectures complement each other, its regionalism deepens and its cases of democratic transitions extend to other states and consolidate. These issues are discussed separately in later chapters of this volume.

Why focus on political (democratic) transitions?

In the general study of political modernisation and political development, the prevailing thought has been that all politics can and should evolve toward some form of democracy. This pattern and/or progression of stages starting from political modernisation → development → democratisation have more or less defined the kinds of approaches and theories that have evolved in the study of comparative politics in the developing world. Moreover, these approaches argue that with industrialisation bringing about rapid economic growth, the social and economic transformations taking place in modernising societies will result in, among other things, the rise of a new middle class who will then push for and play a key role in instituting political change toward liberal democratic political systems.

This line of thought reflects a teleological approach to politics. One of the more current, yet definitive examples of this kind of thinking is found in Francis Fukuyama's *End of History* that speaks about the 'perceived consensus – worldwide' that liberal democracy is the legitimate form of government as against other types of government such as monarchy, fascism or communism. In his book, Fukuyama argues that liberal democracy is the 'end-point of mankind's ideological evolution' and the 'final form of government'. He further argues that despite the daily political setbacks and widespread pessimism about notions of democracy, events during the last quarter of the twentieth century have made clear that there is indeed a 'coherent and directional history' or development of mankind tending toward liberal democracy.[2] The enthusiasm toward democratisation was further boosted in a similar work by Samuel Huntington that described the different processes of democratisation taking place around the world.[3]

Such trends appeared to be applicable to the developing states in Southeast Asia. Indeed, the much celebrated people power movement in the Philippines in 1986, followed by attempts – albeit short-lived – at a people power revolution in Myanmar in 1988, and the 1991/92 democratisation in Thailand reinforced Huntington's claim, ushering in a new sense of hope and confidence that democratisation was to be the end-point of politics. Finally, the collapse of the Suharto government after the 1997 Asian financial crisis sparked more enthusiasm about the future democratic landscape of the region.

Underpinning these dramatic political developments has been the assumption that rapid economic growth brings about drivers of political change that push for democratisation. John Girling, for instance, credits economic growth in the mid-1980s as the 'turning point' in Thailand's political transformation.[4] It leads to, among others, the emergence of a new middle class and civil society organisations that enter the political arena and consequently reconfigure political power in a country.[5] Similarly, Neher and Marlay, writing on Indonesia, have described how a mix of improvement in living standards, access to international news, higher educational levels and resistance to political repression of intellectuals had provided the potent force for regime change in the country, from authoritarianism to democratisation.[6]

However, as noted earlier, the unexpected turn of events in Thailand – which until 2006 had been a model of a promising democratising state with a rapidly developing economy despite being severely affected by the 1997 financial crisis – have certainly raised questions about the nature and trajectory of political developments in the region. Hence, while there has been significant movement in the direction of democratisation, there remain nagging worries of the possible return of the military in politics, who could once again wield power. There also remains concern over tendencies of authoritarian rule among popularly elected leaders. Compounding these authoritarian tendencies are the risks of emerging security threats which are increasingly becoming transnational. These include the threats posed by transnational crimes, infectious diseases and environmental degradation. Against these concerns, a common question raised among policy analysts in the region is: what ails democratisation in Southeast Asia? Are elections and/or changes in political order not enough?

Political transitions and the challenges to democratic consolidation in Southeast Asia

The processes of transitions being examined in this volume go beyond the analyses of elections and/or changes in governments in these selected countries. Of greater salience to the analyses of this study is the impact of the new actors that have entered the political arena and how they may have altered the power configuration within these countries, how these affect the nature of state–society relations, and whether these transitions lead to the establishment of a more liberal political environment.

At the outset, it is, therefore, important to clarify the concept of political transition that is being studied here. One would start by drawing a clear distinction between the meaning of change and transition, with the latter signalling some notion of movement from one defined (political) condition or state of being to another, completely different one. Hence, while one often sees changes in governments after general elections, these may not necessarily lead to political transitions. In Southeast Asia, we have already seen the dramatic political transitions of authoritarian regimes to emerging democracies. The Indonesian case is the latest case in point. We have also seen notable movements push within the so-called semi-democratic regimes toward more open and democratic political systems, like in the case of Thailand, and even in Malaysia and Singapore.[7] Even the case of the Philippines can be described as one of a continuing push to consolidate its democratic system. These transitions from authoritarianism and semi-democratic regimes to democratising ones, or from emerging democracies to consolidated democracies have in fact been areas of enquiry in many recent studies of political transitions.[8]

What then is the value added in examining these transitions further? From a broader perspective, one could argue that the continued salience of examining political transitions is explained by the uneven experiences of democratic consolidation among new democracies in Asia. As mentioned earlier, although scholars and policy makers agree that there are different paths to democratisation, there remains the underlying assumption that political transitions eventually lead to the establishment of democratic regimes. The question however is the extent to which this is borne out in the Southeast Asian experience.

Exploring this issue further actually raises a number of related questions impinging on our understanding of what these transitions mean for political development in this region. This is a salient point given that the various studies on democratisation do in fact indicate that the notion of democratic consolidation remains contested. As argued by William Case, unlike democratic transitions, it is more difficult to ascertain what democratic consolidation really means.[9]

Studies suggest that there are two simple ways of understanding consolidation. First is the minimalist view that looks at democratic consolidation as a process based on the regularity of holding elections or simply, the procedural angle. From this view, one could for instance argue that the institutionalisation of regular elections is already a good indicator of Linz and Stepan's criteria that a democratic regime has to show that 'democracy is (now) the only game in town',[10] provided that these elections meet Samuel Huntington's 'two-turnover test' which, in turn, assesses democratic consolidation to be a case wherein a ruling party loses an election to an opposition party or coalition, and wins it in the next round of elections.

A number of political scientists, however, have noted that electoral processes do not necessarily ensure the establishment of a liberal democratic regime.[11] This second argument falls within the 'maximalist view' of democratic consolidation which argues that in addition to elections, democratic consolidation involves other important processes which include the observance of the rule of law, greater government responsiveness and the existence of various and diverse forms of social equity. Yet, there are also scholars working on democratic consolidation who argue that the meaning we ascribe to the notion of democratic consolidation really 'depends on where we stand – our empirical viewpoints – and where we aim to reach, i.e. our normative horizons'.[12] Understanding democratic consolidation therefore varies according to the contexts and the goals we have in mind.

Notwithstanding the lack of consensus on what democratic consolidation entails, some political scientists offer more definitive views of the processes of democratic consolidation which are not dependent on electoral tests alone, but also, if not more so, on a situation where all political actors take for granted the fact that democracy is the *only game in town*.[13] This 'stage' however comes with five interacting criteria:

- Flourishing civil society – where citizens organise themselves into social groups and movements such as interest groups and trade unions.
- Strong political society – where citizens and polity have respect for the democratic institutions that are in place, and any problems are dealt with within the aforementioned institutions.
- Rule of law – where legal guidelines are provided to maintain stability and allow for civil and political societies to function.
- Strong state apparatus – having a functioning bureaucracy in order to command, regulate and extract tax revenues.
- Strong economic society – to serve as a system to mediate between the state and the market.

Jeff Haynes sums up the processes of democratic consolidation neatly in four ways:

> '[After] a shift from authoritarianism, political actors' behaviour appears decisively to shift toward democratic patterns. There is open admittance of pro-democracy political actors into the system. Political decision-making henceforth proceeds according to what have become legitimately coded procedures. The mass of ordinary people, as well as political leaders and activists, perceive the democratic system to be better than any other possible alternative form of government.'[14]

Against these debates, the other set of questions we had to address was, what set of criteria or conditions would we like to use to examine the nature of political transitions that are taking place or had taken place in the respective case studies? How reflective were these of the context in the region?

The issues raised earlier reflect our working premise that there has been a lack of comprehensive and systematic study in understanding the problems of democratic transitions in Southeast Asia. Instead much of the current work has focused on the problems of democratic consolidation. We argue, however, that one of the consequences of privileging consolidation over transition is the tendency for studies on democratisation to concentrate more on classifying regime-types rather than teasing out the reasons why processes of political change remain stuck in the transition phase instead of moving forward to consolidation. Larry Diamond, for instance, had introduced the concept of 'hybrid regimes' to describe a political system that combines elements of democracy (e.g. elections) and authoritarianism (excessive executive power).[15] Similarly, Levitsky and Way introduced the notion of 'competitive authoritarian regimes' to refer to political systems where democratic institutions are used as a means of gaining power.[16] Thus while competition is made real, state power is abused to suppress civil liberties and severely handicap opposition parties, consequently making the playing field highly uneven.

While regime classification has its usefulness, this study argues that more attention needs to be given to understanding why democratic transitions do not necessarily lead to democratic consolidation. As pointed out by Haynes, despite the fact that dozens of 'Third World' countries (already) went democratic over the 1980–2000 period, only a few were able to 'unequivocally manage to consolidate their democratic status'.[17] By probing further into what takes place during these transitions – i.e. by looking at the dynamics between and among actors (agency) and processes (structures) that drive the impetus for change before and during transitions – we hope to be able to understand the nature of power reconfigurations that emerge within a state, examine their impact on the creation of, and strengthening or weakening of political institutions, as well as define the direction of the political changes that are taking place either forward, toward consolidation, or backward, toward authoritarianism.

The emphasis on the processes and problems of transitions does not, however, disregard the importance of analysing democratic consolidation. As argued by many scholars, analyses of democratic consolidation compel us to examine the extent to which power holders have been 'encouraged by pressure from various external and domestic sources – for example, internationally, from foreign governments and . . . [domestically] from civil and political society – to allow citizens greater participation in the political arena'.[18] Others suggest that democratic progress is primarily associated with an array of domestic factors affecting political outcomes, including level of economic development, quality of political leadership and nature of elite bargaining, political institutions and even political culture.

Between preconditions for democratisation and crafting institutions

An important component in the study on transition is the continuing debate regarding what is more central to the process of democracy: the 'preconditions' that favour democratisation vis-à-vis the need to establish the democratic institutions.

The latter argues that democratising states must have the 'right' institutions in order for democratisation to succeed. These would include: rule of law, flourishing civil society, political parties, elections, etc. On the other hand, the former argues that democratisation can only succeed if it is predicated on particular social, economic and cultural factors within the society.[19]

It is interesting to note that the former approach that emphasised 'preconditions' to democratisation has been challenged in a recent study on modernisation, democracy and the developmental state in Asia. As argued by Clark, Asia's experience in general presents several causes of democratic transitions that are not fully explained by modernisation. For example, in his survey of several 'democratically transitioning' states, he found little correlation between democratic transitions and level of (economic) modernisation, although there is partial support that a lack of modernisation created 'political decay' in earlier periods. Equally significant is his finding that the nature of Asian regimes was instead primarily determined by domestic elite bargaining rather than the prerequisites to democracy.[20]

These debates continue to resonate well in Southeast Asia, given that there are countries that have had an impressive record of high economic growth for several years which have spurred calls for political reform and change, while there are other states where an emerging civil and economic society conducive to democracy have began to develop but where significant challenges remain. These trends, therefore, do not only make analyses of political transitions timely and relevant, but they also raise the need to develop comparative perspectives of both democratising and democratic states.

Moving beyond transitions to democratic consolidation

As noted earlier, a fundamental challenge in consolidating democracy during and after transitions is the development of a more durable basis for political authority, shared political principles, credible political institutions and the development of democratic norms and practices. In brief, an important issue that arises in the analysis of democratic consolidation is how democratic practices can be embedded in these transitioning states to make these democratic regimes more resilient. Conversely, if states have not been able to consolidate democratic gains, we are compelled to examine why and identify some conditions and factors that may explain weak democratic regimes.

In plotting the different milestones of political changes in the region and assessing the trajectory of these transitions toward democratic consolidation, the study takes off from the work of Andreas Schedler who examines what takes place during periods of transitions and democratic consolidation.[21] Schedler identifies a hierarchy of three independent variables that determine the stability and quality of political regimes.

- Behavioural foundations– examines, among others, anti-democratic behaviour during periods of transition, i.e. are people able to behave in accordance with the rule of law and abide with democratic norms, and whether political

actors are actively engaged in the promotion of democratic culture and consensus, as well as the strengthening of state capacity.

- Attitudinal foundations – focuses on the attitudes, convergence of norms on democracy among political elites and the public at large and analyses whether there is enough support for democratic institutions, and whether these can be sustained.
- Structural foundations – examines whether there are socio-economic and institutional bases that support democratic consolidation and analyses whether institutions and structures enhance or obstruct the ability of the political system to facilitate the guarantee of civil liberties, and ensure equality before the law.

Following Schedler's three inter-related variables of transitions: behavioural, attitudinal and structural foundations, the individual chapters in this volume have
attempted to reflect to whatever extent possible whether these variables do help to
explain why democratic consolidation remains elusive to some, if not most, states
in the region, despite their experiences with democratic transitions.

Starting with the chapter on *Political transition and democratic resilience in
Indonesia*, Rizal Sukma examines the events of the May 1998 transition in the
country and its aftermath, which had far-reaching consequences for the country's
political life. According to him, the collapse of the Suharto-led New Order
Government was the most important political change in the country since 1966,
which might have paved the way for Indonesia's transition toward democracy. A
number of significant developments followed which included the amendment of
the country's Constitution that dismantled the military's political role, the devolution of power to the regions and the establishment of new political institutions
which also paved the way for the country's first ever direct presidential election in
2004.

Sukma however cautions that the democratisation process in still very much an
ongoing political negotiation among competing forces. The processes of transition
taking place in the country have therefore evoked a combination of frustration and
optimism, which according to him are defined largely by the character of regime
change and the nature of transition itself. This was due to the nature of political transitions that took place, in which there was a constant stream of political negotiations – it was not merely a replacement of a regime but more an extrication of a
regime.

In examining how resilient the process of democratisation was in the country by
juxtaposing it with the three conceptual indicators – behaviours, attitudes and institutions – used by Schaedler, Sukma noted that Indonesia's experience with anti-
democratic behaviour was the most worrying as seen in the use of violence during
communal tensions, rejection of elections and a transgression of authority
(spawned by a culture of impunity especially in the military). Yet, this anti-
democratic behaviour has failed to reverse the process of democratisation.
However, it was more positive for the second indicator, attitudes. There was the
perception amongst the public that it was only with democracy that various parties

in Indonesia would be able to have a stake in politics. Finally, strong socio-economic institutions are needed to support democratic processes. However, Indonesia is lacking in this aspect, as its existing socio-economic institutions remain weak. Nonetheless, he argues that signs of consolidation and future challenges for Indonesia are already there.

Following the experience in Indonesia is the chapter on Thailand which examines what happened to Thai democracy. Entitled *Confusing democracies*, Pavin Chachavalpongpun begins his analyses with how the military coup of 19 September 2006 brought Thai democracy back to its chequered past of elections, coups and constitutions. What seemed like an inexorable march toward democratic consolidation has ended up as a retreat at best to democratic transition. To many Thais, the more than a decade of political reforms toward democratic consolidation which began in 1992 has come to naught.

While adopting Schedler's three variables in dissecting what happened to Thai democracy, Chachalvalpongpun argues that whatever indicators one would use to measure democratic consolidation in Thailand, it must take into account the fact that there exist different interpretations of democracy. A critical element in his analyses, therefore, is the role of agencies and how they perceive their power position in a changing Thai polity. What is therefore emerging in the rapidly changing political environment in the country as a result of a number of political transitions that have happened, has been the growing competition between the old political players and emerging actors including a number of civil society groups that compete for power with elected officials. This has in turn pitted the old establishment and enduring institutions like the monarchy against 'new' political forces, significantly changing the nature of politics in the country. This was best reflected in the rise and fall of Thaksin Shinawatra's political fortunes. The ouster of Thaksin by the military-led coup and the subsequent short-term regimes that followed reflected the nature of the 'royalists/elitist-defined' democratisation process in the country, which one analyst had described as being anti-1997 constitution, anti-Thaksin, anti-politician as well as displaying contempt toward the rural masses.[22]

Herman Kraft's chapter on the Philippines, entitled *A (not so) funny thing happened on the way to the forum*, examines the travails of democratisation in the country. Despite being the first country in the region to have democratised, the Philippines have been described as having a low-quality democracy.[23] This observation is shared by Herman Kraft who noted that 20 years since the overthrow of the authoritarian presidency of Ferdinand E. Marcos, there is a general sense among political observers and analysts, as well as the general public in the Philippines, that the transition toward democracy has failed to bring about lasting political stability, responsive governance and an economic environment conducive not only to growth but more so to a greater number of people sharing in the effects of that growth.

Thus while democracy remains the preferred system for most Filipinos, it has suffered from the loss of public confidence in the current political institutions and political leadership. Meaningful change is hampered by the persistence of a weak Philippine state. This has made it difficult for various government agencies to formulate and implement policies independently of the powerful vested interest groups in Philippine society. Kraft highlighted two important points in determining the success of political transitions in the country. First is the attitudinal variable – the extent to which democracy spreads and is accepted. This is visible in the Philippines' case. Second, on the structural variable, particularly the extent to which the institutions are able to respond to and appropriately convey what the people want – the Philippines is clearly lacking. Nonetheless, while the Philippines' political institutions remained weak, it would still be possible for personalities to change this, thus highlighting the significance of political elite behaviour in political transitions in the Philippines.

In his chapter on Cambodia, *The challenge for democratic consolidation in postwar societies*, Sorpong Peou argues that despite going through a period of remarkable political transition, Cambodia remains a poor candidate for democratic consolidation. Significant political elite members, especially those within the executive branch of government, did not effectively comply with the democratic procedures, rules, norms, and principles. As of 2003, the country had held elections on a regular basis, but they did not become noticeably freer and fairer. They have violated such democratic rules while rampant corruption remains a critical challenge to these rules. The liberal norms of accountability and nonviolence remain extremely weak. The liberal principle of liberty has also come under constant challenge in recent years. In other words, Cambodian elites still maintain antidemocratic attitudes in that they have sought to pursue power rather than promote democracy. The dominant party – the Cambodian People's Party (CPP) has proved quite successful in consolidating its political power base rather than democracy and is now emerging as the hegemonic party. As a result, the new democratic regime remains unconsolidated.

To Peou, the single most important variable that constrains and impedes democratisation remains its serious institutional weakness at the state, political and civil society levels. Peou therefore argues that in studying the challenge for democratic consolidation in post-monarchical, post-communist and post-conflict countries like Cambodia, attention should be focused on analysing the structural impediments – particularly, the political elites' personal pursuit of all-out domination of economic, political and military power. Bringing in the perspective of what he calls 'complex realist institutionalism', Peou goes further to bring together Schedler's variables and attempts to provide a different theoretical lens in understanding democratic consolidation in Cambodia.

The chapter on Malaysia by Lee Hock Huan and Helen E. S. Nesadurai 'unpacks' the nature of political transition in a country which to them has been one of the few hybrid regimes that has successfully thwarted changes and challenges to its rule, and avoided catching the liberal democratic bug that seemed to spread like wildfire in the late 1980s and 1990s in much of the rest of the world. According to the authors, while the Malaysian regime has variously being described by scholars as quasi-democratic,[24] semi-democratic,[25] statist democratic,[26] repressive-responsive,[27] illiberal democratic[28] and so on, there have been differences in their emphasis. Yet, according to them, all the different descriptions concur that the

Malaysian regime embodied both democratic and authoritarian features, captured in Steven Levitsky and Lucan Way's concept of 'competitive authoritarian' states.

The authors note that the most significant element of political transition in Malaysia has been the leadership change from Mahathir Mohamad to Abdullah Badawi in late 2003. In analysing the nature of the political transition experienced in the country over the past few years, Lee and Nesadurai point to the way that these transitions have led to, or are leading to the continuation, or further consolidation of Malaysia's competitive-authoritarian 'hybrid' regime – although with some degrees of liberalisation. The authors also pay close attention to the results of the 8 May 2008 general election that made significant gains for the country's opposition parties, and for the first time in the country's political history, denied the incumbent coalition – Barisan Nasional – its two-thirds majority in parliament. Among the key questions therefore raised in the chapter is whether the 'political tsunami' represented by the unprecedented event signals the slow withering of Malaysia's hybrid regime and in turn facilitate the slow but steady consolidation of democracy in the country. The chapter further suggests that in the Malaysian experience, the relationship between agency and structure is quite dynamic in that agency has defined the structures in the short term, while structures have influenced the behaviour of agency in the long term.

Finally, the chapter on Singapore by Cherian George provides an interesting contrast to the various studies on political transitions in the region. As noted by George, any survey of political change in the region has always had Singapore as an anomaly given that its 'hegemonic, dominant-party system' has remained in power since the country's independence in 1965. Yet, as argued by George, any analysis of Singapore's seemingly unchanging political system ought to examine the changing, albeit subtle, dynamics between the state and society where the former embeds itself in dense networks to keep it connected to its mass base, to which it remains highly responsive, to elites whom it works hard to co-opt, and to global economic forces with which its policies are kept in tune. It is this 'networked' quality where change takes place at a very gradual pace that is carefully managed which makes the system resilient.

In this chapter, George posits that while frameworks provided by Schedler and other comparativists or transitologists are useful, in the case of Singapore a more suitable framework is required if one is to have a more nuanced understanding of state–society relationships, while at the same time, come up with an objective assessment of the capacity of the state to manage the multiple pressures it faces in governing and being responsive to its people. George therefore offers a novel framework, which he terms as 'networked autocracy'.

To George, while the Singapore political system is not as open in the way democratic systems are generally understood, individual participation in public affairs is actually encouraged, and these connections between the state and its people are painstakingly built. By consciously plugging into various segments of Singapore society, the ruling party can be seen as a fairly disciplined grassroots machine. This is evidenced by its weekly meet-the-people sessions, when citizens are given the opportunity to express their grievances to the Minister of Parliament of their constituency. This makes government officials easily accessible to the public thus ensuring that no one is left out. It is therefore the networked quality of Singapore's authoritarian model that has accounted for its exceptional resilience.

While seemingly incongruous with the rest of the chapters, the inclusion of the Singapore study in this volume on political change is important if one is indeed to have a better understanding of the political dynamics taking place in the region. Hence with the other objective of going beyond labels and mindful of the perils of a minimalist view of democracies, the chapter on Singapore arguably provides readers with some novel insights into the kind of political bargaining and negotiations that take place even in political systems that are less democratic. One could for instance raise the point that regardless of its semi-democratic system, having a government that is responsive to societal needs may also be a useful measurement of the success of the political transition process. By measuring the state's ability to perform and deliver to its people, it would not only create an accountable political system but also increase the probability of creating a stable political system, despite being less democratic.

In conclusion, the study points to some key points in the broad canvas of different experiences of political transitions in Southeast Asia. First, the study notes that democratic transitions and consolidation are two separate processes. As such, it is important to analyse why some democratic transitions revert to authoritarian rule and why in some cases, democratic consolidation can lead to the rise of hegemonic power. In both cases, the adoption of Schedler's variables – to the extent possible – provides useful insights into different cases of transitions of selected states.

Second, the study highlights the key role of institutions in the process of political transitions and democratic consolidation. All the chapters in this volume underscore the fact that institutions matter. At the same time, the different chapters also show that institutions alone cannot guarantee the success or failure of democratic consolidation. These have to be accompanied by behaviours and attitudes that promote democratic norms.

Third, is the critical role of agency. The studies have shown that political elites, political leadership and civil society groups are important but are also competing actors in the political arena. The nature of their interactions could therefore define the outcome of democratic transitions and the prospects for democratic consolidation.

Fourth, in Southeast Asia, the democratic process(es) is most often not linear nor is it seamless. While not necessarily a novel finding, the case studies reinforce a point raised by Thomas Carothers who argued that there can be no real sequence for democratisation.[29] Instead a common pattern was toward 'feckless pluralism' and dominant power politics – both of which cannot be stations to liberal democracy. Democratic regimes can also be eroded.

Fifth, while measuring democratic consolidation is important, we also ought to be mindful of the risk of idealising and reifying what Guillermo O'Donnell calls 'strong teleological favour'.[30] But one could nevertheless argue that we need to address this issue if only to debate the fact that the notion of democratic consolidation should not be confined to one characteristic telos but many. Thus, in analysing the experience of political change and development in Southeast Asia, this should lead us to identify our own concepts of what democratic consolidation is within our own context and capture what 'democracy' and political development have been so far.

Notes

1 Samuel P. Huntington, 'Democracy for the Long Haul', *Journal of Democracy*, vol. 7, no. 2, 1996, p. 3.
2 Francis Fukuyama, *The End of History and the Last Man*, New York: The Free Press, 1992.
3 Samuel P. Huntington, *The Third Wave: Democratisation in the Late Twentieth Century*, Norman: University of Oklahoma Press, 1991.
4 John Girling, 'Thailand in Gramscian Perspective', *Pacific Affairs*, vol. 57, no. 3, Autumn 1984, pp. 385–403.
5 Suchit Bunbongkarn, 'Democracy Under Siege', in James W. Morley (ed.), *Driven by Growth*, pp. 161–75.
6 Clark Neher and Ross Marlay, *Democracy and Development in Southeast Asia: The Winds of Change*, Boulder, Colorado: Westview Press, 1992.
7 Both countries have often been described in existing literature to be 'half-way' houses or semi-democratic states. See for example, William Case, *Politics in Southeast Asia: Democracy or Less*, Richmond, Surrey: Curzon Press, 2002, and the earlier work by James W. Morley (ed.), *Driven by Growth*.
8 See James Hollifield and Calvin Jillson (eds), *Pathways to Democracy: The Political Economy of Democratic Transitions*, New York: Routledge, 2000, and Jeff Haynes (ed.), *Democracy and Political Change in the 'Third World'*, London and New York: Routledge, 2001, pp. 1–20.
9 William Case, *Politics in Southeast Asia: Democracy or Less*, Richmond, Surrey: Curzon Press, 2002, p. 178.
10 Juan J. Linz and Alfred Stepan, *Problems of Democratic Consolidation*, Baltimore: The Johns Hopkins University Press, 1996.
11 See, for example, Fareed Zakaria, 'The Rise of Illiberal Democracy', *Foreign Affairs*, vol. 76, no. 6, November 1997.
12 Andreas Schedler, 'What is Democratic Consolidation?' *Journal of Democracy*, vol. 9 no. 2, 1998, pp. 91–107.
13 Linz and Stepan, *Problems of Democratic Consolidation*.
14 Haynes (ed.), *Democracy and Political Change in the 'Third World'*, p. 11.
15 Larry Diamond, 'Thinking about Hybrid Regimes', *Journal of Democracy*, vol. 13, no. 2, April 2002, pp. 21–35.
16 Steven Levitsky and Lucan A. Way, *Competitive Authoritarianism: The Origins and Dynamics of Hybrid Regimes in the Post-Cold War Era* (mimeo), 2006.
17 Haynes (ed.), *Democracy*.
18 Haynes (ed.), *Democracy;* Larry Diamond, Juan J. Linz and Seymour Martin Lipset (eds), *Democracy in Developing Countries, Vol. 3*. Boulder, Co: Lynne Rienner, 1989; Guillermo O'Donnell and Philippe C. Schmitter, *Transitions from Authoritarian Rule: Tentative Conclusions about Uncertain Democracies*, Baltimore: The Johns Hopkins University Press, 1986.
19 This is an approach that had been extensively covered in modernisation theory and in particular, the relationship between level of economic development and the transition to democracy. See for example, Harold Crouch and James Morley, 'The Dynamics of Political Change', in James W. Morley (ed.), *Driven by Growth*.
20 Cal Clark, 'Modernisation, Democracy and the Developmental State in Asia: A Virtuous

Cycle or Unraveling Strands', in James F. Hollifield and Calvin Jillson (eds), *Pathways to Democracy*, pp. 160–77.

21 Andreas Schedler, 'Measuring Democratic Consolidation', *Studies in Comparative International Development*, vol. 36, no. 1, Spring 2001, pp. 66–92. See also Schedler's 'What is Democratic Consolidation?'.

22 Thitinan Pongsudhirak, 'What happened to Thai Democracy?' Paper presented at the Workshop on Political Transitions and Democratic Consolidation in Southeast Asia, Jakarta, Indonesia, 30–31 July, 2007.

23 Case, *Politics in Southeast Asia.*

24 Zakaria Ahmad, 'Malaysia: Quasi-Democracy in a Divided Society', in Diamond *et al.* (eds), *Democracy in Developing Countries*, Vol. 3.

25 William Case, *Semi-democracy in Malaysia: Pressures and Prospects for Change*, Canberra, ACT, Australia: Political and Social Change, Research School of Pacific Studies, Australian National University, 1992.

26 James V. Jesudason, 'Statist Democracy and the Limits to Civil Society in Malaysia', *The Journal of Commonwealth & Comparative Politics*, vol. 33, no. 3, 1995, pp. 335–57.

27 Harold Crouch, *Government and Society in Malaysia*, St. Leonards: Allen & Unwin, 1996.

28 Meredith Weiss, *Protest and Possibilities: Civil Society and Coalitions for Political Change in Malaysia*, Stanford, California: Stanford University Press, 2006.

29 Thomas Carothers, 'The End of the Transition Paradigm', *Journal of Democracy*, vol. 13, no. 1, January 2002, pp. 5–21.

30 See O'Donnell and Schmitter, *Transitions from Authoritarian Rule.*

2 Political transition and democratic resilience in Indonesia

Rizal Sukma

Introduction

The path towards democratic consolidation in democratising states has never been easy. The prospect of a democratic backsliding often overshadows the process of democratisation in these countries. In Southeast Asia, the process of democratic backsliding has been well demonstrated in the case of Thailand under Prime Minister Thaksin Shinawatra. Democracy in Thailand was even suspended when the military took over power in the bloodless coup of October 2006. The government in Thailand continues to face mounting opposition, and politics in Thailand remains marred by uncertainty and instability. The possibility of a stagnating process of democratic transition should also not be overlooked. In the Philippines, the process of democratisation, which started almost two decades ago, has not yet resulted in a consolidated democracy in the country. Indonesia, which embraced democracy in 1998, also continues to face tremendous challenges in consolidating its democracy despite the apparent progress it has made after ten years of democratic reform. In other words, democratisation in Southeast Asia is still a fragile process and far from complete.

Indeed, one common problem that often accompanies the process of consolidation in democratising states in Southeast Asia is the ability of those states to withstand challenges to the democratisation process. The efforts to preserve democracy and accelerate the process of democratic consolidation in those states are often characterised by the imperative of managing anti-democratic behaviour, broadening public support for democracy, and strengthening socio-economic and institutional bases of democracy. The ability of democratising states to preserve and consolidate democracy in the face of those challenges clearly requires a degree of democratic resilience. Without the ability to develop democratic resilience, a democratising state would easily descend into democratic backsliding and in turn fail to consolidate democracy.

In the case of Indonesia, the possibility of a stagnating political transition process should not be overlooked. Democratic transition in Indonesia is still an ongoing process and will continue to bring about new changes to the country's political landscape in the years to come. Indeed, there have been a number of significant developments in the country's political life since 1998: from the introduction of political liberalisation, the devolution of power to the regions, the amendment of the Constitution, the dismantling of the military's political role, the establishment of new political institutions, to the first direct presidential election in 2004. Even though recent developments in Indonesia's democratisation process have provided some grounds for optimism about the prospect for democratic consolidation in the country, problems remain abundant. This chapter assesses the prospects for democratic consolidation in Indonesia by looking at the nature of political transition and the process of democratisation in the country.

The nature of transition: from authoritarianism to emerging democracy

Democratisation in Indonesia began with the collapse of the New Order Government in May 1998. This government, led by President Suharto, came to power in May 1966 after the fall of President Sukarno who had ruled the country since independence in August 1945. Indonesia entered its post-independence era by experimenting with a liberal parliamentary democracy system. This experiment in democracy, however, was abruptly brought to an end in 1957 when President Sukarno, with the support of Indonesia's military and the now-defunct Indonesian Communist Party (PKI), instituted authoritarian rule. The replacement of President Sukarno by General Suharto was not followed by the re-installation of democracy. Instead, General Suharto continued and even consolidated Sukarno's authoritarianism with greater longevity. When Suharto's New Order collapsed, and a democratic transition began, Indonesia had been under authoritarian rule for more than four decades. Political change that occurred in 1998 did not constitute a complete break with the past. It was the result of political compromise that allowed many characteristics of the regime to remain intact.

The breakdown of authoritarian rule

After more than 30 years in power since its inception in 1966, signs of impending change within New Order Indonesia began to emerge in the mid-1990s. The ability of the New Order Government, led by President Suharto, to control and dominate Indonesia's politics began to erode. The president's supreme authority over Indonesia's politics began to meet overt resistance and open challenges. The people's patience in witnessing Suharto's enormous personal power, exercised by the president, his family and cronies in various forms across the country, was reaching the limit. The authoritarian style of the president, the expansion of his family business in light of perceptions of corruption and cronyism, and the unlikelihood of his stepping down soon, irritated even his loyal followers within the military and bureaucracy. Open criticisms from elite circles, especially within the middle class and intellectuals, were increasingly directed at President Suharto and his family. The fact that Suharto himself had become the direct target of such criticisms – something that rarely occurred since the crackdown on the opposition in 1974 – suggested the extent to which public opposition to him had developed.

Despite such growing resentment, however, few would have thought at the time that the year 1996 signified the beginning of the end of Suharto's era and his New Order Government. That beginning was marked by the regime's move to oust Megawati Sukarnoputri from her position as Chairperson of Indonesia's Democratic Party (PDI) by supporting a rival faction in what looked like an 'internal friction' within the Party's leadership. Megawati, however, chose to fight on by insisting that she was still the legitimate leader of the PDI. The Party's office became the 'headquarters' for those who supported Megawati. When the place turned into a *mimbar bebas* (free podium), where political speeches espousing anti-Suharto and anti-government sentiment were made by opposition forces on a daily basis, Suharto and the military simply took over the Party's office by force on 27 July 1996. Riots ensued in parts of Jakarta and the military quickly resorted to repressive means to suppress the protest.

The situation worsened by the end of 1997 when the economic crisis, which had begun in July 1997 in neighbouring Thailand and also in South Korea, swept Indonesia. Despite growing challenge to his rule, however, President Suharto was re-elected as Indonesia's president for the seventh time in March 1998. When Suharto surrounded himself with a cabinet consisting of members of his family and his cronies, he certainly misjudged the extent of opposition against his regime. Students, who had begun to demonstrate demanding the resignation of Suharto in early 1998, stepped up the pressure. Popular support for their movement, especially among urban professionals, grew rapidly. Active involvement of Muslim groups, especially those under the leadership of Muhammadiyah chairman Amien Rais, increased the pressure on the government.[1] The shooting of four students at the University of Trisakti on 12 May was soon followed by the mass riots of 13–15 May. On 21 May, President Suharto abruptly announced his resignation and Vice-President B. J. Habibie was sworn in as Indonesia's third president. The New Order Government was finally brought to an end.

There have been numerous studies that attempt to explain the reasons for the collapse of the Suharto Government in Indonesia. Liddle, for example, argued that Suharto's fall can be attributed to his old age which impaired his ability to identify and solve the problem of the economic crisis rationally.[2] Smith explains that Suharto's fall was the result of 'a dramatic change in the structures of political authority that began in the mid-1980s with economic reform and led to the weakening in loyalty of his two most important allies, the military and Golkar.[3] Huxley argues that it was the economic crisis that galvanised the political change in Indonesia.[4] Berger observes that:

> Globalisation and the process of uneven capitalist development bring with them formidable challenges to Suharto's New Order. While capitalist development is often seen as the key to political and social stability, historically it has also been central to social diversification and the generation of conflict. The very success of capitalist development under the New Order is central to the crisis and political decline of Suharto's regime since the second half of the 1990s.[5]

Furthermore, 'one aspect of that political decline is the failure of Suharto's New Order to acknowledge and accommodate social diversification and the generation of conflict brought about by the unresolved tension between the state and society.'[6] Others, such as Robison and Hadiz, explain the fall of the New Order in terms of 'the fatal flaws and sources of tension within the Soeharto regime that accelerated its disintegration in the context of economic crisis.'[7] Despite the different emphasis in each analysis, however, most analysts agree that the breakdown of authoritarian rule in Indonesia cannot be attributed to any single factor. Even though the resignation of President Suharto was carefully crafted to suggest a voluntary decision, his downfall was the result of a combination of several factors.

More importantly, with Suharto's resignation, Indonesia entered what was the beginning of a dire period of uncertain democratic transition. Indonesian society was imbued with the sense of 'political freedom' long denied to them by Suharto's New Order regime. In the early years of the *reformasi* era, however, the effect of leadership change on Indonesia's political situation had been 'messy'. The departure of Suharto from power had not meant the complete removal of the political system he had created 32 years ago. For example, many viewed the new government under President Habibie as an extension of Suharto's government. When successive regimes (from Habibie, Abdurrahman Wahid, to Megawati) failed to adequately address many post-Suharto problems, a sense of frustration at the pace of political reform began to creep in. However, a deeper look at the process of political change in Indonesia during 1998–2006 reveals that despite the occasional frustration and disillusionment, Indonesia's democratic transition has also been characterised by 'dramatic breakthroughs and moments of great optimism.'[8] That combination of frustration and optimism in the process of transition resulted from the character of regime change and the nature of the transition itself.

Characteristics of transition: bandwagoning, the absence of alternative power and persistent negotiation

Indeed, regime change in May 1998 did not constitute a collapse of the New Order regime in its entirety. Instead, it was an 'intrasystemic transfer of power' from Suharto to his deputy Habibie that 'avoided the complete destruction of the regime and allowed many of its key components, including the armed forces, to make a relatively smooth transfer into the new polity.'[9] It was a negotiated regime change, especially between the military, the regime and the opposition forces, that 'avoided a sharp break with the political power structure that had underpinned the regime.'[10] The negotiation took place primarily due to the absence of unity among opposition forces. Deep division among opposition forces – especially among three key opposition groups (Amien Rais-led modernist Islam, Wahid-led traditional Islam and Megawati-led nationalist-secular groups) – forced them to compromise and accept the replacement of President Suharto by Vice-President Habibie. In effect, this compromise facilitated political bandwagoning and persistent negotiation in the absence of a dominant alternative opposition force to fill in the vacuum left by Suharto.

The political bandwagoning began when several cabinet ministers deserted President Suharto. As the situation in Jakarta and other major cities continued to worsen since the mass riots of 12–13 May 1998, President Suharto announced on 19 May that he would reshuffle his cabinet, and promised a new one which would be tasked to carry out reform agendas as demanded by opposition forces, including the students. He also promised that general elections would soon be convened. To the surprise of many, however, 14 ministers with economics-related portfolios refused to serve in the next new cabinet. One day earlier, Golkar's Chairman and Speaker of the House of Representatives (DPR) Harmoko, himself a staunch supporter of Suharto, had asked the president to resign. In such circumstances, the military under General Wiranto also tried to persuade Suharto that resignation was indeed the best option for him, his family and the nation. As he became aware that he had lost the support of the two main pillars of his power, President Suharto resigned and transferred power to Vice-President Habibie on 21 May 1998.

Opposition forces, overwhelmed with joy due to the departure of Suharto, were not prepared and were unable to present themselves as a united force that could replace the New Order regime with a new one. Instead they accepted Habibie with the understanding that his government would be a transitional government, which would lay the foundation for new political power structures to emerge through democratic general elections. The period between the time when the compromise was agreed upon and the convening of the general elections scheduled to take place in 1999 provided an opportunity for former supporters of the New Order regime to ride on the public expectation of the dawning of a new democratic era. Indeed, President Habibie appointed most of the ministers who had previously deserted Suharto into his cabinet. Habibie also relied on General Wiranto, who continued to retain his position as Commander of the Armed Forces, to stabilise his rule. In fact, a number of military officers were also accommodated in his cabinet.

President Habibie, amidst mounting pressure from the students and other pro-democracy forces, was eager to demonstrate that his government was not merely a continuation of that of his predecessor. To emphasise this point, he immediately launched a number of political reforms, including releasing political prisoners, removing restrictions on the press, introducing regional autonomy laws that allowed for the devolution of power to the regions, passing a number of political laws that paved the way for the return of a genuine multi-party system, and re-introducing democratic parliamentary elections scheduled in June 1999. Through these significant reforms, the Habibie Government, which consisted of key figures from the previous Suharto regime, attempted to demonstrate itself to be a regime that championed the democratisation process. In reality, however, these measures at the same time allowed elements of the New Order to consolidate their position by bandwagoning into the process of democratisation. President Habibie himself, in his attempt to cling to power, continued to rely on the two pillars of the New Order regime: Golkar and the military. Indeed, it has been noted that this early period of *reformasi* under Habibie had 'allowed for the regrouping of old New Order forces, albeit in new alliances and in a new political environment.'[11]

Within such a political context, elements of the previous regime managed to create a space for a continuous negotiation with the opposition elites 'who had been for years on the fringes of political power.'[12] The opposition forces themselves, plagued by internal frictions, opted to support the interim government-led process of gradual reform for fear of social anarchy and public disorder. The influence and power of the key obstacle to the democratisation process in the previous regime – the military – was left intact and in fact was allowed to determine and shape its own course of reform. In other words, the democratic transition in Indonesia was taking place within the context of persistent negotiation between old elements of the New Order regime and the new aspiring power holders. The promise of democratic elections compelled the opposition forces to immediately turn their attention to the need to organise themselves, either through the establishment of new political parties (in the case of Amien Rais and Abdurrahman Wahid) or by consolidating their existing political vehicles (in the case of Megawati's PDI-Perjuangan [PDI-P] and the United Development Party).

The negotiation process took place not only among contending civilian forces or between the government and opposition forces in the society, but also between the civilian and the military forces. Due to its strong and influential position in Indonesia's politics, the military managed to secure its position as a significant player in that process and, for that matter, played an important role not only in setting the pace of political negotiation but also in influencing the direction of democratic transition. Both military and civilian forces sought to advance their particular views and conceptions of politics in post-Suharto Indonesia. Pro-democracy civilian forces could not just ask the military to simply go 'back to the barracks'. Similarly, it has been increasingly difficult for the military to re-dominate the whole process without facing strong resistance from the resurgence of civilian politics. Both sides would have to negotiate their respective agendas in determining where Indonesia should be heading, what kind of polity and political system should be created, and what type of political arrangements should be formed. It should be noted that the most difficult issue during this negotiation process has been the problem of redefining the function, the place and the role of the military in the post-Suharto new political system.

Therefore, it can be said that when political transition began in May 1998, it did not take place in the form of 'replacement' where 'opposition groups took the lead in bringing about democracy, and the authoritarian regime was overthrown.'[13] It was a process of transition through 'extrication' where the weakened regime – due to the growing economic crisis, regime disunity, external pressure and a standoff with the growing opposition – sought to extricate itself from power but continues to influence the process of democratisation.[14] This process was made possible due to the fact that the opposition forces did not consist of radically different political groups from outside the regime. They were partly derived from within the regime itself. They did not challenge the whole regime, but only its top leadership, namely, President Suharto. The opposition forces also lacked a common platform regarding how a new political system should be constructed, and were plagued by internal disunity, competition and rivalry.

Habibie's experiment in opening up the political system, however, served as a double-edged sword. The political reforms and liberalisation initiated by President Habibie – especially the introduction of a genuine multi-party system, free press, and the devolution of power from the central government to the regions – soon eroded the government's ability to monopolise political power. Even though the two main pillars of Suharto's New Order (the military and Golkar) remained intact and were even able to consolidate, the proliferation of new power centres was also inevitable. The proliferation of power centres also took place within the ruling regime when the leaders of both Golkar and the military were re-positioning themselves in preparing for a new political system after the 1999 elections. Indeed, the outcomes of the 1999 elections resulted in a democratic transition characterised by the amalgamation of old and new political forces within a new political environment in post-Suharto Indonesia. The process of democratisation since 1998, which was characterised by a mixture of progress and obstruction, optimism and frustration, should be understood within the context of such characteristics of democratic transition during the period of 1998–2004.

Preserving democracy (1998–2004): challenges, progress and problems

Even though the elements of the New Order regime managed to retain their place in the new political system, they were not able to stop and reverse the process of democratisation in Indonesia. In fact, as was mentioned earlier, the interim Habibie Government was forced to introduce a series of political liberalisation measures, albeit for its own survival. While the process of democratisation did eventually gain momentum, the transition from authoritarianism was not a smooth one. Indonesia's journey towards democracy has been, and still is, a difficult one. It presents a mixed picture of challenges, progresses, obstructions and even unresolved problems. Nevertheless, democracy continues to survive and, since 2004, has even begun to enter the period of democratic consolidation. Using the framework provided by Andreas Schedler,[15] the following analysis examines the extent to which Indonesia's democratisation process has progressed, and how the country has so far managed to withstand the challenges that could have undermined and threatened democratic continuity and survival.

Three questions are of paramount importance in this regard. First, has there been anti-democratic behaviour during the transition process and to what extent has it or has it not undermined democracy in Indonesia? Second, what is the attitude towards democracy among the political elite and the public at large? Third, are there socio-economic and institutional bases that would support Indonesia's consolidation of democracy? Before these questions can be answered adequately, there is a need to look at the progress in political reform in Indonesia.

Progress in political reform: a promising beginning?

Since 1998, Indonesia's political system has undergone a series of remarkable changes. As mentioned earlier, immediately after he succeeded President Suharto,

President Habibie launched several measures to liberalise Indonesia's political system. Regardless of the real motive behind Habibie's political liberalisation, those measures transformed Indonesia's political system in a number of significant ways. Several reform measures introduced during the presidency of Abdurrahman Wahid, and then Megawati, had also contributed to further political transformation in the country.

First, the most important change has been in the area of electoral reform. The introduction of new political laws has significantly laid down the foundation for the return of democratic general elections. Given the provision that the general elections should now be organised by an independent body, the government was no longer in a position to manipulate the results of the elections.[16] Unlike previous elections, civil servants were now freed from the obligation to vote for the one-regime party, Golkar. Moreover, the general elections were also subject to close monitoring by an official, but more independent, election monitoring body (*Panwaslak*). Unlike during the Suharto period, civil society groups were now allowed to monitor the election process. It is also important to note that the new law on general elections for the first time allows the participation of the international community in the monitoring activities.

Second, progress has also been evident with regard to the party system. A genuine multi-party system soon took root. In the past, only two 'opposition' political parties and a one-regime party were allowed to exist. Political parties were tightly controlled and supervised by the government through the Minister of Home Affairs. Unlike Golkar, they were not permitted to open branches below the municipal level so that their influence at the grassroots level was almost non-existent. In the early years of reform, more than 200 political parties were formed, but only 48 were eligible to compete in the 1999 general elections. However, only a few parties really had mass-based support or constituents. These include Golkar, the PDI-P, the modernist Muslim-based National Mandate Party (PAN), the traditionalist Muslim-based National Awakening Party (PKB), the United Development Party (PPP), the Moon and Star Party (PBB) and the Justice Party (PK). However, as we shall see later, political parties in Indonesia still suffer the problem of institutionalisation, corruption, money politics, and the continuing importance and domination of charismatic party leaders.

Third, freedom of the press clearly represents another significant development in Indonesian politics. The press is no longer subject to tight governmental control. While mass media still needs publication licenses from the government, the right of the government to revoke licenses has been seriously curtailed. The government can no longer unilaterally ban any publication without proper, fair and open trial. A number of previously banned magazines, such as the respected weekly magazine *Tempo*, are now out again in the market. Similarly, with regard to freedom of expression, any public event, including demonstrations, no longer needs special permission from the police. The organiser is now only required to notify the police three days before the public event, or political rally, is held.

Fourth, the withdrawal of the military from politics, though still incomplete and only in a formal sense, has reduced the political role of the military and consequently contributed to healthier civil–military relations in the country. Meaningful efforts to reform the military did not come from President Habibie, but from his successor, President Abdurrahman Wahid. President Wahid moved rapidly to bring more discipline to and assert greater civilian control over the military. Wahid's efforts to discipline the armed forces of Indonesia (TNI) paid off significantly when on 21 April 2000, Commander-in-Chief Admiral Widodo submitted the decision by the military leadership to finally relinquish its social and political functions. The passage of Law No. 3 on State Defense in 2002 under the Megawati presidency further strengthened the foundation for democratic civil–military relations.

Fifth, there was the devolution of power from the central government to the regions. Excessive concentration of power in the hands of the central government during Suharto's New Order rule led to an unbalanced relationship not only between the centre and the regions but also between Java and the outer Islands. Growing regional dissatisfaction with this feature of the New Order had been felt long before the fall of Suharto, but it found more overt expression since the fall of his regime. To address regional grievances, two laws – Law No. 22/1999 on Regional Government and Law No. 25/1999 on financial relations between the central government and the regions – were passed by the parliament. These two laws serve as an integral package meant to give more power to the regions, and brought about significant changes both in the nature of the Indonesian state and the style of governance. The laws brought to an end the functioning of Indonesia as a highly centralised state and reduced the power of the central government over the regions in a significant way. A broad autonomy was given to the regions to manage their own affairs, except in the fields of foreign policy, defence, fiscal and monetary policies, religious affairs and the judiciary.

The sixth significant development in Indonesian politics is the changing relationship between the executive and legislative. The parliament, which once played a role as a rubber-stamp institution under the New Order, has become increasingly assertive. It has been mentioned earlier that as power centres proliferated, no political force could dominate the government. Both Wahid and Megawati became president by relying on the support from a coalition of political forces represented in the parliament. As a result, the stability of the government would largely depend on the ability of the president to maintain the coalition of support within parliament. Within such a highly competitive political system, the executive branch of the government, especially the president, was often put under close scrutiny by the legislature. Moreover, parliament also increasingly exercised its control over the government through its budgetary power. Nevertheless, the nature and the quality of that control remains a subject of debate within Indonesia.

All these developments clearly demonstrate the resurgence of democratic practices in Indonesia. After more than three decades of political suppression and control, Indonesian society is now keen to reassert itself and play a greater role in politics. Initial developments in Indonesia's post-Suharto political system, as discussed earlier, clearly contribute to that process. Political reform undertaken during the transition period of 1998–2004, especially the new laws on politics, has 'put in place an institutional framework for political competition and participation'.[17] However, the overall results of the democratisation process in Indonesia since 1998 present a mixed picture and contradictory trends. On the one hand, there has been some progress in certain areas, especially in the opening up of the political system and the re-designing of democratic institutions. On the other hand, Indonesia's democratisation has also been constantly challenged by the presence of what has been described by Schedler as anti-democratic behaviour. What differentiates Indonesia from some of its neighbours is its ability to exercise a degree of democratic resilience in the face of anti-democratic behaviour that continues to colour the democratisation process in the country.

Withstanding anti-democratic behaviour: violence, the 1999 elections, and transgression of authority

As persistent negotiation among old and new power elites continues to colour Indonesia's transition towards democracy, the occurrence of anti-democratic behaviour during the process was to be expected. Indeed, Indonesia's democratisation process has been described as one of rapid political flux amidst the weakening of state capacity to address difficult problems, especially the outbreaks of communal and separatist violence, and continuing economic hardship. However, by examining three indicators of anti-democratic behaviour outlined by Schedler – the use of violence, the rejection of elections and transgression of authority – it seems that Indonesia has been fairly successful in managing and reducing the impacts of these threats to democratic continuity, thus increasing its chances to consolidate democracy further.

The most problematic manifestations of anti-democratic behaviour during 1998–2004 were in the form of outbreaks of communal and separatist violence in several regions. Communal violence, which had in fact begun during the last year of Suharto's rule, escalated after his departure. The conflicts in Maluku, North Sulawesi and West Kalimantan went from bad to worse during 1999–2001.[18] The rebellion in Aceh, and the demand for independence, grew stronger by 1999. The Habibie Government responded to the problem by launching a security operation. A negotiated political settlement was attempted by President Wahid in 2000, but when that failed, he too resorted to the use of force as a method of conflict resolution. Under President Megawati, the government even imposed a military emergency status on Aceh that allowed a massive military operation to be carried out against the Free Aceh Movement (GAM) rebels.[19] Both society and the state were not able to resort to democratic means of peaceful dispute settlement in resolving differences. When communal violence began to subside by 2003, it occurred more due to a growing sense of conflict fatigue among the involved parties rather than as a result of a well-crafted attempt at democratic conflict resolution.

Post-Suharto Indonesia also witnessed the surge of violence carried out by radical Muslim groups, mostly in the form of destruction of public property. These groups often used violence in carrying out what they perceived as a Muslim duty to fight social vices within Indonesia and in expressing their protests against the United States (US). Demonstrations carried out by these groups, especially against the US, were often accompanied by physical attacks on the US Embassy. There have also been cases of violent protests and physical intimidation against churches and Christians, respectively. While this type of violence served as a legitimate cause for concern, its extent did not reach the level that could disrupt and terminate the process of democratisation. As this type of violence had only been perpetrated by a few radical groups, it largely presented a law and order problem that has not been addressed properly by law enforcement agencies.

Elections-related violence was also reported during the 1999 general elections. While there were few cases of intimidation of voters and candidates, Indonesia did not experience political assassinations and kidnappings. In general, the degree of violence was considered minor, and the elections went on in a relatively peaceful environment. There have been a number of disputes regarding the results of vote-counting in some areas, but the cases mostly involved minor political parties. More importantly, when the court ruled over such cases, the disputing parties often accepted the court's decision. The election itself was seen as free and fair, and the degree of acceptance of the result of the elections – which confers legitimacy – was also high.

A more serious challenge stemming from anti-democratic behaviour was the continuity of the culture of impunity. Government officials, especially those who presided over high government positions, often violated the law without being subject to legal persecution. Even when such cases did go to court, many were acquitted. This problem of transgression of authority was more evident in cases involving military officers. For example, no military officer was punished by the courts for what happened in East Timor after the referendum in 1999. The cases of human rights abuses by the military during the Suharto era, such as in Tanjung Priok, Aceh, Lampung, and several other parts of the country, have never been properly investigated. In other words, government officials and military leaders have not 'give[n] up the habit of placing themselves above the law.'[20] If this type of anti-democratic behaviour continues and develops into norms rather than remain exceptions, 'the prospects of democracy darken.'[21]

However, such anti-democratic behaviour has so far failed to reverse the process of democratisation. Nor did it bring Indonesia back to the path of authoritarianism. The occurrences of violence have been concentrated in specific locations and the trend of violent conflicts continues to decline. The results of elections were accepted by the majority of Indonesians. While the problem of impunity continues to hamper the progress of Indonesian democracy, pro-democracy forces continue to put pressure on the government to exercise a greater degree of control over the military and accelerate judicial and legal reforms. Despite all these forms of anti-democratic behaviour, Indonesia continues to democratise. One of the factors preventing its backsliding into authoritarianism has been the growing positive attitude and preference towards democracy among the political elites and citizens.

Attitude towards democracy

According to Schedler, the continuity of democracy also depends on the attitude – the preferences and perceptions – of the political elite and citizens, which has the capacity to confer a degree of democratic legitimacy, namely the genuine, non-instrumental, intrinsic support for democracy. This 'constitutes the most important, and even defining element of democratic consolidation.'[22] An examination of Indonesia's case suggests that there has been increasing commitment to and support among the people for democracy. Among the political elites, even though the motives for supporting democracy might vary, democracy has also come to be seen as 'the only game in town' that would guarantee their place and role as well as survival within the new political system.

After more than four decades of authoritarian rule by President Sukarno (1957–1966) and President Suharto (1967–1998), most Indonesians celebrate the country's hard-won political freedom and its transition towards democracy. Even though that transition is often described as messy and chaotic, Indonesians continue to pin their hopes on the process. Indeed, a recent survey by Roy Morgan Research, for example, shows that three-quarters of Indonesian citizens believed that 'democracy is working well' in Indonesia.[23] However, the fact that one-quarter of the population still disagree with the way democracy has been progressing clearly suggests that Indonesia's democracy is still far from perfect.

Socio-economic and institutional support

The greatest challenge to the consolidation of Indonesian democracy lies in the persistent socio-economic problems that have plagued the country since the outbreak of the financial crisis in 1997, and worsened after the collapse of Suharto's New Order. The socio-economic bases of Indonesia are not yet adequate to support the effective functioning of democracy. The high rate of unemployment, growing poverty and economic inequality clearly serve as factors that could compromise the quality of democracy, and hence the continuity of democracy itself. These factors, for example, contributed to social tension within society even before democratisation started. The occurrence of violent conflicts in post-Suharto Indonesia has been aggravated by the severe impact of the financial crisis that hit the country in 1997. As demonstrated by Tadjoeddin and Murshed, higher incidence of poverty increases the susceptibility of a society to violence.[24]

Even though 'levels of economic development do translate into important constraints and opportunities for the consolidation of democracy', the lack of socio-economic support for democracy does not 'determine the fate of political regimes'.[25] As suggested by Mainwaring, 'democracy can endure under adverse economic and social conditions if the main actors are committed to democratic rules of the game'.[26] In the context of Indonesia, the continuity of democracy has been determined more by the progress made in re-designing the institutional bases of democracy rather than by the ability of the government to deliver economic progress. It seems that the people tend to evaluate the merits of the democratic system independent of weaknesses in the socio-economic foundations of democracy. In other words, the disappointment with the socio-economic situation in the country has not forced Indonesia to terminate the democratisation process and backslide toward authoritarianism. Democracy continues to be seen by the majority of Indonesians as a viable form of government.

Consolidating democracy: 2004 general elections and beyond

As Indonesia prepares for its second direct presidential election, the key question regarding the country's fledgling democracy is whether it can actually become the 'only game in town'. The year 2004 constitutes an important year for answering such a question. For Indonesia, 2004 constitutes the year of elections. On 5 April, Indonesia held parliamentary elections at national, provincial and district levels. On 5 July, Indonesians once again cast their votes in the first direct presidential election. As none of the five candidates received a majority vote, the second round of the presidential election was held on 20 September, and Susilo Bambang Yudhoyono emerged as the victor to become the first democratically elected president of Indonesia in a direct election. After the first democratic election in 1999 which signified the beginning of the country's transition towards democracy, the 2004 general elections have been seen to mark the beginning of democratic consolidation.[27] Indeed, while some enormous problems remain, there have been developments to suggest that such expectation is not without ground.

The 2004 general elections served as the defining moment for Indonesian democracy. In organising the election, Indonesia managed to complete a long and difficult political process with immense logistical and political challenges. For the parliamentary election on 5 April, the main task for the General Election Commission (KPU) was to administer the elections in almost 2,000 electoral districts for the DPR, the House of Regional People's Representatives (both at provincial and district/city levels) and the Regional Representative Council (DPD). There were about 450,000 candidates from 24 political parties, and 946 candidates for the DPD, competing for the votes of 148,000,369 registered voters.[28] For the presidential election, the KPU is tasked to manage a two-round majoritarian system for the more than 152 million registered voters.

Despite enormous logistical and technical problems, the elections were generally free and fair. In this context, there are seven developments that warrant a closer look. First, contrary to what many foreign pundits expected to be violence-prone elections, the elections demonstrated the readiness of Indonesians to move towards democracy. Although imperfect, the process was smooth and relatively trouble-free. Cases of elections-related violence were few and did not escalate into serious conflicts.[29] When disputes occurred regarding the results, all participants in the elections agreed to refer the cases to the newly established Constitutional Court, which in turn adjudicated the disputes. The maturity of Indonesians in exercising democracy was clearly proven when the decisions by the court were accepted by all parties to the disputes. Indeed, the first and the most important aspect of the 2004 elections in Indonesia has been the willingness of all participants to abide by the rules of the game, and resolve conflicts and disputes through the court of law.

Second, while the majority of voters still claimed emotional allegiance to specific parties and individual leaders, the 2004 elections marked the emergence of a new pattern of voting behaviour among Indonesians. The results of the parliamentary elections, for example, demonstrated the growing number of autonomous voters who played an important role as a block of 'swing voters'. Two new political parties, the Islamic-based Justice Prosperity Party (PKS) and the Democratic Party (PD) of General (Rtd) Susilo Bambang Yudhoyono (SBY), owe their surprising rise to this fact. Most of these swing votes came from the middle class in urban areas. Given this new phenomena, political parties can no longer assume that they can continue to draw support from traditional constituencies based on *aliran* (ideological streams in the society). The voters have now demonstrated that they are able to exercise rewards and mete out punishment in the elections.

Third, as demonstrated by the first round of the presidential elections, Indonesia is witnessing the breakdown of patrimonial and traditional authority in politics. Despite their affiliation with mass-based organisations such as the Nahdlatul Ulama (NU) and Muhammadiyah, a significant number of voters no longer feel compelled and obliged to vote for the candidates whom their parent organisations and leaders officially endorsed. Despite the call by Abdurrahman Wahid that members of the NU should vote for General (Rtd) Wiranto-Salahudin Wahid, it was the Susilo Bambang Yudhoyono–Jusuf Kalla team who won the elections in the NU stronghold of East Java. It is estimated that despite the official endorsement by Muhammadiyah for candidate Amien Rais, less than 70 per cent of Muhammadiyah members voted for Rais. The victory of SBY in the second round was made possible by his ability to attract votes from both Islamic and secular constituencies, evidencing the breakdown of religious or ideological barriers in the Indonesian polity.

Fourth, the 2004 elections reinforced the non-theocratic nature of Indonesian politics. When the combined votes received by Islamic political parties reached only 20.5 per cent, it was clear that theocratic politics remained an unattractive option for the majority of voters. Meanwhile, secular parties such as Golkar, PDI-P, PD and other smaller parties received more than 60 per cent of the vote; 79.3 per cent if the inclusive Islamic-based parties such as PAN and PKB are included. The degree of pluralism within the Indonesian Islamic community makes it impossible for any one Islamic party to claim itself to be the only Muslim party representing Muslim interests. Indeed, Islamic political forces in Indonesia have always had difficulty in translating the religious credo of 'the one community' (*ummatan wahidah*) into reality. Nevertheless, they always try to unite even though such attempts have always ended in failure.[30]

Fifth, the role of the media and civil society organisations was instrumental throughout the election process. The media became the most important instrument through which candidates tried to persuade voters. Mass rallies and public gatherings, while still important, were no longer as dominant as they had been in the 1999 elections. The media also played an instrumental role as a watchdog that exposed and constrained the practices of money politics in the elections. Meanwhile, civil society organisations played a key role in conducting voter education, especially in explaining the complexity of the new election system to the voters in rural areas, and in demonstrating the importance of participating in the elections. In other words, the 2004 general elections were conducted under the close scrutiny of the population.

Sixth, the first direct presidential election also forced candidates to begin devising their campaign by taking into account real issues closer to the people's day-to-day interests. While the majority of voters remained uninterested in policy issues, the growing size of the middle class in urban areas – who increasingly cast their votes based on rational consideration of candidates' platforms – ensured that policy issues become important elements in future campaigns. Unlike the 1999 general elections, candidates in 2004 had also begun to pay more attention to public opinion. This, in effect, required those who run for public offices to take into account people's aspirations, even though post-election developments suggest that this is still limited to campaign-related purposes. Nevertheless, it does point to a very important aspect of democracy: people's views matter.

Seventh, the 2004 general elections also confirmed the military's commitment not to interfere in the electoral process, and thus in politics. The elections brought an end to military representation in the parliament. During the campaign, all presidential candidates promised that military reform would continue once they were elected, and that the principle of civilian supremacy would be upheld. However, it should be noted that the process of reforming the military in Indonesia is far from complete. In fact, there are some grounds to say that the current process of military reform has proceeded at a somewhat much slower pace as compared to during 1999–2002. Some even contend that military reform in Indonesia has stalled, with the problems of the military's involvement in business and military impunity remaining unresolved. This, however, does not negate the fact that the military's role in politics has waned further since 2004. This is confirmed by the fact that many candidates with a military background were defeated in local elections across the country.

Beyond the 2004 elections, there has been further institutionalisation of democratic politics. The majority of Indonesian elites and population has now accepted elections as the only instrument of political succession. Political parties, despite their weaknesses, continue to play a role as a vehicle for power competition and political participation. Violent conflicts that have beset the transition period are now either settling down or have been resolved. Of these, the arrival of peace in Aceh constitutes the most important achievement of the SBY Government. Both the government and the GAM rebels had finally resorted to a peaceful means of conflict resolution. On 15 August 2005, both sides agreed to end the four decades of hostility and violence in the province. Peace has reigned for four years in the province, and democratic politics – which has brought a former rebel leader into the province to become its governor – has increasingly become an accepted mechanism for resolving power contests. In other words, the preference to settle differences and disputes through democratic means has begun to take precedence over the use of force.

Conclusion

Most developments discussed earlier suggest that the year 2004 and beyond constituted the beginning of the end of transition, and paved the way for Indonesia to begin a democratic consolidation phase. However, a number of problems – such as economic hardship, a weak judicial system and law enforcement, a corrupt bureaucracy, incomplete military reform, religious radicalism and intolerance, and now terrorism – will continue to pose challenges to Indonesia's struggle in consolidating its democracy. The ability of Indonesia to address those problems will determine the quality of democracy in the country. In other words, a democracy, to be called 'consolidated', requires not only the capacity of the state to enforce the law and deliver policies[31] but also the presence of a strong democratic culture within society.[32] Indeed, even as its term draws to an end, the democratically elected Yudhoyono Government continues to struggle to address those problems.

Those problems, however, do not yet pose immediate threats to the continuity of democracy in Indonesia. On the contrary, there are signs that the process of democratic consolidation will continue to take place. In fact, recent developments in some areas have been very encouraging. In the anti-corruption drive, for example, progress has been more evident over the last few years. Senior government officials have been prosecuted, including the father of President Yudhoyono's son-in-law. Several members of parliament have been arrested and tried on charges of corruption. The military, previously resisting the attempt by the Parliament to pass a law requiring that military personnel committing common criminal offence be tried in public courts, has now agreed to such a provision. Significant progress has been made in the process of transferring all military business to the government, even though the involvement of rogue military personnel in illegal business activities remains a serious problem.

In the run-up to the July 2009 presidential elections, Indonesia has demonstrated a tremendous ability and resilience to withstand the challenges to its young democracy. However, more measures to consolidate democracy need to be implemented. The ability of the government to address these problems would provide a stronger ground for reducing and eradicating anti-democratic behaviour, encouraging greater public acceptance and support of democracy, and strengthening the socio-economic and institutional bases of democracy. Indonesia's brief record in preserving democratisation amid turbulent economic and political transition since 1998 suggests that there are some grounds to expect that the country would continue to be resilient in facing the threat of democratic regression or backsliding.

Notes

1 Muhammadiyah is the second largest mass-based Muslim organisation in Indonesia with a membership of approximately 30 million. Amien Rais, its chairman, emerged as the most vocal critic of the Suharto regime by early 1998.
2 See William Liddle, 'Indonesia's Unexpected Failure of Leadership,' in Adam Schwarz and Jonathan Paris (eds), *The Politics of Post-Suharto Indonesia*, New York: Council on Foreign Relations, 1999.

3 Benyamin Smith, "'If I Do These Things, They Will Throw Me Out": Economic Reform and the Collapse of Indonesia's New Order', *Journal of International Affairs*, vol. 57 no. 1, Fall 2003.

4 See, for example, Tim Huxley, *Disintegrating Indonesia: Implications for Regional Security*, Adelphi Paper No. 349, London: IISS, 2002, p. 14.

5 Mark T. Berger, 'Old State and New Empire in Indonesia: Debating the Rise and Decline of Suharto's New Order', *Third World Quarterly*, vol. 18, no. 2, June 1997, p. 346.

6 Rizal Sukma, 'The Security Problematique of Globalisation and Development: The Case of Indonesia', in David Dewitt and Carolina Hernandez (eds), *Development and Security*, London: Ashgate, 2003, pp. 233–58.

7 Richard Robison and Vedi R. Hadiz, *Reorganising Power in Indonesia: The Politics of Oligarchy in an Age of Markets*, London: RoutledgeCurzon, 2004, p. 165.

8 Edward Aspinall, *Opposing Suharto: Compromise, Resistance, and Regime Change in Indonesia*, Stanford: Stanford University Press, 2005, p. 269.

9 Marcus Mietzner, 'The Politics of Military Reform in Post-Suharto Indonesia: Elite Conflict, Nationalism, and Institutional Resistance,' *Policy Studies* 23, Washington DC: East-West Center, 2006, p. 5.

10 Ibid., p. 7.

11 Robison and Hadiz, *Reorganising Power in Indonesia*, p. 173.

12 Ibid.

13 Samuel P. Huntington, *The Third Wave: Democratisation in the Late Twentieth Century*, Norman: University of Oklahoma Press, 1991, p. 114.

14 Graeme Gill, *The Dynamics of Democratisation: Elites, Civil Society and Transition Process*, London: Macmillan Press, 2000, p. 69.

15 Andreas Schedler, 'Measuring Democratic Consolidation', *Studies in Comparative International Development*, vol. 36, no. 1, Spring 2001.

16 For the 1999 general elections, the membership of the election commission comprised government officials and representatives of political parties. For the 2004 general elections, however, members of the commission were appointed from outside of the government, and political parties by the Parliament. So, the election commission for the 2004 general elections was considered more independent than the one in 1999.

17 Koichi Kawamura, 'Political reform in the Post-Suharto Era', in Yuri Sato (ed.), *Indonesia Entering a New Era: Abdurrahman Wahid Government and its Challenge*, Tokyo: IDE-JETRO, March 2000, p. 16.

18 For a comprehensive analysis of communal violence in these areas, see Jacques Bertrand, *Nationalism and Ethnic Conflict in Indonesia*, Cambridge: Cambridge University Press, 2004. See also Rizal Sukma, 'Ethnic Conflict in Indonesia: Causes and the Quest for Solution', in Kusuma Snitwongse and W. Scott Thompson (eds), *Ethnic Conflict in Southeast Asia*, Singapore: Institute of Southeast Asian Studies, 2005.

19 For a comprehensive analysis on security and military operation in Aceh under Megawati, see Rizal Sukma, 'Security Operations in Aceh: Goals, Consequences, and Lessons', *Policy Studies* 3, Washington DC: East-West Center, 2004.

20 Thomas Carothers, 'The Rule of Law Revival', *Foreign Affairs*, vol. 77, no. 2, March–April 1998, p. 100.

21 Schedler, 'Measuring Democratic Consolidation', p. 72.

22 Ibid., p. 75.

23 *The Jakarta Post*, 'Public still positive about govt: Survey', 19 June 2006.

24 See M. Zulfan Tadjoeddin and Mansoob Murshed, 'Socioeconomic Determinants of Everyday Violence in Indonesia: An Empirical Investigation of Javanese Districts, 1994–2003', available online at http://www.prio.no/files/manual-import/neps/tindbergen2006papers/Murshed_amsterdam_2006.pdf. Accessed on 6 October 2008.

25 Schedler, 'Measuring Democratic Consolidation', p. 80.

26 Scott Mainwaring, 'Democratic Survivability in Latin America,' in Howard Handelman

and Mark A. Tessler (eds), *Democracy and its Limits: Lessons from Asia, Latin America, and the Middle East*, Notre Dame: University of Notre Dame Press, 2000, p. 60.

27 See, for example, Edward Aspinall, 'Politics: Indonesia's Year of Elections and the End of the Political Transition', in Budy P. Resosudarmo (ed.), *The Politics and Economics of Indonesia's Natural Resources*, Singapore: Institute of Southeast Asian Studies, 2005.

28 Leonard C. Sebastian, 'The Paradox of Indonesian Democracy', *Contemporary Southeast Asia*, vol. 26, no. 2, August 2004, p. 261; and Kevin Evans, 'Hasil Pemilihan Umum 2004' [The Results of 2004 Elections], *The Indonesian Quarterly*, vol. 33, no. 2, June 2004, p. 200.

29 For a comprehensive analysis about elections and violence in Indonesia, see Patrick Barron, Melina Nathan and Bridget Welsh, 'Consolidating Indonesia's Democracy: Conflicts, Institutions, and the "Local" in the 2004 Legislative Elections', *Conflict Prevention and Reconstruction Working Paper* No. 31, December 2005, Washington DC: World Bank.

30 Jalaludin Rakhmat, 'Islam di Indonesia: Masalah Definisi' [Islam in Indonesia: The Problem of Definition], in M. Amien Rais (ed.), *Islam di Indonesia: Suatu Ikhtiar Mengaca Diri* [Islam in Indonesia: An Attempt at Self Reflection], Jakarta: Rajawali, 1986, p. 38.

31 Jusuf Wanandi, 'Indonesia: A Failed State?' *The Washington Quarterly*, vol. 25, no. 3, Summer 2002, p. 135.

32 International IDEA, *Democratisation in Indonesia: An Assessment*, Stockholm: IDEA, 2000, p. 13.

3 Confusing democracies

Diagnosing Thailand's democratic crisis, 2001–8

Pavin Chachavalpongpun

Introduction

Thailand was transformed from an absolute monarchy into a constitutional monarchy in 1932. In the 70 years since, democratisation in Thailand has not been an effortless process, often hampered by periodic military coups and regular returns by power-hungry military regimes. In this military-dominated political structure, especially throughout the Cold War, Thailand continued to see itself as a proud, modern democratic nation. Such a perception could only possibly be constructed because Thailand aligned itself with the Free World. In reality, politics was very much steered by the despots of the day. This condition, as many academics argue, gives rise to a vital question: Is Thai democracy an imaginary exercise for the ruling elite and the general population alike? The question became more pertinent after the first elected government of General Chatichai Choonhavan came into power in 1988. For a moment, the Thais believed that they finally had a chance to taste true democracy, only this was to be taken away in another military coup after Choonhavan's government was accused of widespread corruption. Following a bloody crackdown on protestors in May 1992 and the subsequent fall of the military government, fresh elections in late 1992 and a period of democratic consolidation thereafter seemed to culminate during the governments of Thaksin Shinawatra from 2001–6. Under his rule, however, democracy underwent a series of terminological surgeries, being discursively defined to serve certain benefits of the ruling leaders. It eventually took a sharp turn when the most popular democratic regime in Thai history was toppled in another military coup in September 2006. This period onwards marks the most critical juncture of Thai democracy as the country slipped into a political coma as a result of vicious proxy wars between the pro- and the anti-Thaksin forces.

The so-called democratic movement led by the People's Alliance for Democracy (PAD) came into the picture in 2005 when it first launched an anti-Thaksin campaign, accusing him of abusing political power and exploiting democracy for his own interests. Although Thaksin was forced to retreat from Thai politics, The PAD has continued its crusade against the government of Samak Sundaravej, leader of the People's Power Party (PPP), on the ground that he worked as an agent of Thaksin. Samak and his party won a majority vote in the election of December 2007 and formed a PPP-led Government in February 2008. The tension escalated when

The PAD seized the House of Government in August 2008 and has since remained in the compound despite arrest warrants being issued for the core PAD leaders. After Samak was stripped of the premiership, allegedly for receiving small payments for his television cooking programmes, the PPP nominated Somchai Wongsawat, Thaksin's brother-in-law, to head a new government. Somchai immediately became a target of The PAD for his connection with the Shinawatra family. The situation turned intense on 7 October 2008 when the police violently clashed with The PAD protesters who had been camping outside the parliament in order to obstruct the delivery of national policies of the Somchai Government. The brutal confrontations led to two people being killed and over 400 others being injured. But the sacrifice of lives did not terminate Thailand's political violence. On 25 November 2008, over a week after the funeral of the king's sister, Princess Galyani Vadhana, The PAD launched what they claimed to be their 'final battle' when it seized Bangkok's Suvarnabhumi Airport and the old Don Mueang Airport, demanding an immediate resignation of Prime Minister Somchai. The seizure of the Thai airports cost the country enormous economic loss. Meanwhile, the political violence has become a fact of life. Bomb blasts have taken place at many spots near The PAD's demonstration camps. In a seemingly final twist, the Constitutional Court, on 2 December, dissolved the PPP and banned Prime Minister Somchai from politics for five years – this forced the premier to step down from power. While the court's verdict fulfilled the objective of The PAD, the pro-government protesters expressed their fury. The possibility of this leading to a fresh round of bloodshed became apparent. In the midst of an anarchic atmosphere, the rumour of a new military coup surfaced.[1]

What has happened to Thai democracy? What are the critical hurdles to the democratic development of a country whose name means 'the land of the free'? This chapter diagnoses the condition of Thai democracy and analyses its development path from the assumption of power of Thaksin in 2001 through to the military's seizure of power in 2006, the breakout of violence between The PAD and the police in October 2008, The PAD's seizure of Thai airports on 25 November, and the dissolution of the PPP on 2 December. It also discusses the emergence of non-state actors in Thai politics, particularly the role of The PAD, its political dogma and tactics. The central question highlighted in this chapter is: Why has the democratic consolidation been unsuccessful even while Thailand seemed to practice the rules of democracy, including attaching importance to majority vote and free and fair elections? The study employs Andreas Schedler's theoretical framework in assessing the state of Thai democracy based on the observations of Thai political behaviour, attitudes and structures, while pointing out factors that have led to the unsuccessful consolidation of democracy.[2] As the title suggests, 'confusing democracies' connotes that there is more than one meaning of democracy among those who have claimed to be champions of Thai democracy. Different interpretations of democracy derive from the way in which political actors have perceived their power position in politics. Schedler's measurement of democratic consolidation sits perfectly in the Thai case where struggle for power among various political players within the much-exploited democratic domain has emerged as the root cause of the current crisis.

Rocky path to democracy

Although the departure point of this study begins in 2001 under the Thaksin Administration, it is essential to briefly recount the incident of 1992, an upheaval known as 'Black May', when a series of violent confrontations erupted between army units and protesters in Bangkok in which hundreds were killed, to understand the political order in the pre-Thaksin period. The army strongman, General Suchinda Kraprayoon, also leader of the 1991 coup that removed the government of Chatichai from power, stepped in as premier after Narong Wongwan, leader of the winning party, Samakkhitham, in the March 1992 election, was forced to withdraw from the top position due to his alleged connection with narcotics trafficking. Suchinda's self-proclaimed premiership provoked thousands of pro-democracy protesters, led by the one-time Young Turk member who was at the time leader of the Palang Dhamma Party. The confrontations ended tragically, and for many Thais, this brief period of undemocratic rule served as a sacrifice of democracy.[3] King Bhumibol Adulyadej intervened, fearing that the situation could spin out of control like confrontations at Thammasat University in 1976 had done previously.

The coup of 1991 and the Black May incident explained the existence of certain obstacles in the consolidation of Thai democracy. First, the military remained the major source of destabilisation of democratic elements and was in no way ready to surrender political power for the sake of the country's democratisation.[4] It also defied domestic and international conditions, deemed highly conducive to the materialisation of democracy at the time. Internally, the political transition from an appointed government under General Prem Tinsulanond, which had reigned for eight years, to an elected one under Chatichai signified that the country was on the road to democracy. In the global context, the beginning of the 1990s saw the end of the Cold War and the emergence of a capitalist force that came to conquer almost every part of the world, including Southeast Asia. Francis Fukuyama suggested in his book, *The End of History and the Last Man*, released in 1992, that the advent of Western liberal democracy may signal the end point of mankind's ideological evolution and the final form of human government.[5] The military, having long been a traditional, dominant factor in politics, openly contested the trend toward democratisation to maintain its own political space. The geo-political reality in the post-Cold War, with the communist threat vanishing, was at first glace a fundamental impediment for the military in claiming its hegemonic role in the country's policy making and to keep its hand in politics. The fact that Chatichai implemented the policy of transforming Indochina from battlefield into marketplace strongly hinted that the military had to return to the barracks. However, his elected government, despite extolling democracy, was largely sullied by rampant money politics and corruption, therefore allowing the military to challenge the quality of a democratic regime which, as it argued, must not be judged purely on the basis of elections and majority vote. Undemocratic behaviour like money politics and corruption served to delegitimise Chatichai's democratic regime. The military has since claimed to represent a moral compass with a mission to clean up bad (democratic) governments.

Second, the role of the Thai monarchy has remained immeasurable, albeit contentious, in the discourse of Thai democracy. Royal intervention had been called upon several times in the past as it was considered by the public as a quick-fix tool to unlock political crises. But it has recently become a subject of serious debate as to whether it has deepened the struggle to expand Thailand's democratic space. Giles Ji Ungpakorn of Chulalongkorn University wrote:

> The monarchy in Thailand can cope with either a democratic regime or a military junta. As an instrument of modern ruling class power, the king is neither a victim nor the most powerful man in society. On occasions, the king has supported modern democratic methods. Yet, he has also supported coups and goes along with the myths of ancient powers.[6]

Despite functioning as an extra-constitutional power to resolve bloodletting and confrontations in the past, royal intervention has served to belittle democratic institutions in their process of providing political solutions to crises.

After Black May, the military was depicted as 'democracy's slaughterer', and began to reduce its role in politics gradually, albeit not completely, owing to intense pressure from the Thai public. But subsequent democratic regimes were weak, mainly because they were lacking good governance, transparent public administration and policy making that was efficient and accountable. In 1997, there was an attempt to put forward political reforms among ruling elites through the amendment of the constitution, not only in response to the idea of greater democratisation, but also to the financial crisis that had hit Thailand and other countries in the region. Thailand urgently needed to reconstruct its economy and to rebuild foreign investors' confidence. In doing so, the country had to be able to demonstrate that it promoted political reforms, that the government could implement coherent economic policy, and that its politics possessed a high degree of stability.[7] Thailand took a big step forward in the process of democratic reforms with the events of 1997, and seemed to be well on its way to democratic consolidation. The 1997 constitution was extolled as one of the most liberalised charters; in that it seriously addressed electoral reform and established new bodies to check and oversee corruption and abuse of the political process.[8] The Chuan Leekpai Government (1997–2001), in spite of its overt affection for democracy, had to step down after numerous allegations of corruption were pressed against some members of the ruling Democrat Party. The 2001 election that installed Thaksin in power heralded a new dawn of the country's democratic consolidation. His party, Thai Rak Thai (TRT), won the election and formed a government with strong support at the grassroots level. In adopting Samuel Valenzuela's definition, 'Consolidation of democracy is generally taken to mean a system that is unlikely to break down, that is, we can expect it to last well into the future',[9] one can argue that the efforts at democratic consolidation in Thailand seemed to have been complete in the era of Thaksin regime.

The Peron of Thailand

Gwynne Dyer called Thaksin, 'Juan Peron of Thailand', since he used his power to shift wealth and power systematically from the rich to the poor. Like a latter-day

Peron, Dyer argued, Thaksin made decisive changes in government spending patterns through his famous populist programmes, ranging from debt relief, cheap loans, improved health care and other services that were not previously part of the currency of Thai politics. Certainly this is hardly against the norm in other democratic countries, but in Thailand, Thaksin infuriated the traditional political elite and their mostly urban, middle-class supporters. The peasants, instead of obediently voting for the traditional rural allies of the urban elite, were voting for Thaksin and their own economic interest.[10] For Thaksin, he considered himself a true democrat, having been elected prime minister in 2001, 2005, 2006, promoting capitalist agendas in order to lift the rural poor out of poverty, and educating them about the need to go to the polls to elect their representatives. Thaksin propagated his effort as 'democratising Thai politics'. During his interview in New York in September 2006, when asked to clarify his famous statement 'democracy is not an end in itself, but a means', Thaksin replied:

> You know, sometime you think you understand democracy, you really don't. You have to think about the people. Democracy for what? For the people. If your democratic system is not about bringing happiness to the people, it is no use. I have the people at the center. We do everything for the people. . . . Democratic election process must not be compromised by those who do not like its outcomes. When the people have spoken through elections where – which are judged truly democratic, the people's will must carry the day and must not be compromised by demonstrations in the street. If this were to happen, what can we expect to happen to Asia's democratic future?[11]

Behind the scenes, Thaksin's so-called democratisation was designed to diminish the power of the military. Unlike his predecessors, Thaksin adopted a hard-nosed approach in retrenching the military's role in politics, taking away sources of its prestige such as by appointing his own cousin, General Chaiyasit Shinawatra, as commander-in-chief (2003–4), and spurring on friction between the military and the police especially in the context of competing for power in managing the conflict in the south. Thaksin wrote off the military's reputation as an important enforcer of stability in the past, while elevating himself to become the country's sole source of stability, prosperity and wealth. A growing sense of resentment was felt within the military not only because of Thaksin's role in the demilitarisation of politics, but also some of his policies that were disapproved by the military. For instance, whereas the Thaksin Government forged cosy economic relations with Myanmar, the military, especially in the north, was more concerned with the way the politicians in Bangkok were sidelining other issues of more importance, such as flows of refugees, illegal migrants, drugs trafficking and spread of infectious diseases.[12]

More importantly, what Thaksin also did was to blatantly challenge the royal institution, a traditional source of political power. Despite staying above politics, the Thai monarch has been recognised as holding moral authority in the political domain and therefore remained an influential figure in the country's political landscape. Thaksin was ambitious and abrasive in shifting this old political structure, which he branded as one of the obstacles to developing a true democracy. The battle to attain the ultimate political power was evident in the rural areas where Thaksin successfully won the hearts and minds of the poor with his effective populist programmes. For decades, the poor villagers had relied heavily on the benevolence of the royal family, whose members initiated a myriad of development projects to help uplift their living standard. Thaksin made them realise that the new breed of politicians, like himself, could also bring about a better life in a more tangible and substantial way. The legacy of Thaksin, built in less than a decade, is powerful and has become a subject of nostalgia among those who gained direct benefits from his development programmes.

However, his version of democracy was widely contested as artificial, self-serving and indeed, very authoritarian in its essence. The numerous allegations that surfaced against Thaksin – such as those of corrupt practices, his exploitation of state power to augment personal interests and his exercise of state censorship against the media – seemed to imply that Thai democracy was not really in progression, but rather regression.[13] Thaksin's arbitrary definition of democracy failed to explain his own undemocratic behaviour. A strong government eventually delivered a weak democracy in which political leaders neglected the very fundamental principles of good governance, transparency and accountability. Thaksin's stable democratic regime did not necessarily reflect a democratic quality. First, Thaksin might seem to have engaged in the promotion of democratic culture, but only nominally and selectively in a sense that, for him, 'only the ballot box really counted'. Second, during the Thaksin period, democratic procedures and institutions were bypassed as a result of Thaksin's own assertion, 'think out of the box'. But the boundary of this assertion was never clearly defined, thus, in many ways, permitting political leaders to transcend the realm of legality and decency to get things done.[14] Third, institutionalisation reached a near moribund point in this particular era, reflected through the existence of money politics and corruption, and the absence of strong opposition parties and a vibrant civil society.

It can be said that Thaksin fell into the trap of his own ingenuity. Adored by the poor, Thaksin soon became the target of the old power in Bangkok who exploited his obscure discourse of democracy to remove him. Urban middle class, seen as supporters of the old establishment, began to rally against the Thaksin Government for tilting toward authoritarianism. But his undemocratic outlook was not the only reason behind the rejection of his regime. The old establishment, comprising the royalists, the military, well-educated Bangkokians and parts of the business community, perceived Thaksin's rise to power as a threat to their own power position. Hence, the anti-Thaksin campaign endorsed by the old establishment was never designed to save the democracy that had been tarnished in the hands of Thaksin. It was instead launched to safeguard the old political structure in which the old establishment had enjoyed power for many decades before Thaksin came along.

The coup of 2006

The PAD, widely known as the front army of the old establishment, spearheaded the scheme of deposing Thaksin's elected government for undemocratic

behaviour. Sondhi Limthongkul, leader of The PAD, is a media tycoon and a for-
mer ally of Thaksin before they fell out. The mission to bring down the Thaksin
Government, therefore, not only served to maintain the old structure of power, but
also served as a spectacle of a personal vendetta between the two individuals. The
PAD, establishing itself as a powerful extra-constitutional actor, began its cam-
paign against the Thaksin regime in 2005. The PAD accused the Thaksin
Government of lacking in legitimacy to govern.[15] Being under extreme pressure,
Thaksin dissolved parliament and called a snap election on 2 April 2006. The
PAD's solid backing from the authoritative old establishment helps enlighten why
Thaksin, despite holding a majority rule, had to resort to the dissolution of parliament as a political exit. It also helps explain the condition of Thai democracy in
which an extra-constitutional element has effectively overpowered an elected government, thus interrupting the consolidation process of a democratic system. The
PAD was also given more political weight against the TRT Government after the
opposition – the Democrat Party – boycotted the April election, prompting Thaksin
to resign from the premiership two days after the election. Here, the Democrat Party
was also playing a risky political game where it obviously endorsed The PAD so as
to attain its own political upper-hand. In painting a justifiable image the Democrat
Party leader, Abhisit Vejjajiva, said, 'There is no way out of the crisis unless the
prime minister accepts that the key part of the problem is his own legitimacy'.[16] To
prove that his mandate to rule was still strong, Thaksin, as a caretaker prime minister, called for another election, supposedly to be held on 15 October 2006. Thaksin
was confident that his supporters in the rural regions would render their votes for
the TRT once again.

On 19 September 2006, while Thaksin was in New York attending the United
Nations General Assembly, the military staged the 18th military coup since the
change of political regime from absolute monarchy to constitutional monarchy in
1932. The coup-makers immediately defended their actions as legitimate, stating
that Thaksin was creating an unprecedented rift in society, and was guilty of corruption, nepotism, interfering with independent agencies and insulting the king.[17]
Thitinan Pongsudhirak argued that the coup was in fact due to conflicts between
Thaksin and King Bhumibol Adulyadej.[18] Early in 2006, Thaksin declared on his
weekly radio programme that he would be happy to step down from the premiership
'if the King whispers in his ear' – the statement infuriated royalists who pointed the
finger at Thaksin for treating the monarch disrespectfully and committing acts bor-
dering on *lése majesté*.[19]

General Sondhi Boonyaratglin, leader of the coup, defended his seizure of power
as the military's duty to sustain democracy and promised to return power to an
elected government soon after the political order was restored. Exactly what kind
of democracy the military had in mind was highly ambiguous. The revisit of the
military rule engendered widespread concerns among Western governments, not
because they believed that Thailand could be heading toward bloody confrontations as seen in the 1976 incident. Instead, they were worried that the fact that the
coup was widely supported by the vast middle-class populace seemed to suggest
that part of the Thai understanding of democracy was at odds with that of the

Western world.[20] At a deeper level, the military also had to work under intense pressure from The PAD who conspired to get rid of Thaksin 'hard and fast' before he further challenged the power of the old elites. It was reported that General Prem pulled the strings behind the military coup, purportedly because he believed that Thaksin was increasingly becoming a threat to the throne.[21] For the realists, Prem's decision could have derived from his own power insecurity. As a principal guard of the *ancient regime*, Prem could have been aware that the diminishing power of the royal institution, as a result of Thaksin's growing political strength, could have meant his own diminishing power too.

As the struggle for power has become a natural state of Thai politics, Thaksin's elected government, especially in the second term, was seriously destabilised by the reassertion of the old establishment's power with the backup of the military and The PAD. Thaksin's political enemies, in working under the pretext of saving democracy, pursued an anti-capitalist agenda, while accusing Thaksin of taking advantage of the poor in order to sustain his grip on power. Warsame Galaydh argued that this struggle for power stemmed from the fact that Thaksin made the mistake of expanding upon his personal wealth and strengthening his party by limiting the power of other political factions.[22] Galaydh implicitly suggested that the old establishment was one of the political factions. But the old establishment was not Thaksin's democratic counterpart. In any case, it represented a dangerous subversive force that aimed at defying democratic rules. The military coup of September 2006 was believed to have been endorsed by the monarch, thus signalling the real political order that has very much been dominated by an extra-constitutional actor.[23]

The role of the king in Thai politics is immense and inexorable. In June 2006, Thaksin sent a personal letter to US President George W. Bush, lamenting the undemocratic situation in his home country. He said that

> There has been a threat to democracy in Thailand since early this year. Key democratic institutions, such as elections and their observance of Constitutional limitation on government, have been repeatedly undermined by interest that depend on creating chaos and mounting street demonstrations in Bangkok as a means to acquire political power that they cannot gain through winning elections. Having failed to provoke violence and disorder, my opponents are now attempting various extra Constitutional tactics to co-opt the will of the people.[24]

Critical studies on the role of the Thai king are limited due to the stiff punishment for those who are tempted to damage the dignity of the royal family. The crime of injury to the royalty, *lése majesté*, has been widely employed by various political factions to demoralise their opponents. They accused each other of being disloyal to the king, who is regarded as a symbol of political correctness, in spite of the fact that he is above the political fray. *Lése majesté* is defined by Article 112 of the Thai Criminal Code, which states that defamatory, insulting or threatening comments about the king, queen and regent are punishable by 3 to 15 years in prison. Over the years, *lése majesté* has conveniently become a political weapon used to eliminate any non-conventional views or opinions in society. Thaksin was the first in the current political tug-of-war to be condemned for challenging the institution of royalty. The leaders of previous military regimes justified the coup against Thaksin's elected government based on their need to protect the monarchy from Thaksin's 'arrogance of power'. He was considered to have committed *lése majesté* and therefore deserved to be ousted.[25] The PAD has been exploiting this law to achieve political gains at the expense of its political enemies.

Dyer summed up the precarious condition of Thai democracy as being under attack by non-state, non-democratic actors. Dyer said:

> It's too bad that a figure as divisive as Thaksin was the first to try to open Thai politics up to the concerns of the poor, but a less flamboyant and abrasive politician would probably never have tried. What remains to be seen is whether The PAD can shut the door again, and for how long.[26]

Thaksin might have been half-hearted in his attempt to consolidate Thai democracy, but to a certain extent he opened the door for power contestation within the democratic realm. The PAD has striven to close this contested space, thus purposefully disrupting the process of democratisation.

The final showdown

The rise of the anti-military, pro-democracy forces in the event of Black May was made possible because of the expansion of a well-educated urban middle class that sent out an important message that the military was no longer tenable in the face of increasing demands for democracy. Neil Englehart argued that the middle class protests in 1992 that ejected the junta put Thailand firmly on the path to democratic consolidation.[27] But why has this powerful segment of society fallen out of love with democracy and even acted to sabotage the elected governments of Thaksin, Samak and Somchai? The middle class urbanites of the capital, despite not representing the majority voice of the entire population, have long held a firm political influence, primarily because of Bangkok's domination of political power, finance and commerce. Bangkok is the engine of the country, contributing about 70 per cent of the national gross domestic product. It is also the seat of the government and the powerful monarchy – the key to control the entire country of 63 million. The Thais in general agree that the rural people voted in their leaders who were eventually brought down by the Bangkokians. The PAD has portrayed itself as spokesperson of the Bangkok middle class who stood up against dictators in democratic disguise. Little is known about how The PAD, as the voice of the Bangkok elite, has secured its own interests in getting rid of the Thaksin regime. Defending democracy does not seem to be on the PAD's real agenda even though its name seems to suggest its affiliation with democracy. This study will examine why The PAD, known for its aggressive campaign for democracy, has become one of the main sources of the failure of Thai democratic consolidation.

After the military government of General Surayud Chulanont stepped down and paved the way for the new round of elections in December 2007, Samak Sundaravej, a veteran politician and former Bangkok Governor, assumed the position of leader of a newly established PPP, a reincarnation of the TRT. Following the coup of September 2006, the Bangkok elite began its tactical revenge against Thaksin and his political loyalists. The Thai Constitutional Court disbanded the TRT for its election fraud and barred its 111 executive members, including Thaksin, from entering politics for the next five years. Chaturon Chaisaeng, leader of the TRT at the time said, 'We were not treated fairly. The ruling was made on the basis that those who seize power can decide what's right and wrong even if that power comes from the barrel of a gun'.[28] The Constitutional Court was extolled for its courage in prosecuting the top leaders who abused state power. In the past, top leaders acted as if they were above the law. However, academics were concerned that the Thai judiciary process could have also been manipulated and highly politicised by the Bangkok elite in condemning Thaksin.

Samak, during the campaign period, openly described himself as Thaksin's political nominee. He calculated that in working as an agent of Thaksin, he could be certain of winning votes from Thaksin's supporters at the grassroots level. Samak promised to resurrect Thaksin's populist programmes to help improve the lot of the poor. He even started the 'War on Drugs II' to curb the use of narcotics in the kingdom. The first War on Drugs was launched in 2003 during the Thaksin Administration, which was criticised for the state's heavy-handed measures against drug traffickers, through extra-judicial killings. More than 2,500 people had been killed under the initial campaign. The choice of Samak as a new leader was a little peculiar. Samak, well-known for his sharp tongue, was seen as a 'wild horse' that could challenge the military. Samak's immunity was due in part to his own past credentials as a staunch royalist and a virulent anti-communist; he comes from a family of royal courtiers. In October 1976, Samak, as Minister of Interior at the time, played a key role in stirring up a right-wing frenzy against a purported communist plot to seize power that resulted in the massacre of hundreds of Thais and the return of military rule.[29]

Samak and his PPP won a landslide election in December 2007 and formed a new government in February the next year, leaving the Democrat Party as the only opposition party. Could this be construed as another return to the consolidation of Thai democracy? In theory, the arrival of the Samak Government appeared to insinuate that Thai democratisation was back on track, with the people exercising their rights at the ballot box and democratic institutions being restored. Samak's personal pledge to amend the 2007 constitution, written by those appointed by the coup-makers, infuriated The PAD and the anti-Thaksin forces. Samak said, 'The current constitution is a political trap to destroy this government, so this constitution must be changed and I will propose to amend the constitution once parliament resumes next month.'[30] He believed that the constitution made it easy for political parties to be disbanded by court order, with the potential for creating a dangerous vacuum in the governance of the country. Samak's pro-democracy attitude won him political popularity among voters in the rural area. The fact that The PAD attempted to force the newly elected government out of power also made Samak a 'saint of democracy'. Peter Jenssen wrote, 'Ironically, the PAD's brinkmanship tactics and fuzzy politics have managed to make Samak, a right-wing politician notorious for his crude language and undemocratic methods, look good'. Kraisak Choonhavan, member of the Democrat Party and son of former Prime Minister Chatichai, added, 'It is unfortunate the way things have turned out, with Thaksin and Samak becoming known as the champions of Thai democracy'.[31]

The PAD, seeing Samak as Thaksin's surrogate, kicked off mass demonstrations on 25 May 2008, calling for the resignation of the prime minister. The situation, however, turned more intense on 26 August 2008 when PAD protesters stormed into the state-run television station and damaged government facilities. In the meantime, more than 10,000 PAD members marched into the House of Government and occupied the compound till 1 December. In both incidents, The PAD demonstrators exploited symbolism of the monarchy to justify their course of action. They wore yellow t-shirts, the colour of the king who was born on Monday (yellow is the colour of Monday). They also had in their hands portraits of the king while rummaging through the government's properties. The use of royal symbolism, consciously or otherwise, seemed to signal that the PAD's actions were carried out in the name of the palace. The Samak Government retaliated by requesting the court to issue arrest warrants for nine of the core members of The PAD, including Sondhi and Chamlong, on charges of treason, which could carry the maximum penalty of death.

Yet, at this point, Prime Minister Samak maintained his soft approach toward The PAD protesters, reportedly after he was advised by the king to be 'gentle' with them. Samak later confirmed, 'I was granted an audience with His Majesty the King. His Majesty asked me to enforce the law with extreme caution, to be soft and gentle. I beg all of you to understand and sympathise with me'.[32] His soft approach did not bear fruit. On 28 August, the number of protesters swelled to 40,000 inside the grounds of the House of Government. The fact that the military chief insisted on not getting his hands dirty in this vicious political game raised confidence and perhaps arrogance among PAD members. For example, The PAD exercised its authority by 'ordering' rail workers to stage a partial strike in which 80 trains drivers and mechanics at key rail junctions connecting central Thailand to the north, northeast and south, called in sick, disrupting at least 93 train lines and stranding thousands of passengers. Seventy-six cargo trains also ceased to function. Main airports in the South, Phuket, Krabi and Hat Yai, were shut down. Forty-three unions representing workers at state companies, including water, electricity, telephone and national airlines, threatened to stop services. This partial strike ended with a brief street fight between The PAD and the pro-government force, known as United Front of Democracy against Dictatorship (UDD), leaving one dead and over 40 others injured.[33]

Fearing that the confrontation could develop into a civil war, the government declared a State of Emergency on 2 September, allowing the military to take control of the situation, to police political activities and to suspend certain civil liberties. Meanwhile, the Samak Government had to attend to its own survival after the election commission called for the disbanding of the PPP over claims of vote-buying. The commission made the recommendation to the Office of the Attorney General, and if the prosecutors decide to take up the case, they could ask the Constitutional Court to disband the party and ban its leaders from politics for five years, reminiscent of what the TRT went through.

In a desperate attempt to find the solution to the political deadlock, Samak proposed a national referendum to be held one month later. The national referendum would be introduced with three simple questions: Should the government continue in office? Should The PAD continue or cease its protests? Should the PAD's proposal for 'New Politics', where future parliament should comprise 30 per cent elected and 70 per cent appointed members to revamp the electoral system, be accepted? Samak's idea of holding a national referendum was immediately criticised for further dividing Thai society. The opposition labelled it as 'unconstitutional' and as a means to buy time.[34] Samak's proposal of a national referendum was another attempt to prove his respect of democracy and the will of the people. It also revealed his strategy of engaging people at the grassroots level in this political process, as successfully implemented during the Thaksin era. The national referendum, however, was discarded following the forced resignation of Samak as prime minister. On 9 September, the Constitutional Court ruled that Samak violated Article 267 of the constitution by hosting commercial cooking shows on television while serving as prime minister. All members of his cabinet also had to step down. The PAD for once sensed victory in the 'war'.

In the wake of Samak's downfall, the Thai courts also tried former Prime Minister Thaksin and his wife, Khunying Pojaman, on several charges of corruption. In July 2008, Pojaman was convicted of tax evasion and sentenced to three years in prison. On 21 October 2008, an anti-corruption court also sentenced Thaksin, who is in exile in Britain, to two years in prison for conflict of interest in the purchase of a piece of land in Bangkok.[35] Thaksin, as well as members of the PPP, believed that the judicial system is highly politicised. He once wrote in an open letter from London, 'There is a continuation of dictatorship managing Thai politics, which is followed by interference in the justice system. These are my political enemies. They do not care about the rule of law, facts or internationally recognised due process'.[36] He confirmed this view after learning of his sentence, 'The case is politically motivated'.[37] The Thai judiciary system, having long been perceived as inactive and dominated by rich politicians who often acted with impunity, has repainted its image as more assertive and bold. In his birthday speech of 2006, the king called on judges to sort out a disputed parliamentary election, which was subsequently annulled by the courts. In a deeply polarised nation, however, a more 'muscular' role of judges also raises delicate questions over their political loyalties.[38] The sheer number of court cases against the PPP members has induced the thinking that the revolutionised judicial system could have been too politicised. Furthermore, the acquittal of treason charges of nine core members of PAD has convinced many that the judiciary was influenced by the anti-Thaksin Bangkok elite.

The battles in court and on the streets have intensified following the nomination of Somchai as a new prime minister. He was elected by PPP members to form a government. Somchai has had a long bureaucratic experience, including more than 20 years as a judge. He was a deputy prime minister and education minister in Samak's cabinet. PPP members agreed on his nomination mainly owing to his direct link with Thaksin. Somchai was married to Yaowapa, Thaksin's sister who is believed to hold the real power behind the government. Thaksin, impressed by his sister's talent, once said that if Yaowapa were his brother, she would have taken a ministerial post, and that if Yaowapa had not been banned from politics, it might be her turn now to be Thailand's first female prime minister.[39] By nominating Somchai as a new leader, the PPP party was certain that it would continue to gain strong support from its up-country voters. But the choice of Somchai did not help heal the political wounds. The PAD, with its mission to erase Thaksin's legacy, has renewed its campaign against the Somchai government, and this time, it flatly refused to accept anyone from the PPP as government leader.

On 6 October, PAD leader Sondhi ordered his loyalists to march to the parliament in an attempt to prevent the addressing of national policies of the Somchai Government's new cabinet. They used trucks to seal off the building. But the protest ended tragically when the police, at dawn of the next day, used tear gas to disperse The PAD members, resulting in two protesters being killed and hundreds being injured. The PAD immediately condemned Somchai for the murder of unarmed protesters and continued to call for his resignation. Queen Sirikit decided to attend the funeral of one of the victims. She was greeted by ecstatic anti-government protesters who hailed her rare appearance as a sign of support. Her daughter Princess Chulabhorn, Army Chief Anupong and senior members of the opposition party also turned out to pay their respects at the high-profile event, which took place as the government's woes mounted.[40]

While Prime Minister Somchai was travelling to Peru to attend the 16th Asia-Pacific Economic Cooperation Economic Leaders' Meeting from 22–23 November 2008, The PAD decided to further pressure him to resign by seizing Bangkok's Suvarnabhumi Airport, as well as the old Don Mueang Airport, causing vast economic losses to the country, mostly in the tourism industry and the export sector. The occupation of the two airports had completely paralysed the country, shutting it from the outside world. Foreign tourists and Thais alike expressed their disappointment in the way The PAD held the country hostage and on the government's inability to solve the crisis. Many foreign governments issued travel warnings for Thailand. The US, the UK and the European Union released statements urging anti-government protesters to vacate Bangkok's airports, saying that the rallies were inappropriate and preventing the free movement of peoples and goods. By physically shutting down the airports, The PAD had upped the stakes in Thailand's ongoing political polarisation. It had demonstrated the extent it would resort to in order to achieve its aims. In fact, The PAD had been bent on creating conditions of un-governability and then demanded the ouster of then-Prime Minister Somchai on grounds that Thailand had become ungovernable. Its tactics warped into a blatant street campaign of intimidation and fear, of coercion and force.[41] The un-governability of the political condition in Bangkok drove Somchai to retreat to his stronghold in Chiangmai, where a new base of command was established.

In the aftermath of the airport closure, Army Chief Anupong, on 26 November, suggested the government to dissolve the House, a move seen by the public as in favour of The PAD. In fact, General Anupong previously said that the Somchai Government must take responsibility for the clashes between The PAD and the police on 7 October:

> I am not saying this to pressure the government to resign, but it must take responsibility. No government can survive after the spilling of people's blood, because society can never accept this. There's no point in staying on when the country has already been damaged.[42]

The army chief's strong message signalled a rift between the military and the government. It also signalled that the military did not approve of the state's violent measures against The PAD demonstrators, but somehow felt more sympathetic towards The PAD, which, for many, only confirmed the military's support of the anti-government force. The rift does not only exist between the military and the government. The alignments of the police and the military have never been clearer. It is understandable since Thaksin is an ex-policeman who still has nurtured good connections with high-ranking police officers. In reaffirming this close link, the government refused to rely on the military in handling The PAD protesters who had occupied the airports. Instead, Somchai assigned the responsibility of diffusing The PAD protest and of restoring normalcy at the airports – the areas that were declared to be under the state-of-emergency decree – to the police. To exercise his power over the police, Somchai sacked Police Chief General Patcharawat Wongsuwan on the grounds that he had failed to evict The PAD protesters from the seized airports. But this move could also be interpreted as the prime minister's tactic to remove certain disloyal key figures in the security forces.[43] At the same time, an estimated 4,000 members of the UDD gathered on 30 November in front of Bangkok's City Hall to show their support for the Somchai Government. Leaders of the UDD vowed to protect democracy at all costs and oppose a military coup should it be staged at this critical juncture. This same message was conveyed by Thaksin, who earlier gave an interview to an American journalist in Hong Kong, warning that a military coup would definitely lead to inevitable bloodshed.

On 2 December, just three days before the king's birthday, the Constitutional Court dissolved the PPP and banned Somchai from politics for five years. The court found the PPP guilty of electoral fraud after an executive member was charged with vote-buying. Under the current constitution, if any member of the ruling party is found guilty of vote-buying, the leader of that party and its executive members will have to resign. The court's verdict seemed to fulfil the objective of The PAD whose members had called for the resignation of Somchai for months. But it would not end the political conflict since the pro-government force pledged to fight for justice, maintaining the judicial process to be highly politicised. In the meantime, members of the PPP who have not been barred from politics have begun to move to a shell party called Puea Thai (For Thais) and plan to nominate a new prime minister to be in charge of the country's administration. In response to the court's decision, The

PAD agreed to vacate the airports to ease the transportation crisis in which more than 350,000 travellers had been stranded in Thailand since the closure of the Suvarnabhumi Airport.[44]

As the former members of the PPP search for a new prime minister, the crisis continues because The PAD has pledged to carry on its crusade against the government, in the name of protecting democracy, especially if the new prime minister is proven to be another proxy of Thaksin. There seems to be no solution in sight in the Thai political turmoil. The prolonged uncertainty of politics has the potential to gradually erode the foundation of Thai democracy, which, despite its imperfect nature, had in the past lent itself as a model for other developing countries.

Looking through analytical lens

Democracy in the Thai political context has been interpreted differently, mostly to suit the interests of the leaders of the day. In rejecting the Thaksin-style democracy, The PAD argues that Western-style democracy gives too much power to the rural poor who it sees as being susceptible to vote-selling. The PAD's logic is fascinating in that it likens Thaksin's democracy to that of the West. If everyone would agree on the supremacy of the Western model of democracy, then the question is why it is wrong for Thailand to adopt Thaksin's democracy. At the same time, The PAD has recommended an alternative way, as it has claimed, to achieve democratic development. Criticised as highly controversial, the PAD's New Politics poses a serious threat to democracy when it suggests that future parliamentarians should comprise elected and appointed officials in the proportion 30:70, respectively. Nattahan Sirichotphaisal, a PAD supporter, in defence of the New Politics, said, 'Bangkok people know what is going on. The people in the provinces do not know'.[45] The Thaksin camp counter-argued that the New Politics is designed to keep power in the hands of the educated, urban elites, rather than to decentralise power to the people in the rural areas. Samak, while still in office, even declared that he had a duty to preserve the country's democracy from the undemocratic PAD. The military, recognised as the traditional order-keeper, is being seriously challenged by the ongoing political conflicts of which it has become a part. Despite constantly ruling out a coup as an option, the military has been tempted to intervene in politics in order to, as it often reasons, rescue democracy – yet, for whom does it rescue democracy? The many versions of Thai democracy have served to deepen the divide in an already fragmented society. Some consider this to be the rise of political pluralism. But is the emergent pluralism contributing to the consolidation process of Thai democracy?

It is obvious that, at present, the two poles of power – the Thaksin regime and the old establishment – have been manipulating the political situation behind the scenes. The confrontations have been exacerbated by the many proxies, be they the PPP and the UDD on the one side, and The PAD and factions of the military on the other. Thailand's recent democratic regimes, those of Thaksin, Samak and Somchai, have constantly been under attack from a myriad of non-democratic elements, including the anti-democratic forces led by The PAD and the asserting of military power in order to protect the interest of the old establishment. As Schedler suggested, democratic norms and procedures must be respected so that a democratic regime can enjoy longevity and stability.[46] Clearly, the old establishment, sanctified by the power of the Thai monarch, views the effort towards democratisation made by Thaksin and his successors as a threat to their own political well-being. The PAD, at the same time, has conspired to disqualify the rights of the majority Thais who have lent their support to Thaksin, accusing them of being politically illiterate. A key factor contributing to the unstable democratic regime is the reality in which the old establishment has vehemently defended its position as the sole hegemonic entity in Thai politics. They simply reject the notion that democracy is the most appropriate way to govern collective life. It is therefore essential to assess Thai democracy from the viewpoint of it being a channel to serve the personal and political interests of the power-holders.

Have Thaksin and his successors done enough to consolidate Thai democracy? From 2001–8, they might have worked arduously in pricking people's political consciousness, granting them the right to directly participate in politics, improving their lives through many populist programmes promised during the election campaign, as well as defying the old power and its domination of national politics. Yet, they have also used democracy to fulfil their personal agendas. Thaksin and his successors have failed to promote a democratic culture, such as good governance and accountability. They have often bypassed democratic institutions, curbing the existence of a free civil society, and indulged in rampant money politics and corruption. These non-democratic behaviours have been conveniently employed as a justification for the anti-Thaksin forces to question, or even overthrow, successive democratic regimes since 2001.

Conclusion

From 2001 to 2008, Thailand has experienced many phases of democracy, ranging from the most promising democratic regime to the present state of anarchy where democracy is on the verge of collapse. Thailand represents one unique case in which non-state actors have eagerly competed for power with elected governments, with a sizeable support from expanded middle-class urbanites. The democratic consolidation process was unable to take shape due to the clash between two powerful factions in politics – Thaksin and his loyalists versus the old establishment. What Thaksin and his successors have done is nothing more than an attainment of political power through legitimate means of elections. But Thaksin and his TRT had come to dominate the political space, hitherto jealously guarded by the conservatives. The result has been a persistent struggle for power. Whereas Thaksin has attempted to open up a political space for free and fair contests and involve the people at the grassroots level, the old establishment has sought to close it, maintain its hegemony and defend the power position of the rich middle class. Giles Ji Ungpakorn labelled the coup of September 2006 as 'a coup for the rich'.

In the battle for political power, various factions claim to uphold the principle of democracy even when their behaviour is visibly undemocratic. The need to cling to the notion of democracy serves just one purpose, that is, to gain political legitimacy. But this practice has caused severe damage to Thailand's democratisation process. The contest is no longer about who might best give back power to the people, but about how to preserve power for personal use. If asked if a way out of the political impasse is at the horizon, the answer would be pessimistic. Despite having driven Thaksin into exile, and now turning him into a fugitive, the old establishment finds it difficult to eradicate his influence. The current crisis has been cast upon the competition for power between the two entrenched camps. Thus far, neither has been willing to compromise for the sake of saving real democracy. Politics in Thailand will therefore remain a zero-sum game for some time.

Notes

1 Pavin Chachavalpongpun, 'Is a Coup the Only Option Left?' *Today*, 19 October 2008, p. 19.
2 See Andreas Schedler, 'Measuring Democratic Consolidation', *Studies in Comparative Development*, vol. 36, no. 1, Spring 2001, pp. 66–92.
3 William Case, 'Thailand: An Unconsolidated Democracy', in *Politics in Southeast Asia: Democracy or Less*, Richmond, Surrey: Curzon Press, 2002, p. 176.
4 Chai-Anan Samudavanija argues that in Thailand, the military, alongside civilian bureaucracies, have been the most important forms of organisation and collective action, in fact since the Ayutthaya period (Ayutthaya is the old capital of Siam, 1351–1767). Formerly, the state was concerned with organising methods for combining its military and civil structures and functions. At the same time, it structured the relations between the elite and commoners, and within the elite itself. In Chai-Anan Samudavanija, 'The Military, Bureaucracy and Globalisation', in Kevin Hewison (ed.) *Political Change in Thailand: Democracy and Participation*, London and New York: Routledge, 1997, p. 46.
5 Francis Fukuyama, *The End of History and the Last Man*, New York: The Free Press, 1992.
6 Giles Ji Ungpakorn, 'How Much Power Does the Thai King Really Have', *Asia Sentinel*, 29 January 2008. The following statement also appears in *Asia Sentinel*: 'On January 28, Thailand's Special Branch officially banned the sale of *A Coup for the Rich* by Associate Professor Giles Ji Ungpakorn of the Political Science Faculty of Chulalongkorn University in Bangkok. The book criticises the 2006 military coup and the liberals who supported it. Ungpakorn says "The emergence of a PPP government lead by Samak Sundaravej is not encouraging. As Interior Minister in 1976, Samak banned around 100 academic books and ordered their removal from libraries throughout the country. The banning of academic books by governments or bookshops is a gross infringement of democracy and academic freedom."'
7 Amy L. Freedman, *Political Change and Consolidation: Democracy's Rocky Road in Thailand, Indonesia, South Korea and Malaysia*, New York: Palgrave Macmillan, 2006, p. 47.
8 See Duncan McCargo (ed.) *Reforming Thai Politics*, Amsterdam: Nordic Institute of Asian Studies, 2002, p. 3.
9 See Samuel J. Valenzuela, 'Democratic Consolidation in Post-Transitional Setting: Notion, Process, and Facilitating Conditions,' in S. Mainwaring, G. O'Donnell and S. Valenzuela (eds), *Issues in Democratic Consolidation: The New South American Democracies in Comparative Perspective*, Notre Dame: University of Notre Dame Press, 1992, pp. 57–104.
10 Gwynne Dyer, 'Thaksin Shinawatra Could be the Peron of Thailand', 5 September 2008, available online at http://www.straight.com/article-160848/gwynne-dyer-thaksin-shinawatra-could-be-peron-thailand. Accessed on 12 September 2008.

11 Transcript, *A Conversation with Thaksin Shinawatra, Prime Minister of Thailand*, Council on Foreign Relations, US, 18 September 2009, available online at http://www.cfr.org/publication/11482/conversation_with_thaksin_shinawatra_prime_minister_of_thailand_rush_transcript_federal_news_service_inc.html. Accessed on 14 September 2008.

12 In an email interview with Bertil Lintner, the author of *Burma in Revolt: Opium and Insurgency Since 1948*, Chiangmai: Silkworm Books, 1999.

13 For example, Thaksin was accused of abusing state power (his wife, Khunying Pojaman Shinawatra, was reported to have bought 'under-priced' state land, and of granting Bt 4 billion soft loan to the Myanmar junta to in turn invest in his telecom company, and of tax evasion in the event that he sold his Shin Corp to Singapore's Temasek Holdings).

14 Thaksin also promoted the slogan 'Think New, Act New' which was resonated with a reformist emphasis on the need for considerable changes in ideas and ways of workings. In Duncan McCargo and Ukrist Pathmanand, *The Thaksinisation of Thailand*, Copenhagen: Nordic Institute of Asian Studies, 2005, p. 13.

15 Pavin Chachavalpongpun, 'In Thailand with The PAD: "New Politics" of New Communists?' Available online at http://www.opinionasia.org/InThailandwiththePAD. Accessed on 1 October 2008.

16 Abhisit gave this interview to *The Taipei Times*, quoted in John Roberts, 'Snap Election Heightened Political Crisis in Thailand', available online at http://www.wsws.org/articles/2006/mar2006/thai-m03.shtml. Accessed on 2 October 2008.

17 'Thaksin Feels Heat After Chilly London', *The Nation*, 17 November 2006; 'Sondhi Outsmarted Thaksin at the Eleventh Hour', *The Nation*, 22 September 2006; 'We Did It For the People: Sondhi', *The Nation*, 25 November 2006.

18 Kate McGeown, 'Thai King Remains Centre Stage', *BBC NEWS Asia-Pacific*, available online at http://www.news.bbc.co.uk/2/hi/Asia-pacific/5367936.stm, 21 September 2006. Accessed on 29 September 2008.

19 See Duncan McCargo, 'Toxic Thaksin', *Foreign Affairs*, 27 September 2006. Available online at http://www.foreignaffairs.org/20060927facomment85575/duncan-mccargo/toxic-thaksin.html. Accessed on 6 October 2008.

20 See Sirivalaya Kachatan, 'Democracy and the Military Coup in Thailand', paper presented at the Annual Meeting of the Southern Political Science Association, Hotel Intercontinental, New Orleans, LA, 9 January 2008.

21 Michael H. Nelson, 'Thaksin Overthrown, Thailand's Well Intentioned Coup of September 19, 2006', in *Eastasia.at*, vol. 6, no. 1, June 2007, p. 9. Available online at http://www.eastasia.at/vol6_1/article01.pdf. Accessed on 12 August 2008. See also Thongchai Winichakul, 'The Kingmakers', *Krungthep Thurakit*, 18 October 2006, p. 13.

22 Warsame Galaydh, 'Thailand and the Region of Southeast Asia: Transitioning to Liberal Democracies', unpublished thesis, Carleton College, USA, 2008, p. 21.

23 Sulak Sivaraksa, a social critic currently being charged with *lése majesté*, said, 'If the King did not give a nod, this never would have been possible', *Associated Press*, 20 September 2006, quoted in Nelson, 'Thaksin Overthrown, Thailand's Well Intentioned Coup of September 19, 2006', p. 13.

24 McCargo, 'Toxic Thaksin', *Foreign Affairs*, 27 September 2006.

25 Pavin Chachavalpongpun, '*Lése majesté* in Thailand: Do not Insult the Royalty!' Available online at http://www.opinionasia.org/DonotinsulttheRoyalty. Accessed on 15 October 2008.

26 Dyer, 'Thaksin Shinawatra could be the Peron of Thailand', 5 September 2008.

27 Neil A. Englehart, 'Democracy and the Thai Middle Class: Globalisation, Modernisation and Constitutional Change', *Asian Survey*, vol. 43, no. 2, March–April, 2003, p. 253.

28 Seth Mydans, 'Thai Court Disbands Former Prime Minister's Political Party', *The New York Times*, 31 May 2007.

29 'Samak Sundaravej: Thailand's Surrogate Prime Minister?' *Asia Pacific News*, 28 January 2008.

30 'Thai Prime Minister Vows to Amend Constitution', *International Herald Tribune*, 13 July 2008.

31 Peter Janssen, 'PAD Demonstrations Raise Concerns over Democracy', *The Nation*, 6 September 2008.

32 'Our Tolerance is Limited: Samak', *The Nation*, 27 August 2008.

33 The UDD had announced its plan to take up arms and stage running battles with the army on the streets of Bangkok if the military attempts to stage a coup against the Somchai Wongsawat Administration. In Wassana Nanuam, 'Pro-Govt Groups Warn Against Coup', *Bangkok Post*, 19 October 2008.

34 'Thailand's Political Crisis: PM Samak Resorts to Referendum', available online at http://www.aseanaffairs.com/thailand_political_crisis_pm_samak_resorts_to_referendum. Accessed on 15 October 2008.

35 Thomas Fuller, 'Thai Court Sentences Thaksin to 2 Years in Jail', *International Herald Tribune*, 21 October 2008.

36 Pavin Chachavalpongpun, 'Thaksin Saga: More Urgent Matters Beckon', *The Straits Times*, 25 August 2008.

37 Nirmal Ghosh, 'Thaksin Gets 2 Years' Jail for Graft', *The Straits Times*, 22 October 2008.

38 Simon Montlake, 'Critics Slam Thailand's Activist Judges', available online at http://news.yahoo.com/s/csm/20081006/wl_csm/ojudges. Accessed 10 October 2008. Montlake also reported that the military-backed constitution gave the judiciary and other state agencies an enhanced role in curbing the power of elected officials. But the pendulum has swung too far in the opposite direction, said Rungrawee Chalermsripinyorat, an analyst in Bangkok for the International Crisis Group. 'The 2007 Constitution now restricts the executive to the point that governing is almost impossible. There is a need to strike a balance between giving the executive sufficient power to govern and ensuring effective checks and balances,' she said.

39 Kornchanok Raksaseri, 'New First Lady Yaowapa Wongsawat', *The Nation*, 19 September 2008.

40 'Thai Queen Attends Funeral for Anti-Government Protester', available online at http://afp.google.com/article/ALeqM5gOnmGa0M_MkEz3_xsI9qgHViQQ0A.

41 Thitinan Pongsudhirak, 'Bangkok Protests: Where is The PAD Going with This?' *The Bangkok Post*, 27 November 2008.

42 Wassana Nanuam, 'Accept Responsibility or There Will Be Chaos', *Bangkok Post*, 17 October 2008.

43 Tim Johnston, 'Thailand Police Chief Removed', *Financial Times*, 29 November 2008.

44 'Thai Court Bans PM, Flights to Resume', *AFP*, 2 December 2008, available online at http://sg.news.yahoo.com/afp/20081202/tap-thailand-politics-protest-c8d5519.html.

45 Janssen, 'PAD Demonstrations Raise Concerns over Democracy'.

46 Schedler, 'Measuring Democratic Consolidation', pp. 70–72.

4 A (not so) funny thing happened on the way to the forum

The travails of democratisation in the Philippines

Herman Joseph S. Kraft

Introduction

This chapter looks into the factors that have influenced the democratisation process in the Philippines. Twenty years since the overthrow of the authoritarian presidency of Ferdinand E. Marcos, there is a general sense among political observers and analysts, as well as the general public in the Philippines, that the transition towards democracy has failed to bring about lasting political stability, responsive governance, and an economic environment conducive not only to growth but more so to a greater number of people sharing in the effects of that growth. Democracy remains the preferred system for most Filipinos; but democracy in the Philippines has suffered from the loss of public confidence in current political institutions and the political leadership. Why has the democratisation process in the Philippines apparently fallen so short of expectations? What makes democracy in the Philippines so vulnerable to political exigencies within and outside the country? Does this portend a revival of non-democratic forces in the country?

Mired democratisation?

In his seminal work entitled *The Third Wave: Democratization in the Late Twentieth Century*, Samuel Huntington pointed to the 'People Power Revolution' in the Philippines as the start of the third wave democratisation process in Asia. Since then, the progress of the democratisation process in the Philippines has become mired in political scandals involving the highest office in the government, continued political violence, and diminished public confidence in the country's political institutions. These coincide with public dissatisfaction over the inability of past and current administrations to raise the level of economic development in the Philippines.

Interestingly, public opinion polls in the Philippines continue to indicate a general preference for democracy as a political system. At the same time, however, there are indications that there is also a compelling preference for 'strong' leadership to come to the fore. Anecdotal evidence indicates that a number of Filipinos believe that a leader in the mould of a Lee Kuan Yew is what the current situation in the country calls for. In this context, it is the current political leadership across the spectrum of Philippine politics that has lost the confidence of the Philippine public.

The diminution of public confidence in the current political leadership, however, has been mistakenly taken by some opposition groups as an opportunity to change the political system itself. Former University of the Philippines President Francisco Nemenzo proposed the establishment of a transitional government (this was actually first presented as a 'revolutionary' government) that would stay in place for a limited period to oversee the implementation of necessary reforms in the country. The proposal posits that the first step in this process is the resignation of the current administration, and the suspension of the Constitution. The public has generally taken very little note of this proposal, though there have been constant public demonstrations by activists from the Left in support of it.

Perversely, the call for political change has galvanised the administration of President Gloria Macapagal-Arroyo to look into the possibility of changing the structure of the political system, i.e. shifting from the current presidential system to a parliamentary one, from a unitary system to a federal one. This prospect is strongly supported by local political leaders and much of the support for President Gloria Macapagal-Arroyo's Administration from the political elite stems from her promise to ensure changes in the country's political structures, initially by 2007, or, failing that, before 2010. The attempt in 2007 was led by a Presidential Commission headed by another former President of the University of the Philippines, Jose V. Abueva, which held nationwide consultations on this issue. A number of criticisms against this proposal revolved around the sense that shifting to a parliamentary system and, even more so, to a federal system will only consolidate the powers of existing political clans. If this is the case, change in the political structure will not lead to any meaningful political change.

Meaningful change is hampered by the persistence of a weak Philippine state. This has made it difficult for various government agencies to formulate and implement policies independently of the powerful vested interest groups in Philippine society. In particular, the exercise of economic and political power in the country continues to be mediated by family relationships and 'kinship networks'.[1] The influence of powerful political families is historically rooted in the still predominantly agrarian nature of Philippine society. At the same time, non-traditional political forces have also emerged since the collapse of the Marcos dictatorship whose interests are also affected by political reform issues. Civil society groups have increasingly become more active in pushing for reform – a development which is generally seen as positive for democracy. A number of these groups, however, are not inclined towards liberal democratic reforms – a condition that makes their emergence as a political force in the country a problem for democratisation in the Philippines.

There is extensive literature on democratisation. Fundamentally, it is seen as a process that passes through different if not mutually exclusive stages:[2] (1) decay of authoritarian rule; (2) transition; (3) consolidation; and (4) maturing of a democratic political order. As a complex historical process, these are empirically overlapping conditions. In a logical sequence, democratisation may run in a smooth path starting from the disintegration of the authoritarian regime and the emergence of the new democratic system, through the consolidation of that regime, to its maturity. However, the process is not that linear or rational in actual application. Some democracies abort as soon as they emerge, while others erode as much as they consolidate.[3]

Democratic consolidation, however, is another concept that defies clarity. Thomas Carothers basically described it as

a slow but purposeful process in which democratic forms are transformed into democratic substance through the reform of state institutions, the regularisation of elections, the strengthening of civil society, and the overall habituation of the society to the new democratic 'rules of the game'.[4]

Or, to put it more simply, it refers to the completion of the transition from authoritarianism to democracy.[5] This is not to imply that all democratisation processes eventually end with the 'consolidation' of democracy. As noted earlier, the process can always be reversed. Neither should it be taken that the successful holding of more or less free, fair and competitive elections signals the 'inevitable' continuity of democracy. Andreas Schedler points out that central to the meaning of democratic consolidation is 'reducing the probability of [democracy's] breakdown to the point where [actors] can feel reasonably confident that [it] will persist in the near (and not-so-near) future.'[6] This means that democratic consolidation at its most basic is associated with two principal issues: improving the quality of democracy and democratic deepening. Schedler contends that these issues, however, are difficult to pin down in terms of what constitutes them. Both do not have fixed meanings, and are open to re-interpretations depending on the mores of time periods. In this context, no democracy will ever be 'fully consolidated'.

The vagueness of what a consolidated democracy is, however, has led to an entirely different set of explanations for cases such as the Philippines wherein the establishment of democracy has not led to expected outcomes, particularly in terms of effectiveness, accountability, and the preservation of civil liberties. Instead of putting the blame on the lack of completion of the democratisation process, the presumption is that a democratic system is in place but is not performing up to expectations of what a democratic system should accomplish. In this context, William Case describes the Philippines as a 'stable, but low quality democracy'.[7] He explains this by noting four principal characteristics of Philippine politics: (1) the tendency of political figures to test the limits of its democratic institutions; (2) the limited options open to the electorate during elections; (3) the tendency of the elite to pay no more than rhetorical consideration to addressing the welfare of the people; and (4) the continuing widespread use of violence as a tool of politics.[8] This generally fits into conceptions of what constitutes 'good quality' democracy which can be defined as 'one presenting *a stable institutional structure that realizes the liberty and equality of citizens through the legitimate and correct functioning of its institutions and mechanisms.*'[9] Thus, the quality of a democracy is determined in terms of its ability to satisfy the needs of citizens, ensure their enjoyment of liberty and equality, and guarantee that citizens themselves can check and evaluate whether government and political actors perform their functions (and perform them well) under the constraints of the rule of law.

Whether the case of the Philippines can be analysed in terms of being an 'unconsolidated' democracy or a 'low quality' one, there is a clear idea that democracy in the Philippines, after 20 years of development, has not quite provided peaceful, stable, and effective governance. It in fact exemplifies what Schedler alluded to when he noted that the consolidation of democracy must take into consideration the existence of uncertainties that could weaken or erode it. In this context, the different efforts at trying to determine standards along which the 'quality' of democracy is measured as well as the degree to which the members of society are socialised into the values of democracy serve a necessary and a not-so-useless function. In Southeast Asia, these questions began to be raised at the first ASEAN People's Assembly (APA), a meeting that put together government and non-government actors in one forum to discuss issues that were central to the future work of ASEAN.[10] The APA sessions involved intense, rich, and stimulating deliberations which eventually led to the decision to institute an APA Action Plan for Democratisation Assessment. The key premise is that the consolidation of democracy is a complex and difficult process requiring widespread agreement on 'the rules of the game' (*a la* Carothers). It was proposed that oversight activities include the development of instruments that look into the presence or absence of 'democracy promoting indicators' and/or 'democracy eroding indicators'. All participants were conscious that during the critical period of democratic transition in Southeast Asia, a period when empowerment tends to be diluted, it is vital to have a people-initiated, concerted, and in-depth assessment.

This project, which became known as the 'ASEAN Democracy Scorecard', eventually tried to identify a number of themes and variables which the project team felt were crucial to ensuring the strengthening of the democratisation process in the region. While it did run into the difficulties identified by Schedler, it eventually focused on three components with 10 themes to look at the processes of democratisation in Indonesia and the Philippines.[11] The findings of that project on the Philippines are telling. It noted that

> [w]hile it has been more than 17 years since the "redemocratisation" process have [*sic*] started with the Aquino transition regime, severe limitations and deficits on the performance of democratic institutions can be seen. While the country had generally adopted into laws and institutions the various principles of democracy like representation and accountability, they are frequently pervaded with the culture of impunity, particularism, and patronage. While provisions for the participation of citizens are very much recognised, they are not implemented or certain informal norms had [sic] the tendency to obscure the democratic intentions of such laws and institutions.[12]

The prospects for democracy in the Philippines: diminishing expectations or popular resignation?

Schedler, though cognisant of the weaknesses inherent in the conceptualisation of democratic consolidation, noted three factors, embedded in society itself, that are key to assessing why consolidation progresses, stalls, or even backslides: behavioural foundations, attitudinal foundations, and structural foundations. Schedler argued that most scholars try to assess the health of a democracy based on the behaviour of political actors in the system. Thus the principal indicator of consolidation is the increasing absence of what he refers to as 'anti-democratic behavior'.[13] This is primarily seen in the degree to which resorting to violence is utilised as a political instrument, the degree to which the results of elections are accepted or rejected, and the extent to which the rule of law is internalised by political actors. At the same time, the extent to which democracy is able to deliver on freedom and civil liberties is an important factor in strengthening popular support for a country's democratic institutions. In other words, more democracy strengthens democracy.[14] Popular support, however, is also contingent on the extent to which the socio-economic conditions help to strengthen or weaken public confidence in democracy, and the extent to which the institutional design of the form of government and electoral system of the country reflects the people's preference.

The indicators presented by Schedler are paralleled by Morlino in his assessment of what constitutes 'good' or 'bad' democracies.[15] Democratic quality is supposed to be determined by five dimensions. The first two have to do with the extent to which decisions and their implementation are based on the rule of law, and the extent to which those in government are held accountable for ensuring that these decisions are enforced and enforced on the basis of the supremacy of the law over any other considerations. The third dimension brings in the effectiveness of the government in responding to the public's demands. This entails not only coming up with policies that directly address these demands but ensuring the consistent implementation of these policies. The government, when making decisions, must always keep in mind that the substantive content of a democracy is based on the two values of freedom and equality. Rule-making, government responsiveness, and the implementation of these dimensions must necessarily be founded on these substantive values. Overall, the quality of democracy is differentiated by the extent to which these dimensions are realised.

The elements of each set of assessments largely overlap. Both fundamentally argue that democracies must:

1　behave in accordance with rules that are clearly presented, strictly observed, and equally and consistently enforced. Non-observance of any of these aspects should render the officials involved (no matter how high the office) accountable to the people.
2　ensure that popular support for democratic institutions is sustained by addressing the socio-economic needs of citizens. This requires institutional mechanisms that will be responsive to the needs of the citizenry regardless of vested interests within society that might oppose policies along these lines.
3　guarantee the civil liberties of citizens and residents, and ensure that, regardless of identity, all citizens and residents will be treated equally before the law.

As the APA's Working Group on a Democracy Scorecard noted in its preliminary report, the case of the Philippines shows a dangerous surfeit of characteristics that create 'severe limitations and deficits on the performance of democratic institutions', an observation that coincides with the assessment of William Case. A careful assessment of Philippine democracy using the general categories noted earlier will allow for a more nuanced look at the essential issues.

Behavioural foundations: the rule of law and the supremacy of law

In 1992, a study conducted by a group of political scientists under the aegis of Social Weather Stations (SWS) identified the weakness of the Philippine state as the critical issue that any political leadership in the country must first contend with.[16] The cogency of that observation, and the apparent lack of response to it from those in authority, was affirmed when ten years later President Gloria Macapagal-Arroyo pointed to the problem of the weak Philippine state as the principal reason for the country's continuing malaise. She blamed this weakness in state institutions on 'dominant classes or sectors [that] control . . . or shape government policies, especially those dealing with the economy.'[17] This has resulted in the wide gap between the rich and the poor, a political system based on patronage that has helped breed corruption in government service, and a preoccupation with politics that has subordinated legal rules to political exigencies in cases involving the aforementioned dominant classes and sectors.

The reference made by President Arroyo to the culpability of 'dominant classes and sectors' points to a long-standing pattern of elite politics in the Philippines dominated by entrenched political clans.[18] Aside from the traditional elite, however, other emerging forces have become a factor in influencing the state. These include major commercial and industrial conglomerates, an active civil society, and even the bureaucracy itself. The period immediately following the Marcos era was the opportune time to put in place reform programmes necessary for economic, political, and social development. Very little along these lines actually materialised and the most important programmes were certainly noticeable for their lack of sustained success. A comprehensive agrarian reform programme was diluted by a legislature dominated by members of the landed elite. Tax reform never took off because of manipulation by a number of major corporations. Attempts to push economic liberalisation and industrialisation have been hampered by a strange alliance between leftist ideologues and the self-serving protectionist interests of local capitalists.[19]

The issues confronting the Philippine state do not only have to do with vested interests seeking to influence the state for personal advancement. This is also evident in the inability of the government to face up to interests within the bureaucracy and the military. Cartels in the bureaucracy have institutionalised corrupt practices. Raul Roco, a candidate for the presidency in the 2004 elections, was appointed as the Secretary for Education during the first term of the Arroyo Administration. His reform agenda for the Department of Education ran against entrenched interests. In a rather unusual situation, the Department of Education during this period was considered to be one of the most corrupt agencies in government. Cartels operating there had control over the issuance of rights to publish textbooks, as well as the purchase of school materials used in public schools. Roco's reform programme threatened the interests of cartels and other groups within the Department which then led to the Department's employees clamouring for his removal. Two other reformers placed in charge of other agencies also suffered the same fate. All of them were asked to resign by the president and replaced.

The most serious examples, however, of the way the rule of law has been stretched and manipulated in the Philippines involved the highest political office. The entry of Joseph Estrada into the scene was generally perceived upon his accession as an indication of popular rejection of traditional politics and an assertion of the political empowerment of the masses. He became president due to the overwhelming number of votes he received from the poorest classes in the country. His administration, however, became noted for three main points. First, was the lack of competence at the highest levels of political leadership in the country. His management style was based on *compadre* relations, or loyalty to and from close friends. Dong-Yeob Kim made the observation that the policy-making process in the Philippines is traditionally highly personalised rather than institutionalised.[20] This was particularly so in the case of Estrada. His 'style', however, also evoked images of the Marcos-era crony capitalism that turned the Philippine economy on its head. This opened the way to the second characteristic of the Estrada Administration: its tolerance of corruption at different levels of government, most of the time involving the president's cronies.[21] While seeming to continue the liberalisation and reform programmes of the Ramos Administration, the influence of close friends, business and political associates and supporters slowed down the process. The highly touted anti-poverty programme of the Estrada election campaign never got off the ground.[22] Finally, the widespread perception of corruption and incompetence led to his term in office being truncated to less than three years by another EDSA (Epifanio de los Santos Avenue) uprising, His term of office was completed by his vice-president, Gloria Macapagal-Arroyo. Even as the reform programmes of the Ramos Administration were limited by opposition from established interests both within and outside the political system, the Estrada Administration saw the more direct influence of similar vested interests in the decision-making processes of the government.[23] This badly affected business confidence in the country and led to a slow recovery from the effects of the financial crisis – this in spite of the Philippines having been the least affected among those hit by the Asian contagion. Carl Lande made the observation that considering 'the perilous condition of the economy, the country could not have tolerated three more years of Estrada.'[24] The case of Estrada, however, also showed dangerous characteristics that again illuminated the weakness of the Philippine state and how this in turn was exacerbated by the lack of competent political leadership. His election to the presidency, as noted, showed an increasing cynicism on the part of the people towards the country's political institutions. Again, this was reflected in the attitude of the poorer classes (shown in polls) towards Estrada even after he had been removed from office. He continued to retain much of these classes' support. This again is a consequence of the political elite's historical neglect of the poor.[25] More importantly, his removal from office through street demonstrations was seen as a further sign of the erosion of Filipinos' trust in their political institutions – in no small way a reaction to what is generally perceived to be predatory and power-hungry behaviour on the part of the political elite.

The challenge to Philippine democracy perhaps reached renewed heights with President Gloria Macapagal-Arroyo's Administration. In June 2005, the Arroyo Administration faced the biggest scandal of its unique two-term existence. An audio tape which purportedly had the president talking to Election Commissioner Virgilio Garcillano at a time when the results of the 2004 Presidential Elections were still in doubt was made public. If it was indeed the president's voice that could be heard in the tape, her discussion with a member of the Commission on Elections regarding election returns when the results were as yet unknown was in violation of election laws. The situation was exacerbated by the admission of the president a few weeks later that she had indeed talked to a member of the Commission on Elections even as returns were being tabulated. She did not, however, admit that the voice on the tape was hers nor did she say that the member of the Commission on Elections whom she talked to was Garcillano. The episode prompted a political crisis which saw the opposition attempt to mobilise a people power revolt through a series of daily mass actions intended to force Arroyo to step down. The Arroyo Administration managed to survive that particular crisis because the Catholic Bishops' Conference of the Philippines chose not to become involved and did not make any statement that explicitly supported or condemned the president. Support from local government officials and the House of Representatives eventually killed any momentum that the opposition might have built towards forcing President Arroyo to resign.

The survival, however, of the Arroyo Administration did little to assuage a public that was already polarised by the claims of the opposition that government resources had been used by Arroyo in order to gain an advantage during the 2004 elections. SWS issued the results of a nationwide poll on 10 September 2005 which showed that large majorities across the country (except in the Arroyo bailiwick in the Visayas where sentiments were split) 'called for GMA's impeachment'.[26] A more telling statistic was that 51 per cent were in favour of using people power to oust the president in the event that she remained in power as opposed to only 26 per cent opposed. Following the Garcillano tape revelations, some officers from the Armed Forces of the Philippines defied the chain of command and came out in public to report that the military was used to help Macapagal-Arroyo win the 2004 elections. The opposition has since then been trying to build a coalition of forces that could give muscle to what has been described as 'a growing perception that "GMA will be ousted through a combination of mass actions or people power, and some form of military intervention."'[27]

This came to a head on 24 February 2006 when key officers in the elite Scout Rangers and Philippine Marines announced the withdrawal of their support for the chain of command – a euphemism for what was in fact a coup attempt. As with most failed coup plots in the past, however, this did not have the support of the upper echelons of the military and eventually collapsed.[28] The involvement of the political opposition in the attempted coup was supposed to be in the form of mobilising popular support for the coup when it was launched. The quick response of the government, however, isolated the coup plotters early in the process and the intended melding of popular and military forces against Arroyo was not realised.[29] The issuance of Proclamation 1017 declaring a State of Emergency in the Philippines when the coup plot was uncovered provided the legal mechanism for the government to act against both the military officers involved in the plot and the civilians who supported them. Despite claims made by the opposition that the State of Emergency was unconstitutional, it was upheld by the Supreme Court albeit with the injunction that the declaration did not grant the president the right to take over facilities. This was a reference to the takeover of the office of the *Daily Tribune*, a paper well-known for its critical reporting on the Arroyo Administration. The State of National Emergency was raised on 3 March 2006.

These developments illustrate the difficulties facing Philippine democracy. Case had pointed out that while the country's political elites express their support for constitutionalism and the rule of law, they do tend to test its limits and often get away with it. The very fact that the president has admitted to having talked to an official from the Commission on Elections, although she very well knew that this was against the electoral code, shows that this is an attitude of the political elite that is carried and acted upon even at the highest levels. Attempts on the part of the government to block legal channels of complaints and seeking of redress against the actions of the president skim the borders of legality. More importantly, they have long-term consequences for democracy in the country. A critic of the president from the business sector very clearly pointed this out when he said that even as the business community did not want to see or support unconstitutional avenues of forcing Arroyo out of office, 'the government has shut down all the options . . . [forcing] people to look at more desperate means.'[30] The preparations made by the opposition in trying to mobilise a people power action against Arroyo both in the aftermath of the Garcillano tape unveiling and in support of the military coup of 24 February 2006 indicates that extra-legal means of forcing Arroyo out from the Presidency are not just a last resort of the desperate, but has become a principal option. Reports of similar action planned in conjunction with the 2003 Oakwood mutiny only show how the political elite of the country have become more cynical about the country's democratic institutions and turn more easily to non-constitutional means of forcing the president out.

This cynicism is further illustrated by the fact that the case against the Arroyo Administration goes back to the results of the 2004 elections. Even before the revelations (whatever it might have revealed) of the Garcillano tape, the opposition was already unwilling to accept the victory of Arroyo in the presidential polls.[31] This is illustrative of how election results in the country are not always taken to be final. Hence, the Commission on Elections is bombarded with appeals for a recount. In some cases, winning candidates are threatened with violence by their opponents. This tendency in the political elite to see election results as always contestable makes it difficult for winning candidates at all levels of politics, but especially those involved in presidential elections, to take office with the security provided by the knowledge and assurance of the legitimacy provided by the results of the elections. In the case of the Arroyo Administration, the need to secure her power base even in the aftermath of her victory in the 2004 elections, and again (and arguably with greater desperation) in the aftermath of the Garcillano tape revelations hindered her ability to meet the expectation as expressed by one of those who voted for her of 'finally [being] able to steer the country toward a brighter future.'[32]

It is, however, the continued presence of political violence that is arguably at the heart of the tendency of the democratisation process in the Philippines to proceed in fits and starts. The involvement of the military in opposition plans to overthrow the Arroyo Administration shows the key role played by force in Philippine politics. It has given the military undue influence over political outcomes and has made the Arroyo Administration particularly vulnerable to pressure from the military hierarchy on policy issues. The influence of the military, however, is also exacerbated by the continued presence of armed challenges to the government. The Communist Party of the Philippines (CPP) and its armed wing, the New People's Army, have proven to be very resilient and remain an active threat to the current political structures of the country. The ongoing peace talks between the CPP and the Philippines government have been characterised by bad faith on both sides that the prospects for progress are low. The Moro Islamic Liberation Front (MILF) remains the largest threat to peace in the country as it is the best organised and well-armed opposition to the government. Peace talks between the MILF and the Philippine government, however, have begun to make advances as both sides decide on the basic framework for peace in Mindanao. The issue of terrorism, however, clouds the situation as the relationship between the MILF and the Abu Sayaff Group (ASG) continues to create trouble for the Philippine government. The ASG's alliance with the Jemaah Islamiya, a Southeast Asian terrorist network with links to Osama bin Laden's Al-Qaeda, has been the centre of the security concerns of the Philippine government. The military confrontation between the Philippine government and these armed groups have been instrumental in colouring relations between the armed forces, or segments of it, and the civilian government.

Cognisant of Schedler's caveat about thresholds on anti-democratic behaviour, these issues point to not just isolated events but also trends and patterns of increasing cynicism amongst the country's political elites (including the Left in both mainstream politics and in the underground) regarding the country's political institutions. It has not helped that both the supporters of the Arroyo Administration and the opposition have resorted more to methods that circumscribe the law to resolve political issues in their favour rather than allow political processes to continue to their intended ends. As indicated earlier, these have consequences in terms of public perceptions and attitudes towards these same institutions.

Attitudinal foundations: sustaining popular support for democratic institutions

What is perhaps most surprising is that amidst all these manoeuvres taking place among the country's political elites, popular support for democracy has remained constant. According to Jorge Tigno, this is perhaps the main factor that has helped keep the embattled Arrroyo Administration in power.[33] It is this aspect of democracy in the Philippines that is at the same time a source of good tidings and also an indication of the vulnerability of the democratisation process. In a number of public opinion polls, it is clear that the Philippine public is still able to discriminate between their attitude towards the Arroyo Administration, particularly President Arroyo, and their support and preference for democracy. To what extent this state of affairs will last, however, is not so clear.

The March 2002 survey of SWS showed that there was still strong opposition to an authoritarian regime. The preference for democratic rule was clear with most of the respondents rating the present form of government as better than the system under Marcos even as it was considered to be less than ideal.[34] As indicated in Table 4.1, this trend of a greater preference for democracy than an authoritarian form of government among Filipinos has remained consistent over the Arroyo Administration with 64 per cent of respondents still giving unconditional preference to democracy in the December 2005 survey of SWS. Only 15 per cent said that under certain conditions they would prefer an authoritarian form of government. This shows that even in the aftermath of the Garcillano tape revelations, the support for democracy among the people remained strong. There is also more residual confidence expressed in the public's opinion of the country's political institutions. As opposed to sentiments expressed among the political elite about the lack of competence of Vice-President Noli De Castro to take over as president in the event of President Arroyo's removal, there is actually a strong majority among respondents in an SWS survey that expressed confidence in his ability to govern the country.[35] A solid majority is opposed to initiatives to change the constitution and would vote 'No' if a plebiscite were to be held. This is a sentiment that cuts across political lines in the country and included those who supported the president.[36]

In comparison with the continuing support for democracy and the country's democratic institutions, the president herself received a –30 net satisfaction rating

Table 4.1 Preference for democratic v. authoritarian government, March 2002–June 2007

Surveys	Democracy is Always Preferable (%)	Authoritarianism is Sometimes Preferable (%)
March 2002	64	18
June 2003	57	23
November 2003	58	20
March 2004	52	26
June 2004	52	25
December 2004	57	24
August 2005	58	19
December 2005	64	15
September 2006	49	23
June 2007	53	19

Source: Social Weather Stations surveys

Table 4.2 Net satisfaction ratings for President Gloria Macapagal-Arroyo, March 2002–June 2008

Surveys	Net Ratings
March 2002	+16
June 2003	+14
November 2003	−3
March 2004	+30
June 2004	+26
December 2004	−5
August 2005	−23
December 2005	−30
June 2006	−13
November 2006	−13
February 2007	−4
June 2007	−3
December 2007	−20
March 2008	−26
June 2008	−38

Source: Social Weather Stations surveys

in the survey done in the fourth quarter of 2005 (see Table 4.2). In fact, the Arroyo Administration had been taking a beating in opinion polls with President Arroyo herself having negative net ratings (i.e. a greater number of those surveyed being dissatisfied with her performance than those satisfied) *since* December 2004.[37] A survey conducted in the first quarter of 2006 showed that the strong dissatisfaction with President Arroyo had led to strong support for her removal either through another people power action (48 per cent in agreement, 23 per cent in disagreement) or through her resignation (44 per cent in agreement, 27 per cent in disagreement).[38] As far as support for democracy goes in the country, the greatest danger posed by the strong and protracted sense of dissatisfaction with President Arroyo lies in the extent to which this has allowed people to accept the possibility of a coup d'etat in order to remove her from office. Thirty-six per cent of those surveyed thought that it would be good for the country if the president was removed by means of a military coup as opposed to 35 per cent who disagreed. The fact that 23 per cent were undecided has potentially grave implications for democracy in the country. These figures reflect the increasing desperation of a people, a strong majority of which will always prefer democracy to an authoritarian system of government, but at the same time with a strong plurality willing to accept military action if the intention is to remove President Arroyo from her office.

The fragility of the current state of democracy in the Philippines can be gleaned from the satisfaction rating of how democracy works in the country. Despite the consistency of the popular support for democracy indicated in the SWS surveys, there has always been some concern with its lack of performance (see Table 4.3). The difference between the high preference for democracy and the middling satisfaction rates with the way democracy has worked in the Philippines can be attributed to popular expectations (arguably even unrealistic ones) of what a democracy

Table 4.3 Satisfaction with the way democracy works in the Philippines, March 2002–June 2007

Surveys	Satisfaction Rating (%)	Preference for Democracy (%)
March 2002	44	64
May 2002	35	N/A
September 2002	42	N/A
November 2002	37	N/A
March 2003	33	N/A
June 2003	45	57
June 2004	44	52
December 2004	40	57
August 2005	44	58
December 2005	48	64
September 2006	45	49
February 2007	44	52
March 2007	49	48
April 2007	46	53
June 2007	54	53

Source: Social Weather Stations surveys

should be able to accomplish. It is therefore normal that satisfaction rates should be lower than the percentages reflecting popular preference for a democracy. At the same time, however, the case of the Philippines indicates the effects of an under-performing government that unfortunately reflect on its democratic institutions.

In a media release distributed on 26 January 2006 and written by SWS President Mahar Mangahas, dissatisfaction with the Arroyo Administration was attributed principally to inflation and corruption, and perceptions of the lack of assistance given to the poor.[39] Similarly, Felipe Miranda of the Department of Political Science at the University of the Philippines noted that the Philippines is experiencing a crisis of governance as seen in the 'ambiguity of political leadership in a time of deepening crisis, exacerbated public safety/public order concerns dramatized by terrorist acts, increasing criminality and military restiveness.' This ambiguity of political leadership is further evident in the worsening of basic needs provision and other equity issues which has created 'a problematically high level of public scepticism'.[40]

In 2002, Pulse Asia surveys showed that the issues which worried respondents most and where President Arroyo had failed to earn majority approval are essentially economic, particularly the questions of economic recovery, widespread poverty, prices of commodities, and low wages. In March 2006, an SWS survey showed that the top three issues facing the country were inflation, the general state of the economy, and corruption. In a refrain of the 2002 Pulse Asia survey results, the 2006 SWS showed that 62 per cent of the respondents rated the performance of the government, particularly the president, in addressing these issues as bad or very bad.[41] In 2002, the most important issue facing the Arroyo Administration was a fiscal crisis borne out of the state's inability to generate revenue. The introduction of austerity measures (not really felt in the legislature), the expanded value added tax measure, and fundamental improvements in collection capacity has made the Arroyo Administration fairly confident about its ability to initiate an extensive infra-structural development programme intended to attract investors and tourists, and to create jobs in the country. In her State of the Nation Address in 2006, President Arroyo unveiled an extensive plan that focused primarily on public works (roads and airports) which Dr Benjamin Diokno of the University of the Philippines School of Economics pointed out would easily cost P500 billion. Criticisms of the president's proposed programme revolved around whether or not the government had the finances for this and predicted that this would again increase the debt situation of the country causing more problems for ordinary Filipinos. The Arroyo Administration's supporters on the other hand argue that the improved fiscal situa-tion of the country has allowed the government to build the needed seed capital for the president's plan. Lower public deficits, a function of reduced spending and increased revenue collections, provide optimism in this regard.

The socio-economic picture of the country has been improving since 2004 but its implications remain somewhat mixed. Macroeconomic numbers for the Philippines have been experiencing modest improvement with GDP growth at 6.2 per cent in 2004 and 5.5 per cent in 2005. In 2007, the Philippines recorded a GDP growth rate of 7.3 per cent, the highest it had achieved in more than 30 years.

What is of great concern to analysts is what the president did not talk about in her 2006 State of the Nation Address. There was very little mention of issues concern-ing education, health and welfare – issue areas that greatly concern Filipinos and which remain largely unaddressed in the public eye. Since 1999, there has been a contraction in government spending in these sectors, particularly with government austerity measures since 2004. All these issues, however, have been largely due to the uneven economic performance of the country over the last few years.

In a region noted for high economic growth rates, the Philippines has always been an outlier. Its economic performance has ranged from modest at best to mediocre at worst. In the aftermath of the Asian financial crisis, the Philippines fell behind its neighbours in terms of economic recovery.[42] In a speech she gave in Singapore in 2004, President Arroyo noted that about 4 million Filipinos were out of jobs, compared to only 2.5 million four years before. It is officially estimated that 40 per cent of the population was mired in poverty in 2006 compared to about 30 per cent in 2000. The prospects for a turnaround in this context over the short term are not good. The 2002 Corporate Performance Survey conducted by the Wallace Business Forum showed that most multinational corporations no longer see the Philippines as an attractive investment prospect because of the shaky peace and order situation and deteriorating infrastructure.[43] Two-thirds of the respondents rated the Philippines as worse than other Southeast Asian countries as an invest-ment destination, giving it a low priority in expansion or new investment pro-grammes within the region.[44] This has improved over 2006 with stock markets seeing an increase in trading. These are, however, mostly portfolio investments and do not really translate into investments in the real economy. Consequently, unem-ployment and underemployment (mainly short-term contractual jobs) remain high at 11.7 per cent and 23.5 per cent, respectively. The slowdown in the global economy, brought about by the credit crisis in the United States and the consequent shaky condition of global financial markets, has made the economic conditions facing the Philippines even more difficult. The International Monetary Fund (IMF) reduced its economic growth estimate for the Philippines in 2008 to 5.2 per cent from its earlier announced figure of 5.8 per cent.[45]

The unemployment picture means that many Filipinos prefer to try their luck overseas. In Pulse Asia survey results released in the middle of 2006, approximately three out every 10 Filipinos indicated their willingness to go overseas if given the opportunity.[46] It has been estimated that between 8.4 million to 12 million Filipinos are working overseas. The country's economy is supported to a large extent by the remittances provided by overseas Filipino workers. In 2007, these reached an officially estimated US$14.45 billion.[47] In the first six months of 2008, a total of US$8.2 billion had already been sent to the Philippines, an increase of 17.2 per cent from the last year for the same period. In 2008, the global economic slowdown effected by the global financial crisis has had a debilitating impact on the Philippine economy. Official reports have shown an increase in the country's unemployment rate from 7.4 per cent in January 2008 to 7.7 per cent in January 2009. Unofficial estimates present an even gloomier picture of unemployment. There were likewise expectations of drops in remittances from overseas Filipino workers by the second quarter of 2009 as the continued recession, especially in the United States, has led to job losses or reductions in income. Remittances from overseas workers are estimated to be the equivalent of 11 per cent of the country's gross domestic product.

Democratisation and its ultimate success places a high premium on the extent to which the socio-economic conditions of the people are addressed. In this context, the mixed picture in the Philippines only highlights the vulnerabilities of democracy in the country. The improved macroeconomic situation has not really translated into an improvement in the day-to-day situation of the people. Poverty remains high and the weakness of the job market provides little avenue for the lower classes to improve their conditions in life. Reliance on the overseas labour market, while of great importance over the short term, creates psychological trauma for the families involved and constrains the autonomy of the government on foreign policy matters. Overall, even as democracy remains the preferred system of government for most Filipinos, there is a sense that it has not been able to provide basic services that could upgrade the people's quality of life. This is not just based on high expectations of what a democracy is supposed to be able to accomplish but on real lack of performance especially on the socio-economic front. While at the moment, this has been instrumental mainly in the negative net satisfaction ratings of the Arroyo Administration, the possibility of it affecting, over the medium and long term, people's confidence in the country's democratic institutions cannot be underestimated.

Structural foundations: protecting freedom and equality

The weak state factor has been an issue that the democratisation process in the Philippines has had to contend with since the accession of Corazon Aquino to the presidency in 1986. Only the reform-oriented administration of President Fidel V. Ramos was able to at least partially institute wide-ranging reforms particularly in infrastructure development and the economy. It, in summary, 'improved the peace and order situation, enhanced external defence capabilities, liberalized the economy, brought macroeconomic stability, more foreign investments, a larger role for the private sector, and better economic infrastructure'.[48] While the economic benefits from these reforms proved to be short-lived, they were at least partially responsible for largely insulating the Philippines from the effects of the 1997 Asian financial crisis.[49] Montes was less sanguine and argued that

> the less intrusive government role in the economy – erected as a result of economic reforms and political democratisation interacting with the long-standing private sector preeminence in the economic sphere – dampened the potential for hothouse, Asian-style growth processes. This prevented the Philippines from growing too fast before the 1997 regional crisis.[50]

De Dios and Hutchcroft agreed with Montes and noted that the success of the Ramos reforms were uneven at best in terms of their overall result.[51] They pointed out that the most important contribution of the Ramos Administration was in economic liberalisation, but it was less successful in putting in place stronger institutional foundations for development, redistributive policies, and political reform intended to enhance participation of and government responsiveness to marginalised groups in society.[52] In fact, the continuing problem of the weak state was evident in the inability of the Ramos Administration to pursue its reform programmes without having to resort to traditional pork-barrel politics. In the end, Presidential Security Adviser Jose Almonte had to admit that even as 'hard reforms requiring greater administrative capacity [were] attempted [during the Ramos period] . . . the weaknesses of the Philippine state [started] to show'.[53]

An attempt to address these issues is part of the planned Charter Change initiative of the Arroyo Administration where the economic provisions which limit foreign participation in the economy is under review. The Consultative Commission led by former University of the Philippines President Abueva emphasised the need to address these issues and consider less restrictive foreign participation in the economy. The initiative on Charter Change itself, even as a majority of Filipinos are opposed to it, is an attempt to address institutional weaknesses in the political system. The proposal to shift to a parliamentary system (without really defining what kind of parliamentary system it is) is supposed to get around the policy gridlock that has been the result of the co-equal status of the executive and the legislature. Put another way, a parliamentary system facilitates more harmonious executive–legislative relations that could more efficiently dispose of policy issues. This fundamental assumption, however, of the inherent superiority of a parliamentary system over a presidential system has already been questioned by academic studies.[54] In the context of the Philippines, institutional limitations make the prospect of a parliamentary system no less problematic than the presidential system. Central to this is poor political party institutionalisation among Philippine political parties. Poor party discipline, lack of accountability of candidates to their parties, lack of coherent party platforms and programmes, and vote-maximisation goals all contribute to poor political party institutionalisation.[55] Political parties are essential to a parliamentary system and party institutionalisation is a prerequisite to an effective parliament, and not the other way around. The Consultative Commission included political party reform in their recommendations but there is really very little incentive on the part of politicians to strengthen political parties at this point. The situation is made worse by the way the party-list system in the Philippines is currently structured. A low threshold of 2 per cent and low limit on seats that each party-list organisation can have regardless of the number of votes they get (three) does not in any way contribute to the strengthening of the party system in the country. The low threshold, while favourable to party-list organisations which more often than not do not really have extensive resources for campaigning, creates a disincentive to strengthening party structures since the number of votes needed to win a seat is relatively low.[56] At the same time, the low ceiling for seats that can be won by party-list organisations means that there is no need to strengthen the political party beyond what is needed to capture these few seats. While the party-list system is really the main venue for the construction of progressive legislation in the House of Representatives, these limitations hinder it from becoming the catalyst for strengthening political party institutionalisation in the country. What makes the situation even more questionable is the presence of a number of party-list representatives in the House of Representatives which have known ideological and institutional ties with organisations that seek to replace the country's democratic system through armed conflict.

As important as these debates and discussions on institutional design are, they overlook the underlying reasons for why Charter Change should be considered in the first place which De Dios and Hutchcroft so perceptively raised: the need to enhance participation and government responsiveness to marginalised groups in society. In a democratic system, institutional and structural reforms are undertaken to enhance and better facilitate the enjoyment of freedom and equality. As noted in the previous section, improved macroeconomic numbers have not really affected the quality of life of ordinary Filipinos. This may be a function of time, but time may be of the essence. Even as the support for democracy remains strong, the continued underperformance of the government in terms of providing for the basic needs of the people, and thereby addressing their socio-economic rights, may lead to widespread disenchantment with the country's democratic institutions.

The question of whether institutional and structural change will enhance the ability of Philippine democracy to facilitate the greater enjoyment of freedom and equality becomes more significant in the face of reports of violations of human rights which involve the government to some degree. This is related to the continued tendency of political actors to use violence to settle differences or grievances. This is seen to have a particular effect on freedom of the press as the Philippines has gained a reputation for being among the most dangerous places in the world for journalists or news reporters due to the number killed since 2001.[57] Accusations have been made by the National Union of Journalists in the Philippines that some ranking police officers may be involved.[58]

Violence and the lack of regard given to due process and human rights have also affected debates regarding the country's security. The passage of an anti-terrorism law was stalled by debates in the Senate over the powers of arrest that it would give the executive. According to Senate Minority Leader, Aquilino Pimentel Jr., the proposed anti-terrorism legislation will be taken advantage of by 'unscrupulous elements of the administration to harass and trample upon the rights of the political opposition'.[59] He cited the arrest of five members of the Estrada-allied Union of the Masses for Democracy and Justice for allegedly planning to assassinate key government officials. The police had initially denied that the five were in their custody. The arraignment of 23 people, including former University of the Philippines President Francisco Nemenzo, on rebellion charges even as the documents and charges against each individual were not clear was also cited by critics of the government as a testament to the increasing tendency of the Arroyo Administration to resort to measures that threatened human rights in the country.

The passage of the anti-terrorism bill into legislation has also been linked to the issue of political killings of the militants of the Left by the military.[60] The Human Rights group Karapatan has recorded that from January 2001 to June 2007, 724 extra-judicial killings have transpired, mostly involving journalists, left-leaning activists, or those critical of the current administration. According to the Bayan Muna Party-list representative Teodoro Casino, the number of activists who have been killed increased dramatically with the entry of the Left in mainstream politics.[61] Most of the killings occur in areas where left-wing party-list representation is strongest. What is curious is that these killings are taking place at a time when the communist insurgency across the country, though proving to be resilient, has seen a drop in the recruitment of guerrillas for the New People's Army. At present it is reported to have around 5,000 guerrillas across the country, 20 per cent of its heyday number of 25,000 during the Aquino Administration. While it is not clear who is responsible for these deaths, the Philippine Commission on Human Rights has pointed to a trend that shows the victims are all somehow associated with groups which are either anti-government or anti-Arroyo.[62] An anonymous military officer was quoted as saying that killing these people is retribution for the abuses committed by the Left on the democratic space that they have been given.[63]

The development of institutional support for democracy is important to sustaining the process of democratisation. The case of the Philippines, however, shows how institution building and development intended to support democratisation can lose sight of its purpose. Procedural concerns for these institutions should be addressed by clear laws and rules that govern their operation. This presumes a certain degree of consistency with which these rules are applied across the citizenry. The problem in the case of the Philippines in this context is that procedures are observed selectively. This is made worse by the absence of observance of the substantive aspect of democracy – the protection of rights and civil liberties. Even as the Philippines is a signatory to all major international human rights instruments, and to a large extent has put into effect national laws that support these commitments, the implementation of these laws and the effective observance of human rights and civil liberties that their implementation connotes has, during the second term of the Arroyo Administration, become less of a deterrent to government abuses. While it is difficult to prove (and therefore legitimately claim) that these abuses have become part of official policy (especially with regards to critics of the administration), the lack of action on the part of the administration to check their occurrence and bring their perpetrators to justice creates an environment of impunity. This only contributes to the growing scepticism that, as per Miranda, has become the general attitude of the public towards the Arroyo Administration, and the consequent effect that this scepticism has on the country's democratic principles.

Conclusion: some thoughts to ponder

The discussion in the previous sections points to three key and interlocking issues that underpin the problem of democracy in the Philippines: a weak state, lack of political stability, and discredited political leadership. Implicit in the context of these three issues are a myriad of factors that influence these key issues and in turn contribute to the 'low quality' of democracy in the Philippines (*a la* Case) or the lack of completion of the country's process of democratic consolidation. These are all interrelated as the weakness of the Philippine state contributes greatly to the political instability of the Philippines and inability of the political leadership at the highest levels to gain credibility from the electorate. At the same time, the inability of a discredited political leadership to mobilise political support for much-needed institutional reforms that could address the weakness of the Philippine state only further exposes the ineffectuality of both. This can be observed in the absence of consistency in the adoption and implementation of policies. As one bureaucrat pointed out, economic policy in the Philippines, for instance, can be characterised as *urong-sulong* (going by fits and starts).[64]

These are the structural constraints with which democratic consolidation in the Philippines has had to contend. It is no wonder then that a brief look at categories by which the degree of democratic consolidation can be assessed shows a disconcerting picture. The most important factor in favour of democracy in the Philippines is the continued preference for it shown in the results of public opinion surveys. As noted in this chapter, there is still a residue of public trust in democratic institutions (even the questionable one of 'people power'). It is this preference which has sustained democratisation, no matter how tenuous, in the Philippines. On the other hand, anti-democratic behaviour especially involving the political elites of the country (regardless of their ideological persuasion) has been key to the stalling of the democratisation process. The prevalence of political violence, the clear-cut disregard for legalities, and the lack of respect for the results of electoral competition (though there is reason for this) have all hindered the strengthening of democracy in the country. Structural constraints only contribute further to the problems of the democratisation process. Democracy's minimum standard is supposed to be the holding of fair, free, competitive, and regular elections. To be able to do so, however, requires a support infrastructure that would ensure that elections are exactly that. This would mean an electorate that is educated and able to make unfettered and intelligent choices, a bureaucratic structure that supports not only the holding of elections, but also its aftermath, and a legal system that is upheld by all. The entire government structure is losing the confidence of its citizens because of a simple issue – the state's inability to look out for their welfare. This includes the inability to deliver services properly and consistently, and the inability to guide citizen behaviour through the largely impartial and consistent implementation of the law. From an economic standpoint, the problem is that inconsistency brings with it a certain degree of unpredictability. Investors would like to know that when they invest, the rules of the game are not going to change overnight.

The law is supposed to provide structure to relationships within a polity. The case of the Philippines has always been less an issue of an absence of the law as the lack of seeing it implemented consistently and impartially. The issue evident here is the extent to which class divides make the law work one way for one group of people and another way for others. Corruption factors strongly in the inconsistent implementation of the law. The very existence of corruption, and its existence at different levels of government, is seen as the epitome of a lack of state control over its own. Even as the administration of Estrada, for example, was rejected by the people through massive street action because of its perceived corrupt nature, other administrations have had to deal with and were tainted by the presence of corruption from the lowest levels of government. The presence of cartels that prevented the successful implementation of bureaucratic reform is testament to this. Yet, corruption is also a function of poverty and lack of material well-being. The existence of a large proportion of the population at or under the poverty line raises the question of the quality of political participation in society.

Again, in the end, democracy is about participation in the political process. Democratic consolidation is dependent not on the quantity of participation (how many people are voting), though that is certainly important, but more so on the quality of it (are they able to make intelligent choices, and are they able to continue doing so beyond elections). All these factors contribute to the problem of democracy in the Philippines. Democracy is supposed to be the best system for getting the concerns of the people to the government. This may be so – and in the Philippines there is no question about what these concerns are or whether people are hesitant to speak about them. The problem is the lack of either political will (especially in the face of vested interests) or capacity to do something about it (the weak state syndrome). The latter part of the Aquino Administration and the period of the Ramos Administration are always seen nostalgically as eras of reform, when political leadership sought to push those policies that were needed to ensure economic growth within a democratic framework. It has been quite a few years since then and the Philippines continues to look for a political leadership that could put it back on the right track.

Notes

1 See Temario C. Rivera. *Landlords and Capitalists: Class, Family, and State in Philippine Manufacturing*, Diliman, Quezon City: University of the Philippines Press, 1994, p. 2. Rivera's book remains relevant in terms of the analysis about the centrality of these family and kinship networks in both the economic and political life of the Philippines.

2 Doh Chull Shin, 'On the Third Wave of Democratisation: A Synthesis and Evaluation of Recent Theory and Research', *World Politics* 47, October 1994, p. 143.

3 Larry Diamond, 'The Globalisation of Democracy: Trends, Types, Causes, and Prospects', in Robert O. Slater, Barry M. Schutz and Steven R. Dorr (eds), *Global Transformation and the Third World*, Boulder: Lynne Reinner, 1992.

4 Thomas Carothers, 'The End of the Transition Paradigm', *Journal of Democracy*, vol. 13, no. 1, January 2002, p. 7.

5 David G. Becker, 'Latin America: Beyond "Democratic Consolidation"', *Journal of Democracy*, vol. 10, no. 2, 1999, p. 139.

6 Andreas Schedler, 'What is Democratic Consolidation?' *Journal of Democracy*, vol. 9, no. 2, 1998, p. 95.

7 William Case, *Politics in Southeast Asia: Democracy or Less*, Richmond, Surrey: Curzon Press, 2002, pp. 201–44.

8 Ibid., pp. 242–43.

9 Leonardo Morlino, '"Good" and "Bad" Democracies: How to Conduct Research into the Quality of Democracy', *Journal of Communist Studies and Transition Politics*, vol. 20, no. 1, March 2004, pp. 6–7.

10 The 1st APA was held in Batam, Indonesia in 24–26 November, 2000. Nearly 300 representatives of think tanks, NGOs, grassroots leaders and activists from various part of the region attended this historic event. In 30 August–1 September, 2002, the 2nd APA followed and this time over 300 participants came to Bali, Indonesia to contribute to the discourse.

11 See Christine Susanna Tjhin, Aries A. Arugay, and Herman Joseph S. Kraft, 'Assessing Democratisation in Southeast Asia: Towards Grassroots Empowerment Regional Grassroots Empowerment', *CSIS Working Paper* 51 (1 March 2004). Available online at http://www.csis.or.id/publications_paper_view.asp?id=44&tab=0 (accessed 17 August 2006).

12 Ibid., p. 25.

13 Andreas Schedler, 'Measuring Democratic Consolidation', *Studies in Comparative International Development*, vol. 36, no.1, Spring 2001, pp. 70–71.

14 Ibid., p. 76.

15 Morlino, '"Good" and "Bad" Democracies', pp. 9–21.

16 Felipe B. Miranda *et al.*, 'The Post-Aquino Philippines: In Search of Political Stability', Quezon City: Social Weather Stations, September 1992.

17 *Philippine Star*, 2 November 2002, 1; *Manila Standard*, 29 November 2002, p. 2.

18 Among the most recent and arguably one of the best discussions on this topic can be seen in Sheila S. Coronel, Yvonne T. Chua, Luz Rimban and Rooma B. Cruz. *The Rulemakers: How the Wealthy and Well-born Dominate Congress*, Quezon City, Metro Manila: Philippine Center for Investigative Journalism, 2004. See especially pp. 44–117.

19 For an analysis of this phenomenon, see Rivera, *Landlords and Capitalists*.

20 Dong-Yeob Kim, 'The Politics of Market Liberalization: A Comparative Study of the South Korean and Philippine Telecommunications Service Industries', *Contemporary Southeast Asia*, vol. 24, no. 2, August 2002, p. 356.

21 See Aries A. Arugay, 'The Accountability Deficit in the Philippines: Implications and Prospects for Democratic Consolidation', *Philippine Political Science Journal*, vol. 26, no. 9, 2005, p. 76.

22 Emmanuel S. De Dios and Paul D. Hutchcroft, 'Political Economy', in Arsenio M. Balisacan and Hal Hill (eds), *The Philippine Economy: Development, Politics, and Challenges*, Diliman, Quezon City: University of the Philippines Press, 2003, p. 60.

23 The 'midnight cabinet' that was common knowledge in the country referred to the evening meetings that eventually turned into gambling and drinking sessions which continued till early in the morning between Estrada, his cabinet members, and some close associates. It was during these 'meetings' that some important decisions were supposed to have been made. For an insider's account on the foibles of the Estrada presidency see Aprodicio A. Laquian and Eleanor R. Laquian, *The ERAP Tragedy: Tales from the Snakepit*, Manila: Anvil Publishing, Inc., 2002. See also Amando Doronilla, *The Fall of Joseph Estrada: The Inside Story*, Pasig and Makati: Anvil Publishing, Inc. and Philippine Daily Inquirer, Inc., 2001.

24 Carl Lande, 'The Return of "People Power" in the Philippines', *Journal of Democracy*, vol. 12, no. 2, April 2001, p. 100.

25 See Ibid., p. 101; and De Dios and Hutchcroft, 'Political Economy', pp. 63–64.

26 See results of 26 August–5 September, 2005 Social Weather Stations Survey in SWS Events (10 September 2005). Available online at http://www.sws.org.ph/pr050910.htm (accessed 17 August 2006).

27 Isagani De Castro Jr., 'Itsy-Bitsy Spiders and Little Ms GMA: A Gallery of anti-Arroyo forces,' *Newsbreak*, 27 February 2006: 12.

28 Marites Danguilan Vitug and Glenda M. Gloria, 'Failed Enterprise', *Newsbreak*, 27 March 2006: 12–15.

29 Miriam Grace A. Go, Aries Rufo, and Carmela Fonbuena, 'Romancing the Military,' *Newsbreak*, 27 March 2006: 18–21.

30 Guillermo Luz of the Makati Business Club as quoted in Ibid., p. 18.

31 One of her critics worked with return figures made available to the National Movement for Free Elections (NAMFREL) and pointed out that it was statistically improbable for Arroyo to have won by the margins that emerged in the final count in Congress or by even the smaller margin that was claimed by the NAMFREL Terminal Report. By implication, there was not only manipulation in the tabulation but also collusion on the part of the Congress and NAMFREL to ensure an Arroyo victory. See Roberto Verzola, 'The True Results of the 2004 Philippine Presidential Election Based on the NAMFREL Tally', *Kasarinlan: Philippine Journal of Third World Studies*, vol. 19, no. 2, 2004, pp. 92–118.

32 Minguita Padilla, 'Business as Usual', *Philippine Daily Inquirer*, 29 July 2004.

33 In a presentation he gave at the Philippine Political Science Association annual conference in Zamboanga City in October 2006, Tigno pointed out that the consistency of the popular preference for democracy has helped sustain President Arroyo's political capital. This has enabled her to fend off the challenges from the political opposition, rebel military forces, and the underground Left. This is in spite of her personal unpopularity.

34 See 'Proceedings: Policy Dialogue Series 2004: Academe Meets the Party-List Representatives', *Kasarinalan: Philippine Journal of Third World Studies*, vol. 19, no. 2, 2004, 119–48.

35 26 August–5 September, 2005 Social Weather Survey (13 September 2005). Available online at http://www.sws.org.ph/pr050913.htm (accessed 17 August 2006).

36 June 2006 Social Weather Survey (13 July 2006). Available online at http://www.sws.org.ph/pr060713.htm (accessed 17 August 2006).

37 Second Quarter 2006 Social Weather Survey (11 July 2006). Available online at http://www.sws.org.ph/pr060711.htm (accessed 17 August 2006).

38 First Quarter 2006 Social Weather Survey (3 April 2006). Available online at http://www.sws.org.ph/pr060403.htm (accessed 17 August 2006).

39 Mahar Mangahas, 'The 2006 SWS Annual Survey Review: A Year of Great Trials,' media release distributed on 26 January 2006.

40 Felipe B. Miranda, 'Alternatives: The People's View,' a presentation for the Philippine Political Science Association's national conference held in Zamboanga City, October 2006.

41 Jorge Tigno and Linda Luz Guerrero, 'Political Capital: The Politics of Leadership Resilience in the Philippines, Thailand, and the United States', presentation given at the Philippine Political Science Association annual conference at Zamboanga City in October 2006.

42 Countries which were harder hit by the 1997 Crisis, like Malaysia and Thailand, have been better able to re-start their economies. Even Indonesia was already recording modest growth rates in 2000 despite the serious deterioration in political and social cohesion the country had experienced since 1997. See *ASEAN Statistical Yearbook 2001*, Jakarta: ASEAN Secretariat, 2001, p. 27.

43 *Manila Standard*, 20 November 2002, p. 1.

44 The Philippines has traditionally been a low priority recipient of FDI within Southeast Asia, but more so in the aftermath of the Asian financial crisis. See *ASEAN Statistical Yearbook 2001*, 152–63. In an interview with Mr Eric Teo, an investment risk analyst based in Singapore, the author was told that the Philippines had not only 'dropped off the radar screen of most investors looking to invest in Southeast Asia', they have actually consciously taken the Philippines out of their list of options. Interview conducted in Singapore on 21 June 2004.

45 *Philippines Daily Inquirer*, 2 November 2008 (downloaded on 2 November 2008).

46 Felipe B. Miranda, 'Alternatives: The People's View,' a presentation for the Philippine Political Science Association's national conference held in Zamboanga City, October 2006.

47 Filipino overseas workers are mostly in the Middle East but are in countries as varied as Guinea-Bissau, Italy, Mongolia, Saudi Arabia, Canada, Singapore, the United States, and Uzbekistan. Official estimates of the remittances sent by overseas Filipino workers is probably an underestimate considering that there are several unofficial avenues by which money is sent to the Philippines from overseas.

48 Daniel Joseph Ringuet and Elsa Estrada, 'Understanding the Philippines' Economy and Politics since the Return of Democracy in 1986', *Contemporary Southeast Asia*, vol. 25, no. 2, August 2003, p. 239.

49 Gerardo Sicat, as cited by Ringuet and Estrada, claimed that strong economic fundamentals allowed the country to weather the crisis at its onset. See ibid., p. 245.

50 Manuel F. Montes, 'The Philippines as an Unwitting Participant in the Asian Economic Crisis', in Karl D. Jackson (ed.), *Asian Contagion: The Causes and Consequences of a Financial Crisis*, Boulder, Colorado: Westview Press, 1999, p. 255.

51 De Dios and Hutchcroft, 'Political Economy', p. 57.

52 Ibid., p. 58.

53 Cited in Ringuet and Estrada, 'Understanding the Philippines' Economy and Politics since the Return of Democracy in 1986', p. 240.

54 See in particular Crisline Torres, 'The Philippine Pro-Parliamentary Position and the Comparative Constitutional Design Literature', *Philippines Political Science Journal*, vol. 25, no. 48, 2004, 59–63.

55 Edna E. A. Co, Jorge V. Tigno, Maria Elissa Jayme Lao and Margarita A. Sayo, *Philippine Democracy Assessment: Free and Fair Elections and the Democratic Role of Political Parties*, Diliman, Quezon City: Friedrich Ebert-Stiftung and the National College of Public Administration and Governance, 2005, 75–110.

56 See 'Proceedings: Policy Dialogue Series 2004: Academe Meets the Party-List Representatives', *Kasarinalan: Philippine Journal of Third World Studies*, vol. 19, no. 2, 2004, 119–48.

57 According to *Karapatan*, a human rights group, 44 journalists have been killed as of May 2006 in the country since 2001. See *Business World*, 29 May 2006, p. 11. See also the Report of The Independent Commission to Address Media and Activist Killings.

Created under Administrative Order No. 157 (s. 2006). This was submitted to the Office of the President of the Philippines in June 2007.

58 *The Philippine Star*, 5 May 2005, p. 4.
59 *Business World*, 29 May 2006, p. 11.
60 *The Philippine Star*, 14 August 2006, p. 1.
61 Carmela Fonbuena, 'Seeing Red', *Newsbreak*, 3 July 2006, p. 16.
62 Ibid.
63 Glenda Gloria, 'Free for All,' *Newsbreak*, 3 July 2006, p. 19.
64 Interview with Mr Deo Reyes, Philippine Trade Attaché to Singapore, 2 July 2004.

5 Toward democratic consolidation in Cambodia? Problems and prospects

Sorpong Peou

Introduction

Cambodia began its democratic transition toward liberal democracy on 23 October 1991 when four armed factions (and 18 other states) signed the Paris Peace Agreements to end the war, held a constituent assembly election in May 1993, and subsequently formed a coalition government, which then formally adopted a fairly liberal constitution for the country. Between then and today, Cambodia had approximately 14 years to consolidate its newfound democracy. The question is whether the new liberal democratic regime has now been consolidated.

The quick answer is as follows: Cambodia remains a poor candidate for democratic consolidation. As of 2008, the country had held several elections on a regular basis, but they did not become noticeably free and fair enough to qualify the new political regime as liberally democratic. Significant members of the political elite, especially those within the executive branch of government, did not effectively comply with liberal democratic procedures, rules, norms, and principles. They still maintain anti-democratic attitudes after they have succeeded in personalising power rather than institutionalising democratic power. There exists an extremely weak system of institutional checks and balances among the three branches of government, as well as between government and civil society. The dominant Cambodian People's Party (CPP) – led by Prime Minister Hun Sen – has proved quite successful in consolidating its political power base rather than institutionalising democracy and is now emerging as the hegemonic party.

What theory best explains the challenges to democratic consolidation in this country? The problem of national identity, as suggested by some scholars,[1] has not posed a critical challenge to this political process. Ethnic problems have existed in Cambodia, but have not raised serious questions about its national identity.[2] Based on Latin American democratic experiences, other scholars focus on the utility of 'pacting' through compromise-induced bargaining between democratic and autocratic elites. Without their political compromises, no democracy can be consolidated.[3] The Cambodia case study, however, suggests that the warring factions did sign a democratic peace agreement through compromise, but the newly elected government ended up behaving in an increasingly autocratic fashion soon after. After 1997, the CPP successfully consolidated power at the expense of its former coalition partners in particular and the opposition in general. This democratic erosion associated with growing autocratic behaviour shows the limits of political compromise based on good intentions alone and partly confirms the post-communist experience that democratic consolidation moves forward only when the democratic opposition takes a radical step to sever its ties with defenders of the old socialist order.[4]

Cambodia as the case study presented in this chapter, however, reveals more complexities than what other post-communist countries in Eastern Europe experienced. Cambodia made a political transition not only from communism but also from monarchism and war; even the opposition was made up of monarchists (who claimed to have democratic credentials and to have fought in defence of democracy) and former armed rebels. The country thus experienced all of what the countries in Latin America, Southern Europe, and post-communist Eastern Europe experienced: a long history of monarchical and colonial rule, socialism, poverty, and war.[5]

The overall experience of Cambodia suggests that a history, a culture, and an ideology that stand against democracy no doubt significantly constrain the process of democratic consolidation, as some have suggested.[6] But this case study further sheds light on the argument that the shifting balance of political power between democratic forces and defenders of the former dictatorial order matters far more significantly. As ruling elite members become more successful in controlling the military and security apparatus, the economy and the political arena, the short-term and medium-term prospects for democratic consolidation grow dimmer.

It may thus be useful to study the challenge for democratic consolidation in post-monarchical, post-communist, and post-conflict countries by looking at how political elites battle for political supremacy through adopting different strategies and tactics (electoral and non-electoral) to consolidate power by personalising it and by preventing or weakening the institutionalisation of democratic power. By focusing its analytical attention on structural impediments (particularly, political elites' personal pursuit of military, economic, and political domination), this chapter seeks to advance a new theoretical perspective called 'complex realist institutionalism'.[7]

Elites' anti-democratic politics: power monopolisation versus democratic consolidation

Democratic transition did take place in Cambodia, beginning with the signing of a democratic peace agreement by four warring factions:[8] the Royalists known as FUNCINPEC, the Khmer People's National Liberation Front (KPNLF), the Khmer Rouge or Democratic Kampuchea (DK), and the State of Cambodia (SOC). The transition process ended with the first election of a Constituent Assembly in May 1993. The peace agreement provided a framework whereby the four Cambodian signatories would compete for power though the ballot box rather than bullets in a free and fair political environment. The 1993 election, judged by the United Nations as a qualified success, led to the expected defeat of the former communist party, the CPP (offspring of SOC) and a victory for the opposition party,

FUNCINPEC. Critics of the UN were largely proven wrong at the time. Personalised politics appeared to have given way to institutionalised politics in the form of liberal democracy. A Constituent Assembly came into existence and was subsequently transformed into the National Assembly (whose members then numbered 122), which adopted a liberal democratic institution[9] and approved the formation of a new coalition government made up of four political parties (the peace signatories).[10]

The new two-headed coalition government (with Prince Norodom Ranariddh of FUNCINPEC as First Prime Minister and Hun Sen of the CPP as Second Prime Minister) had its defects and flaws, but was perhaps the best the country could get under the circumstances at the time. The arrangement overcame the CPP threat of territorial secession and maintained political stability, at least until the mid-1990s.

Whether Cambodia has since 1993 moved in the direction of democratic consolidation or power monopolisation remains a subject of debate. For some scholars, Cambodia has now moved toward democratic consolidation. Robert Albritton, for instance, regards the country in 2003 as being 'on the road to democratic consolidation'.[11] According to this optimistic perspective, democratic consolidation simply means the holding of a third national election in July 2003, judged largely as 'relatively free of violence and corruption, compared to previous balloting' and representing 'a significant step toward a multi-party democracy'.[12]

This premature optimism faces a number of difficulties. The author provides no clear definition of democratic consolidation, leading to a flawed analysis and a prediction not substantiated by much empirical evidence. While relying on the concept of democratic consolidation, he makes several observations that seem to contradict his logic and conclusions. Does relative freedom from violence in election times signal democratic consolidation? National elections in Singapore, for instance, have shown high degrees of nonviolence, but no one would say democracy in this Southeast Asian country has now become consolidated. It remains a non-competitive authoritarian state dominated by one near-hegemonic political party.[13]

If we define democratic consolidation as the maturing process extending beyond democratic transition moving toward the ideal type of the democratic regime, we assume that consolidation has much to do with *compliance with* the democratic decision-making procedures (the formation of government through electoral procedures, policy making, and policy implementation), democratic rules (such as representation), liberal norms (such as peaceful conflict resolution or nonviolence and accountability), and liberal principles (most notably liberty). But if one of the significant political elites refuses to comply with most of them by personalising power and institutionalising personal power,[14] then the political process can be defined as power monopolisation. Monopolising power refers to a process in which a group seeks to acquire power by establishing and strengthening repressive institutions either to weaken development of other institutions designed to check its power or simply to deinstitutionalise them.[15] We thus need to distinguish between two opposite forms of power acquisition: democratic consolidation as the process of institutionalising democratic power and power monopolisation as the process of personalising power.

In reality, Cambodian democracy remains largely unconsolidated. Underneath the new electoral politics in recent years, as noted, lay a shaky political foundation for democratic consolidation. Within the electoral realm, the CPP under the leadership of Hun Sen has worked its way to consolidate power at the expense of the winner of the 1993 election and other parties. Hun Sen first sought to personalise rather than institutionalise power by working with Prince Ranariddh in their joint attempt to weaken the other coalition partners. As the political opposition weakened, Hun Sen began to adopt the next strategy to weaken FUNCINPEC. The process of democratisation finally broke down when Hun Sen staged a violent coup in July 1997, ousting his main coalition partner: Prince Ranariddh. Although the new First Prime Minister, Ung Huot (from FUNCINPEC) was installed, Hun Sen was the man in charge.

After that, political stability increased and three elections were subsequently held (in 1998, 2003, and 2008), but democracy seems to have given way to autocratic politics. The CPP also kept gaining more seats (from 51 in 1993, to 64 in 1998, to 73 in 2003, and to 90 in 2008). After the 2008 election, the opposition has weakened, with the exception of the Sam Rainsy Party (SRP) with 26 seats. FUNCINPEC was badly split and received only two seats. Prince Ranariddh who formed a new party after his name – the Norodom Ranariddh Party – performed badly: it received only two seats (one seat less than what the Human Rights Party received).

Moreover, the CPP has all but monopolised the commune seats since the local council election in 2002. The CPP has since held tight control of close to 1,600, or nearly 99 per cent, of all commune chiefs.[16] The second local council election for 1,621 communes and sub-districts, held on 1 April 2007, gave the CPP another landslide victory, as it retained most of the commune councils, collecting 1,591 council chief positions. The other parties, combined, received only 30 positions.

Cambodia has now moved toward a hegemonic party system, one 'in which a relatively institutionalised ruling party monopolises the political arena, using coercion, patronage, media control, and other means to deny formally legal opposition parties any real chance of competing for power.'[17] It has not yet evolved into a system that may be characterised as 'electoral dictatorship' under which one party dictates the electoral process and does not allow the opposition to compete in elections.

The non-observance of the rule of transparency remains a serious challenge to future prospects for democratic consolidation. This does not mean that no progress has been made. Report after report indicates that the electoral process is becoming increasingly transparent. Still, decisions made by governmental and electoral authorities, and policy actions were not transparent enough. During election times for instance, transparency was often compromised when electoral officials refused to implement complicated regulations and procedures, investigate complaints, and were reluctant to issue sanctions, preferring instead to rely on conciliation.

The electoral rules of freeness and fairness remain subject to violation. Political intimidation and violence, while becoming less widespread and frequent, continues. The CPP has put to the test the rule of free elections by subjecting other political parties to intimidation, violence, and all kinds of legal restrictions. Lest we forget, the CPP has been in power since 1979. The party has engaged in the politics of co-opting and weakening members of the opposition. Hun Sen has succeeded in consolidating his power by relying on both frontal attacks on his opponents as well as a 'divide and conquer' strategy. Between January and August 2004 alone, 11 SRP members were reportedly assassinated by unidentified gunmen. The prime minister also turned against the opposition by supporting and relying on FUNCINPEC's quarrels with the SRP to cause divisions. Early in 2005, three SRP Members of Parliament (MPs) had their parliamentary immunity lifted. One of them was arrested, jailed, and sentenced to seven years in prison, while the other two (Sam Rainsy and Chea Poch) fled the country and have not yet returned. Hun Sen had threatened to arrest them and warned that he would shoot down the plane that would carry Sam Rainsy if the latter returned home. The SRP leader was publically accused of treason. Other political critics were subjected to threats, lawsuits, and imprisonment.

The 2008 election saw no substantial improvement in terms of freeness and fairness. Although the level of political violence was low compared to the previous elections, the political environment did not become any freer and fairer. The CPP changed its strategy from using such methods as direct physical violence and intimidation to applying pressure on people to become its members. A report by the UN Office of the High Commissioner for Human Rights in Cambodia reported that 'since the beginning of the year [2008] OHCHR . . . observed an apparent campaign of pressure, threats, intimidation and inducements against political activists at every level in an attempt to persuade them to change parties.'[18] My discussions with numerous individuals in Cambodia confirm that they were under pressure to support or join the CPP if they wanted to enjoy security and benefits.

Opposition parties have also had limited opportunities to make their voices adequately heard. After the coup in 1997, the CPP moved to dismantle their media outlets and still restricts their access to the media sector. The SRP has not even been authorised to open a radio station. Because Cambodians watch television and listen to radio more than they read newspapers, the CPP has thwarted any attempts to level the playing field by maintaining its domination over the country's broadcast media.[19] The situation has not improved much. The CPP still controls the media, making it difficult for the opposition to conduct an effective election campaign. Prior to the 2008 election campaign period, for instance, opposition party candidate and editor Dam Sith of the newspaper *Moneaksekar Khmer* was arrested and detained because of his report on a speech by Sam Rainsy. The SRP leader himself received a threat because of that speech. The OHCHR issued a statement after the 2008 election, expressing its concern 'about deeply entrenched inequalities among the political parties in their access to, and control of, both electronic and print media, and the consequent effect upon the voters' right to an informed electoral choice'.[20]

The rule of representation also remains weak. Corruption as one key indicator suggests that the regime has violated this democratic rule. In 2005, for instance, Transparency International ranked Cambodia 132nd out of 159 countries. Cambodia scored extremely low: 2.3 out of a clean score of 10, identifying corruption as a very serious problem.[21] The World Economic Forum (WEF) also classified the country as the third most corrupt among 117 countries. Cambodians themselves also regarded corruption as widespread and did not perceive corrupt practices as socially acceptable. They regarded government at all levels as untrustworthy.[22] In addition, they 'express[ed] the need for more transparency in both local and national level bureaucracy' and wanted to 'increase awareness and information on "right" procedures'.[23]

In short, the new democratic regime remains unconsolidated to the extent that its ruling elite members have failed to comply with the electoral rules of transparency, freeness, fairness, and representation. Elections have now become 'the only game in town', as shown by the fact that they have been held more or less on a regular basis. None of the country's significant elites, including the opposition, has now given serious thought to any other alternatives. No one is prepared to take up arms and start a war, although coup attempts may still be a possibility in the foreseeable future. When measured by the degree of elite compliance with these rules, however, the current regime remains electoral (to the extent that political parties are allowed to exist and compete for power), but undemocratic because the ongoing hegemonic party politics has sought to undermine free and fair elections.

The legal norm of accountability still remains under threat. Accountability within the decision-making machinery has shown little improvement. Government and electoral authorities have shown little accountability for their actions, particularly those related to intimidation and violence during election times. The investigation of criminal acts, including politically motivated killings by local police and CPP elements, has stalled.[24] Few such killers, if any, have been brought to justice. The pursuit of criminal justice against surviving Khmer Rouge leaders (accused of having committed crimes against humanity during their reign of terror between 1975 and 1978) is now under way. But of the few Khmer Rouge leaders who have been tried, none had been punished by 2008.

The illiberal norm of violence has diminished but not disappeared. On the surface, trends show a degree of steady progress toward nonviolence. As noted, the level of political violence before, during, and after the elections has decreased over time. Political parties resorted to less and less violence. Violent protests against election results declined from 1993 to 2008. If violence has become less widespread and frequent, one factor may help explain this positive development: the security apparatus has shown considerable success in suppressing any challenges to the CPP regime. The Ministry of Interior showed more willingness to ban peaceful demonstrations, strikes, and any form of protest against the regime. Before the 2003 election, for instance, National Police Chief General Hok Lundy made it clear to the public in general and the electorate in particular that post-election protests and violence would not be tolerated. There still exists an atmosphere of insecurity, as people have become increasingly hesitant to raise voices critical of government policies. Hun Sen has even threatened on several occasions to abolish the monarchy whenever the king signalled that he would not go along with any of his major policy decisions. Less violence, therefore, does not necessarily mean more CPP compliance with the democratic norm of peaceful conflict resolution; it means the

CPP's growing ability to silence critics and dissents without resorting to violent means.

The extent to which the CPP has complied with the principle of liberty remains difficult to measure. Cambodians have enjoyed more freedom than they did under the SOC regime, but these fundamental freedoms – expression, assembly, and demonstration – have faced growing restrictions in recent years. Freedoms of expression and assembly have come under severe restrictions.[25] Pro-government or anti-opposition demonstrations have been encouraged, but anti-government activities have, since 2003, been banned for the sake of peace and stability. Liberty has become more of what accords the executive branch of government the power to protect 'liberty' as it sees fit (i.e., through the lens of national security by way of restricting individual freedom). This form of liberty looks more ancient than modern: it rests on the idea that the electorate entrusts its representative government with the power to command its obedience rather than promote its freedom.[26]

We can thus roughly 'measure' the process of power monopolising by showing how Hun Sen has both become less compliant with democratic procedures, rules, principles, and norms by consolidating power at the expense of other political forces. As the CPP under his leadership consolidated its despotic and infrastructural power (the power to decide and the power to implement), it succeeded in co-opting and silencing opposition elements. Even within his own party, Hun Sen has succeeded in weakening his intra-party opponents led by CPP President Chea Sim and Interior Minister Sar Kheng. He made subsequent moves to establish personal control over the party's decision-making machinery. The overall trend tells us little, if we ignore the growing degree of silent repression underneath the new electoral politics.

In short, the new democratic regime remains unconsolidated, not so much because the ruling political elite in Cambodia have now stopped playing the electoral game, but because they have adopted strategies and tactics to consolidate power by personalising power and weakening the opposition. Although we still know little about the conditions under which political elites pursue power through adopting electoral but undemocratic means or may still have a limited understanding of whether they sequence their strategies and tactics,[27] the Cambodian experience shows that they tend to use all strategies or tactics that are available, simultaneously. As shall be shown next, one condition that encourages the ruling elites to pursue power through electoral means is the fact that the country's institutional structure has always been too weak to guarantee their security and to constrain them.

The persistence of weaknesses in the system of institutional checks and balances

If the overall trend in Cambodian politics points to the process of power monopolisation rather than democratic consolidation, the persistence of weaknesses in the system of institutional checks and balances fundamental to democracy offer the best explanatory variable. The process of institutionalisation in the context of democratisation began in the early 1990s, but has since the mid-1990s failed to mature. This chapter defines democratic institutionalisation as the process in which organisations and procedures become more politically independent (no interference from the outside), organisationally effective and influential (capable of performing efficiently and achieving goals), and sustainable (when regarded as legitimate and financially self-sufficient).[28] With this definition, one can speak of Cambodia's extreme institutional weakness at the state, political, and civil society levels.

New state, political, and civil society institutions in Cambodia sprang up after the 1993 election, but most of them remain extremely weak. At the state level, one unfortunate fact about democratic erosion or stagnation in Cambodia is that personal power still triumphs over the power of democratic institutions. State institutions remain quite weak. The WEF's *Global Competitiveness Report* (2005–6) ranks Cambodia's public institutions 114th among 117 countries.[29] According to one study published in 2008, Cambodia ranks 34th among 141 developing countries in terms of state weakness – weaker than Timor-Leste (43rd) but stronger than North Korea (15th) and Myanmar (17th).[30] These rankings may not be accurate (Cambodia, for instance, seems institutionally stronger than Timor-Leste), but they still reflect a high degree of state institutional weakness in Cambodia.

There is no doubt that the Cambodian state has now become more institutionalised, but it remains under-institutionalised in terms of the requirements of a good-quality democracy. According to a report,

> Inefficient, opaque procedures create confusion and impatience and encourage firms and individuals to pay "speed money" and bribes . . . procedural mistakes are common in the Customs Department, creating clear invitations to bribe. Despite a 2001 law requiring environmental and social impact studies before forest and agricultural concessions are approved, "inefficiency" in the Ministry of Agriculture has essentially waived this requirement.

The report states that, 'Inefficiency . . . helps to limit information resources, maintain Government control and justify shoddy administrative procedures'. Moreover,

> Inefficiency of the Ministry of Finance in carrying out its duty in reviewing major government contracts means sloppy procedures and overpriced contracts go unquestioned. Inefficiency so extreme that veterans' pensions aren't paid for three years enables unscrupulous ministry employees to 'buy' pension rights from their rightful owners.

And 'Inefficient procedures in the judiciary ensure reports of investigating judges and trial court judgments are difficult to access, or are not accessible at all. Inefficiency in passing internal regulations for parliamentary operations hamstrings opposition parties'.[31]

By the first decade of the twenty-first century, limited progress has become more and more evident in the area of institution building within the legislature and judiciary. The bicameral legislature has not become politically independent and organisationally effective enough to withstand executive interference. The National Assembly and the Senate have grown subservient to the interests of the Hun Sen Government. In August 2004, for instance, CPP and FUNCINPEC MPs agreed in a majority vote to exclude the opposition SRP from positions in the nine assembly commissions. In February 2005, the two ruling parties succeeded in lifting three SRP MPs' parliamentary immunity using a show of hands in direct violation of the parliamentary rule of secret ballot.

The judiciary remains institutionally too weak to uphold the interests of democracy. This state institution remains weak and often subservient to the interests of executive members, most notably the prime minister and his cabinet members. The CPP appointed most of the current judges. The Supreme Council of Magistracy (SCM) still has little power to select and discipline judges. The Cambodian Bar Association has become increasingly politicised, having admitted politicians without any legal credentials (such as Prime Minister Hun Sen) as its members enjoying the full right to practice law. The legal community remains small: the whole country has a little over 100 judges, 100 prosecutors, and about 250 private lawyers.

Comparatively, the executive has emerged as the strongest of the three branches of government (including the legislature and judiciary). Still, government leaders have generally proved unable to make effective policy decisions and implement them successfully. Hun Sen, for instance, pledged to press for the adoption of an anti-corruption law in June 2003, but has so far failed to make good on his promise. In another instance, the prime minister declared a 'war against land-grabbers' in March 2007, but proved unable to win the war. Land-grabbing continued unabated. According to a long-time observer of Cambodian politics, Lao Mong Hay, 'forestry land-grabbing has been on the increase in almost all provinces'.[32] State institutions remain deeply corrupt and highly politicised. Not much evidence shows genuine progress in the area of military and police institutional reform, either. A series of surveys during the first half of the 2000s showed that Cambodians regarded the police forces as one of the most dishonest and corrupt institutions.[33]

Political society (particularly political parties) has not become evenly institutionalised, either. Beneath the appearance of party institutionalisation within the multi-party system lurks a growing grip on personal power. The CPP – the country's most institutionalised political party because it has enjoyed the longest history of party building and successes in the subsequent elections, when compared with other political parties – more and more resembles a hegemonic party.

The opposition has grown weaker politically over the years. FUNCINPEC, increasingly fractured, can no longer play the role of an effective party. After 1997, FUNCINPEC lost almost all of its muscle and disintegrated. The SRP has now emerged as the main opposition party capable of challenging the CPP, but remains highly under-institutionalised, as the party is known for its heavy dependence on the personal charisma of Sam Rainsy. As for the other smaller opposition political parties, during the past elections they lacked internal institutional accountability and transparency, were organisationally ineffective, and operationally unsustainable. Political party under-institutionalisation deeply reflects their inability to compete effectively in the elections. Most of them were newly established, under-funded, and highly dependent upon individual party leaders' personal skills and wealth. The declining number of political parties registered to compete in elections reveals another negative trend: the opposition is more likely to weaken than to grow stronger. During the 1998 election, 38 parties competed with the CPP, but the number shrank to seven in the 2002 election. In 2003, 23 parties registered to compete in the election. In the 2008 election, only 11 parties were registered to compete for power.

Between the state and political society stands the Election Administration (EA) made up of the National Election Committee (NEC), 24 Province Election Committees (PECs), and 1,621 Commune Election Committees (CECs), whose role and capacity include organising and administering elections. The EA became more institutionalised over time in technical and organisational terms, especially after the 1998 election, but its legitimacy remains subject questionable. A report by the International Republican Institute, for instance, states that

> the NEC's accomplishments appear to have been largely technical in nature. Many NEC actions – and just as frequently its inaction – reinforced concerns regarding the NEC's political neutrality and contributed significantly to the climate of impunity that allowed for widespread political violence, election law violations, and intimidation of voters.[34]

The NEC has hardly enforced the electoral laws and its own directives. Often based on appeals from its chairman, the NEC issued directives, but has hardly imposed sanctions on violators. According to a report by the UN Special Representative, 'While the 2003 elections saw the first application of sanctions by the National Election Committee and its provincial commissions, the electoral authorities were largely ineffective in dealing with serious breaches of the "Electoral Law".'[35] Prior to the 2008 election, observers had remained sceptical about the institutional independence of the more technically competent NEC, because its members were still appointed by a few political parties, especially the CPP; the NEC headquarters were still located within the CPP-controlled Ministry of Interior; the NEC had no sub-national structure and still relied on commune councils, which were dominated by the CPP and took orders from the Ministry of Interior.

Civil society organisations grew in number during the 1990s and reached more than 1,500 in the mid-2000s. They look 'vibrant' and capable of undertaking tasks the government has not performed. Civil society has been considered 'life-supporting'. To a large extent, they have taken responsibility from the state in meeting social needs and enjoy greater legitimacy than the latter. The pagoda and NGOs have enjoyed the highest level of trust among Cambodians.[36]

In general, civil society organisations remain institutionally weak. Most local NGOs have not engaged in politics (because of their active involvement in delivering services and providing assistance in areas such as food, health, and education) and not developed effective democratic governance for themselves. They also seem to have had difficulty building solid financial systems and putting together credible boards of directors. According to one consultant, 'there are no examples here and there is a shortage of neutral and educated people who can act on boards'. She added that, 'there are plenty of examples of boards that only exist on paper – they don't actually meet or have a role that has been defined.'[37] Even the best boards of directors had to take the need for political balance into account.[38] According to a report put out in 2003, 'In many aspects the civil society in Cambodia must be regarded as weak'.[39] The report further reveals that many civil society organisations were highly politicised, had limited capacity for long-term strategic planning, did not become a credible force in fostering a democratic culture, and remained unsustainable because of donors' short-term and project-oriented support.

Although some NGOs were established by the government to counter-balance NGOs established to monitor government policies and activities, politically independent NGOs remain institutionally weak. A look at the Election Monitoring Organisations (EMOs) and human rights NGOs, for instance, provides empirical support for this claim. The EMOs' institutional weaknesses abound. The Coalition for Free and Fair Elections (COFFEL) was dissolved soon after the commune election in 2002. The Committee for Free and Fair Elections (COMFREL) and the Neutral and Impartial Committee for Free Elections in Cambodia (NICFEC) have managed to avoid the problems experienced by COFFEL. In spite of their generally excellent efforts, these EMOs still lack political influence over the electoral process.

Local human rights NGOs have advanced the causes of human rights, but have not become highly institutionalised either.[40] There exists a trend in the process of institution building in the field of human rights. Initially, there were several independent human rights NGOs, such as the Khmer Institute of Democracy (KID), Cambodian Institute for Human Rights (CIHR), Cambodian League for the Promotion and Defense of Human Rights known as LICADHO, the Cambodian Human Rights and Development Association known as ADHOC, and the Cambodian Center for Human Rights (CCHR). The CCHR, founded in 2002, fell into corruption scandals, and its president, Kem Sokha, formed the Human Rights Party in 2007. In reality, only two (LICADHO and ADHOC) look steady enough to perform their duties.

Overall, civil society organisations have played a positive role in Cambodian politics; however, they have not become institutionally strong enough to help consolidate the democratic gains after the 1993 election. Civil society institutions have shown few signs of institutional development that equips them with the ability to become politically independent, influential, and sustainable. They have not proved useful as an agent of democratic consolidation in terms of their ability to reverse the process of power consolidation by the political and economic elites in the country. There thus exists a question that needs to be answered: why did state, political, and civil society institutions, designed to strengthen a system of checks and balances, continue to remain weak? Structural explanations can help make sense of this.

Structural impediments to democratic institutionalisation

Cultural authoritarianism has existed in Cambodia for centuries and has no doubt worked against modern institutional development.[41] Its political culture does not promote compromise, 'an alien concept'.[42] The monarchy remained highly centralised. Cambodians viewed their kings as divine. Khmer soldiers in ancient Cambodia historically fought to serve their emperor. Civil society existed, when we take religious Buddhist institutions into account; however, social institutions generally remained politically passive or even subservient to state interests.

Cultural authoritarianism has also challenged the process of democratic institution building in a direct way. Cambodian leaders still behave in an autocratic fashion. Even Sam Rainsy, leader of the SRP (the only opposition party capable of posing a challenge to the CPP), for instance, is known for his inability to work with others in his party. Some executive leaders of institutions, including those within civil society, often behave in an autocratic manner. Many of the human rights NGOs with autocratic leaders appear to remain institutionally weak. They have also resisted decentralisation and tend to score low in institutional accountability and transparency. Their staff appear less active and feel alienated from their leaders.[43]

Although it has some merit, the idea of authoritarianism as a cultural constraint on democratic institution building does not hold much weight. Cultural determinists tend to exaggerate the role of authoritarian culture as the independent variable. In my view, traditional culture resists the introduction of liberal values, but it does not explain why democracy has been consolidated in societies where traditional values persist.[44] Culture seems more dynamic than static.[45]

The ideological legacy of socialism offers further explanatory power. Cambodia came under the revolutionary totalitarian rule of Maoists, who sought to break free from its centuries-old cultural traditions perpetuated by monarchism. The Khmer Rouge revolutionary regime, having abolished individualism (a key ideological foundation of liberal democracy)[46] quickly sought to rebuild a new classless society based on collectivism by centralising its communist power through violence.

The People's Republic of Kampuchea (PRK), renamed the State of Cambodia (SOC) in 1989, remained a socialist dictatorship. The political report of the Fourth National Congress of the Front, for instance, stated the Party had 'a line and policy based on the creative application of a genuine Marxism-Leninism to the specific conditions of Cambodia'.[47] Critics have attributed the lack of democratisation to the fact that 'the CPP is tightly disciplined along classic Stalinist lines – a structure that it has used to its advantage'.[48]

Overall the ideological power of socialism as an anti-liberal ideology remains indeterminate. While Cambodia as a single case study may validate ideological determinism, cross-country analyses point to variations in post-communist states that have moved in different ways. Although post-communist states did come from similar starting points in terms of ideology, single-party systems, and state-controlled economies, they have moved in diverse and radically different directions, 'ranging from prosperous social democracies to sultanistic or even dynastic regimes'.[49]

One of the great difficulties facing the process of democratic institution building in Cambodia after the first national democratic election in 1993 resulted from the fact that any institutions that survived the decades of war and the Khmer Rouge regime were left underdeveloped, and the newly established ones hardly had time to develop. Cambodia has a long history of institutional weakness, most notably after the Khmer Rouge Empire began to decline. French colonial rule undermined traditional political institutions, but did not contribute much to the process of modern state institution building. The civil war and extensive destruction throughout the 1970s culminated in the disappearance of many modern institutions. The Khmer Rouge regime (1975–78) destroyed almost all existing institutions. The Pol Pot Government brought down all the pre-1975 bureaucratic institutions, and even eradicated Buddhism and other religious institutions.

This does not mean the Khmer Rouge regime never sought to build any new institutions, but its efforts to do so focused on building state and party institutions in a highly centralised fashion. The Communist Party of Kampuchea (PKK) emerged as the dominant political institution, seeking to control the cooperative but apparently unable to do it effectively. The PKK members numbered only 14,000 and found it impossible to control the population, but the new institutions had no chance to develop as internal struggles for power grew intense,[50] and the war with Vietnam preoccupied Khmer Rouge leaders and led to their downfall in early 1979.

The new socialist regime, the PRK, came to power in 1979 and had to start building new institutions, virtually from scratch. But all new institutions served as the collective political instrument of the PRK regime. The military and police in particular existed to ensure regime security. The National Assembly played a role 'limited to a ratification of the decisions of the government, both for the election of high-ranking officers and for the adoption of laws'.[51] The judiciary enjoyed no political independence: 'the local people's committees (which in turn report to the Council of Ministers), the Party, the Front and other mass organisations . . . exercise[d] a large degree of influence and control' over it.[52]

Electoral institutions were established, but remained rudimentary. The PRK established electoral procedures and electoral authorities (the highest of which was the Electoral Council) to hold the first and only National Assembly election in May 1981. This election administration never evolved into a politically independent institution. Representatives of the Central Committee of the People's Revolutionary Party of Kampuchea, the United Front for the Construction and Defence of the Kampuchean Motherland (whose role was to provide 'solid supports of the state' and to follow the Party as the Front's 'leading core'), and the mass organisations (which came under the auspices of the Front), all made up the Electoral Council.

Structural impediments – poverty and hegemonic party politics – have more explanatory power than the other ideational constraints discussed so far. Modern democratic institution building depends on human and material resources. To achieve institutional development, Cambodia must have a capable, stable, and well-functioning capitalist economy. There seems to be a correlation between lack of institutionalisation and economic underdevelopment. Poor countries cannot afford to build and sustain modern institutions essential to democratic politics.

Key indicators show that Cambodia's overall level of economic development remains extremely low. The number of people living below the poverty line

(50 cents per day) grew from about 36 per cent in the late 1990s to about 43 per cent (about 5.6 million) in the early 2000s,[53] and was once predicted to increase to 45 per cent (5.8 million) in 2005.[54] Real unemployment rates evidently remain very high and may keep rising.[55] Growth of per-capita income has only slightly improved (US$247 in 1998, US$264 in 1999, US$261 in 2000, US$259 in 2001, slightly over US$300 in 2005, and about US$480 in 2006).

The overall trend in economic growth has been positive (with high GDP growth rates: 6.2 per cent in 2002, 8.6 per cent in 2003, 10.0 per cent in 2004, 13.4 per cent in 2005, 10.7 per cent in 2006, and 10.1 per cent in 2007), but long-term prospects for economic development look uncertain. The economy has benefited from growth in a few sectors (mainly construction, garment, and tourism), low inflation (although it rose to 4.4 per cent in 2007), and generally balanced budgets, but has experienced trade deficits and increased foreign debts. The economy remains uncompetitive (with the global competitive index of 105 out of 134 countries in 2006–7, 110 in 2007–8, and 109 in 2008–9)[56] and cannot meet the fast-growing demands of the labour force.

Poor socio-economic conditions also have had limiting effects on institution building. Not enough resources have been available for institution building. Political parties remain under-institutionalised partly because their members are too poor to provide support. Political parties must get rich (even by corrupt means, if they could), become personalised (leaders are providers), and remain unlikely to become highly institutionalised. When in trouble economically, politicians are under pressure to look for scapegoats, such as opposition parties and critical groups, seek to strengthen their power, and make claims about the negative effects of democracy.

Hegemonic party politics, however, remains the severest structural impediment to democratic consolidation. The CPP has sought to consolidate political power, as noted earlier, and become a hegemonic party. After the coup in 1997, the party system in Cambodia resembles more and more a hegemonic party system. With the weakening of opposition parties, mass mobilisation capable of working against the Hun Sen regime also weakened. Mass protests took place after the 1998 and 2003 elections, but have since weakened considerably. The former communist party has made a bold move to restore the old hegemonic order.

Why did the CPP under the leadership of Hun Sen succeed in consolidating personal power at the expense of democratic institutional power? The prime minister and his party seem to have shifted their strategy from relying on politically motivated uses of force (such as grenade attacks, the coup in 1997, and killings) to one based on politically motivated lawsuits (suing political opponents in pro-CPP courts) and other forms of institutional control. Hun Sen has taken advantage of institutional underdevelopment by seeking to dominate other state institutions such as the legislature and the judiciary. The process of decentralisation has not gone well, as commune councils still lack the power to make effective decisions. The Ministry of Interior maintains control over them. Hun Sen also succeeded in getting business tycoons with close personal ties to him elected to the Senate, which saw a reduction of non-CPP seats to 12 from 28 out of the 61 senators (four of whom were appointed by the National Assembly and the king). His political party also funded 'satellite parties' to ensure its electoral victory. His strategy to consolidate power seems to validate conventional theory holding that the personalisation of power works best before institutions capable of checking executive power come unto their own.[57]

Hun Sen has also managed to build and strengthen his own institutions that have helped reinforce his executive power. According to one United States Agency for International Development (USAID) report, his regime 'developed a full array of outside institutions – captive firms, controlled media, party-affiliated NGOs and unions – as well as the police, military, judiciary and parliament to support the corrupt system'.[58] Hun Sen has created other private networks to defend his regime. He succeeded in building an armada of institutions, such as a bodyguard force of 3,500 well-armed soldiers who would protect his life at all costs and the Pagoda Boys who serve his political interests. Known for their staunch defence of his regime, the Pagoda Boys are prepared to launch counter-attacks on any anti-CPP demonstrations. He also proved capable of tightening control over the national police by building a family alliance with top officials, most notably police chief General Hok Lundy, through marriage of their family members.

Overall the CPP has been successful in consolidating political power by adopting a strategy to consolidate its power base by weakening the opposition and by doing as little as possible to strengthen the process of democratic institutionalisation. Bent on maximising its political and security interests, the CPP elite show no real intention of consolidating any democratic gains. This is not to suggest that Hun Sen and other CPP leaders are worse than any other Cambodian politician when in power, but to point out that they all are the by-products of ideational and structural constraints that require them to behave as they did.

Conclusion

Cambodia has now proved unable to consolidate the democratic gains it made after the 1993 election, thus invalidating the argument that regards democratisation as a linear process. There exists one reason for Cambodia's democratic breakdown and erosion: extreme institutional weakness. State institutions such as the executive, military and police, the legislature and the judiciary remain subservient to the ruling elite's interests. The opposition has weakened. Civil society organisations remain too weak to constrain or limit executive power, which is unlikely to become more dispersed. The durability of the CPP regime also lies in its strategy to tighten its grip on political power and to prevent other institutional forces from becoming capable of checking it. The regime's overall success owes to the fact that it could effectively move one step ahead of democratic institutionalisation before it began to solidify. Hun Sen and his loyalists have become the villains, but blaming them alone would not help promote the cause of democracy, for they too operate under the constraints of cultural, ideological, historical, economic, and political structures.

What does the future hold for Cambodia's democracy? As I argued in 2000,[59] the best Cambodia could hope for would be political stability. This chapter validates this prediction. The country will remain stable for some time to come, but this type of stability seems to be fragile. The country might be moving in the direction of electoral dictatorship, with a hegemonic party system on the political horizon. Without a powerful opposition effectively pushing for change, military, police, legislative, and judicial reform efforts remain valiant: it is not in the hegemonic party's interest to voluntarily loosen its control over the state and society.

This case study further shows the limits of democracy assistance. While Cambodians must bear responsibility for the problems their country has faced, the donor community needs to find a more effective way to make things work better. This task – given the CPP Government's successful consolidation of power and good external relations with non-democratic states, especially China and some ASEAN members, such as Vietnam and Burma – may prove rather daunting. The CPP can only be expected to become more and more defiant. This does not suggest that the donor community has played no useful role in democracy promotion. The limits simply mean that donors' efforts have not turned their noble visions into a full reality. Still, donors must continue to stay actively involved: for without their continued assistance, their pressure is unlikely to bear any fruit and Cambodia would have remained highly unstable. However, donors must mean business in the way they put pressure on the CPP. Donors must find a more potent method to apply pressure, especially when CPP leaders seek to silence critical voices. Most importantly, donors must pay special attention to structural impediments to institution building, especially growing poverty and the emergence of a hegemonic party system.

From a theoretical perspective, the Cambodian case study shows that normative, historical and rational choice institutionalisms are inadequate in terms of explaining why democratic consolidation failed in Cambodia. These institutional theories are useful to the extent that they help explain continuity in Cambodian politics. Authoritarian culture, ideology, and a history of violence help make sense of hegemonic party politics. Rational choice institutionalism in particular sheds light on the political parties' pursuit of self-interest in politics under certain cultural, ideological, and historical constraints.[60] But this institutionalism cannot explain why political actors have failed to overcome collective action problems, why they have not effectively cooperated in building democratic institutions that may help mitigate their conflict-prone behaviour, and why the CPP under the leadership of Hun Sen has battled for political supremacy. There are thus limits to how much these institutional perspectives can explain hegemonic party politics. Only complex realist institutionalism can shed much light on this.

Notes

1 Dankwart Rustow, 'Transitions to Democracy: Toward a Dynamic Model', *Comparative Politics*, vol. 2, April 1970, pp. 337–63; numerous countries like Russia continue to face this crisis though.
2 See, for instance, Chou Meng Tarr, 'The Vietnamese Minority in Cambodia', and Ramses Amer, 'The Ethnic Vietnamese in Cambodia: A Minority at Risk?', in Sorpong Peou (ed.), *Cambodia: Change and Continuity in Contemporary Politics*, Aldershot, Burlington, USA, Singapore and Sydney: Ashgate, 2001.

3 See, for instance, John Higley and Richard Gunther (eds), *Elites and Democratic Consolidation in Latin America and Southern Europe*, Baltimore: The Johns Hopkins University Press, 1992.

4 Valerie Bunce, 'Rethinking Recent Democratisation: Lessons from the Postcommunist Experience', *World Politics*, vol. 55, no. 2, January 2003, pp. 167–92. Bunce, for instance, wrote: 'the transitions in the postcommunist region that combined pacting with demobilised publics . . . were precisely the transitions that were most likely to continue authoritarian rule in the postcommunist region,'(2003: 173). Some analysts regarded power sharing between democrats and the former communist party as being the obstacle to democratisation in Cambodia. Julio Jeldres sees 'the pitfalls of power-sharing' in 'Cambodia's Fading Hopes', in Sorpong Peou (ed.), *Cambodia*, p. 350.

5 See Bunce, 'Rethinking Recent Democratisation' and Valerie Bunce, 'Comparative Democratisation: Big and Bounded Conclusions', *Comparative Political Studies*, vol. 33, nos. 6–7, August–September 2000, pp. 703–34; Michael McFaul, 'The Fourth Wave of Democracy and Dictatorship: Noncooperative Transitions in the Postcommunist World', *World Politics*, vol. 54, no. 2, January 2002, pp. 212–44; Timothy Frye, 'The Perils of Polarisation: Economic Performance in the Postcommunist World', *World Politics*, vol. 54, no. 3, April 2002, pp. 308–37.

6 See Zbigniew Brzezinski, 'The Primacy of History and Culture', *Journal of Democracy*, vol. 12, no. 4, October 2001, pp. 20–6; Samuel P. Huntington can be seen as a cultural determinist. He, for instance, makes reference to Chinese Confucianism, asserting that, 'Confucian heritage, with its emphasis on authority, order, hierarchy, and supremacy of the collectivity over the individual, creates obstacles to democratisation', in his *The Clash of Civilisations and the Remaking of World Order*, New York: Simon & Schuster, 1996, p. 238.

7 For more details, see Sorpong Peou, *International Democracy Assistance for Peacebuilding: Cambodia and Beyond*, Hampshire and New York: Palgrave Macmillan, 2007.

8 Steven Ratner, 'The Cambodia Settlement Agreements', in Sorpong Peou (ed.), *Cambodia*.

9 Stephen P. Marks, 'The New Cambodian Constitution: From Civil War to a Fragile Democracy', in Sorpong Peou (ed.), *Cambodia*.

10 The literature on Cambodia's democratic transition is quite rich and controversial. See, for instance, Sorpong Peou, *Conflict Neutralisation in the Cambodia War: From Battlefield to Ballot-Box*, Kuala Lumpur, New York and Singapore: Oxford University Press, 1997; Steve Heder and Judy Ledgerwood (eds), *Propaganda, Politics, and Violence in Cambodia: Democratic Transition under United Nations Peace-keeping*, Armonk, New York, and London, England: M. E. Sharpe, 1996; Michael Doyle, *UN Peacekeeping in Cambodia: UNTAC's Civil Mandate*, Boulder and London: Lynne Rienner Publishers, 1995; Hugh Smith (ed.), *International Peacekeeping: Building on the Cambodian Experience*, Canberra, Australia: Australian Defence Studies Centre and Australian Defence Force Academy, 1994.

11 Robert B. Albritton, 'Cambodia in 2003: On the Road to Democratic Consolidation', *Asian Survey*, vol. 44, no. 1, January/February 2004, pp. 102–9.

12 Ibid., p. 102.

13 Dan Slater, 'Iron Cage in an Iron Fist: Authoritarian Institutions and the Personalisation of Power in Malaysia', *Comparative Politics*, vol. 36, no. 1, October 2003, 81–101.

14 Some scholars define democratic consolidation as the process that 'meets all the procedural criteria of democracy and also in which all politically significant groups accept established political institutions and adhere to democratic rules of the game', in J. Higley and R. Gunther (eds), *Elites and Democratic Consolidation in Latin America and Southern Europe*, p. 3. I prefer to stress that democratic consolidation moves forward when none of the politically significant groups rejects the agreed-upon collective democratic decision-making procedures, democratic rules, principles, and norms.

15 The Malaysian experience shows that Prime Minister Mahathir Mohamad sought to personalise power by establishing institutions supportive of his rule in order to de-institu-
tionalise those armed with the potential to challenge his autocratic rule. See Slater, 'Iron
Cage in an Iron Fist'.

16 For more details, see UNDP, *Report on the Elections of the Commune Councils*, Phnom
Penh: March 2002; National Democratic Institute, *The 2002 Cambodian Commune
Elections*, Washington DC: National Democratic Institute for International Affairs,
2002, p. 22.

17 Larry Diamond, 'Thinking about Hybrid Regimes', *Journal of Democracy*, vol. 13, no.
2, 2002, 21–35 at p. 25.

18 UN Office of the High Commissioner for Human Rights in Cambodia, 'Public
Statement, 29 July 2008, p. 1.

19 According to an EU report, 'The CPP largely dominates Cambodia's broadcast media:
apart from the state-owned TVK and the recently established CTN, the 5 other national
TV stations are CPP-owned or affiliated. TVK can reach almost 90 per cent of the population, and TV5 (Royal Armed Forces Television, privately owned) almost 80 per cent.
The other stations are: TV3 Phnom Penh, TV9 Khmer, TV Bayon and TV11 Apsara',
EU Election Observation Mission, *Members of the National Assembly Elections*, 27 July
2003, p. 41.

20 UN Office of the High Commissioner for Human Rights in Cambodia, 'Public
Statement', 29 July 2008, p. 2.

21 Transparency International, *Transparency International Corruption Index 2005*, Berlin,
Germany: Transparency International Secretariat, 18 October 2005.

22 Christine Nissen, *Corruption and Cambodian Households*, Phnom Penh: Center for
Social Development, March 2005, p. 46.

23 Christine Nissen, *Living Under the Rule of Corruption*, Phnom Penh: Center for Social
Development, March 2005, p. 3.

24 Special Representative of the Secretary-General for Human Rights in Cambodia, *The
2003 National Assembly Elections*, New York: United Nations Cambodia Office of the
High Commissioner for Human Rights, December 2003.

25 Ibid., pp. 11–12.

26 For the difference between the ancient and modern forms of liberty, see Pierre Manent,
'Modern Democracy as a System of Separations', *Journal of Democracy*, vol. 14, no. 1,
January 2003, 114–24.

27 This point is raised by Andreas Schedler in his 'Elections Without Democracy: the Menu
of Manipulation', *Journal of Democracy*, vol. 13, no. 2, April 2002, 36–50 at p. 46.

28 This study does not accept the definitions of institutionalisation provided by Samuel
Huntington, who argues that 'Institutionalisation is the process by which organisations
and procedures acquire value and stability'. See his *Political Order in Changing
Societies*, New Haven, Conn.: Yale University Press, 1968, p. 12, cited in Scott
Mainwaring and Timothy R. Scully, 'Introduction: Party Systems in Latin America', in
Scott Mainwaring and Timothy R. Scully (eds), *Building Democratic Institutions: Party
Systems in Latin America*, Stanford, CA: Stanford University Press, 1995, p. 4. Both
Mainwaring and Scully define institutionalisation as 'a process by which a practice or
organisation becomes well established and widely known, if not universally accepted.
Actors develop expectations, orientations, and behaviour based on the premise that this
practice or organisation will prevail into the foreseeable future', in *Building Democratic
Institutions*, p. 4.

29 World Economic Forum, *Global Competitiveness Report 2005–2006*, Palgrave
Macmillan, 2006.

30 Susan Rice and Stewart Patrick, *Index of State Weakness in the Developing World*,
Washington DC: Brookings Institution, 2008, p. 11.

31 Machiel Calavan, Sergio Diaz Briquets and Jerald O'Brien, 'Cambodian Corruption
Assessment', Washington: report prepared for USAID/ Cambodia, 2004, p. 7.

32 Lao Mong Hay, 'Hun Sen's ineffective war on land-grabbing', UPI Asia Online. Available HTTP: <http://www.upiasia.com/Human_Rights/2008/03/05/hun_sens_effective_war_on> (accessed 5 November 2008), p. 2.

33 Christine Nissen, *Corruption and Cambodian Households*, p. 2 and 48.

34 International Republican Institute, *Cambodia 2003: National Assembly Elections*, Washington DC: International Republican Institute, 26 September 2003, p. 7.

35 Special Representative of the Secretary-General for Human Rights in Cambodia, *The 2003 National Assembly Elections*, pp. 4–5.

36 Christine Nissen, *Corruption and Cambodian Households*, p. 2.

37 Cited in *The Phnom Penh Post*, 29 March–11 April 2002, p. 8.

38 The Cambodian Development Resource Institute (CDRI) is probably the best example of an NGO that has a well-organised board of directors. Its board of directors has been made up of prominent individuals, including politicians, bureaucrats, NGO workers, former diplomats, and a few academics, both national and international. CDRI holds regular board meetings, especially the annual one. For more analysis of board and accountability, see John L. Vijghen, *Cambodian Human Rights & Democracy Organisations*, Phnom Penh: Experts for Community Research, April 2001, pp. 21–22.

39 Sida Advisory Team on Democratic Governance, *Civil Society and Democracy in Cambodia*, Stockholm and Phnom Penh: Swedish International Development Agency, March 2003, p. 14.

40 It is helpful to note that rights organisations have been adopting two prong strategies: (1) advocate and (2) training. For example, LICADHO and CIHR employ both strategies to promote human rights awareness. LICADHO, on the other hand, focuses on human rights monitoring and has an extensive network with other rights organisations such as OUTREACH and VIGILANCE. Moreover, LICADHO seeks to raise rights awareness through projects and workshops. Kassie Neou, Executive Director of CIHR has been undertaking the training approach to educate government officials and ordinary citizens on rights and civil liberties. Lao Mong Hay, former Executive Director of KID, focused on monitoring and assessing the progress of democratisation in Cambodia. The KID study emphasised: (1) process and procedure; (2) due process of law; and (3) criminal penal code.

41 For cultural explanations, see Steve Heder, 'Cambodia's Democratic Transition to Neoauthoritarianism', *Current History* 94, 1995, 425–29; David Roberts, *Political Transition in Cambodia 1991–99: Power, Elitism and Democracy*, Richmond, Surrey: Curzon Press, 2001.

42 Abdulgaffar Peang-Meth, 'Understanding Cambodia's Political Development', in Sorpong Peou (ed.), *Cambodia: Change and Continuity in Contemporary Politics*, Aldershot, Burlington USA, Singapore and Sydney: Ashgate, 2001, p. 333.

43 Vijghen, *Cambodian Human Rights & Democracy Organisations*, p. 21.

44 For critiques of cultural determinism and relativism, see Hahm Chaibong, 'The Ironies of Confucianism', *Journal of Democracy*, vol. 15, no. 3, July 2004, pp. 93–107.

45 Culture does not always determine political behaviour, but can also be seen as constructed by elites to justify their authoritarian rule. The debate over 'Asian values', for instance, resulted from the strategy of Asian elites to maintain their autocratic regimes. See Fareed Zakaria, 'Culture is Destiny: A Conversation with Lee Kuan Yew', *Foreign Affairs* 73, March–April 1994, pp. 109–26; Bilahari Kausikan, 'Asia's Different Standard', *Foreign Policy* 42, Fall 1993, pp. 24–51 and 'Governance That Works', *Journal of Democracy*, vol. 8, no. 2, April 1997, pp. 24–34; Kishore Mahbubani, 'The Pacific Way', *Foreign Affairs* 74, January–February 1995, pp. 100–11.

46 According to Kenneth Quinn, 'What Pol Pot sought to achieve was the obliteration of individualism, for just like Mao, he believed that for communism to succeed it must eliminate individualism . . . Pol Pot saw that to achieve the full socialist transformation he had to strip the concept of individualism from the collective Cambodia psyche. It appears he believed that only by destroying every root, every vestige of individualist

thought could a new society emerge consisting of persons totally dedicated to, and knowing only, a collectivist regime.' See his 'The Pattern and Scope of Violence', in Karl Jackson (ed.), *Cambodia, 1975–1978: Rendezvous with Death*, Princeton, NJ: Princeton University Press, 1989, p. 193.

47 Cited in United Nations, *Report of the United Nations Fact-Finding Mission on Present Structures and Practices of Administration in Cambodia*, New York: United Nations, 24 April–9 May 1990, p. 86.

48 Julio A. Jeldres, 'Cambodia's Fading Hopes', p. 350.

49 Charles King, 'Post-Postcommunism: Transition, Comparison, and the End of "Eastern Europe"', *World Politics*, vol. 53, no. 1, October 2000, p. 168.

50 Even the PKK itself did not become institutionalised, as purges within the party intensified and led to self-destruction. See Timothy Carney, in Karl Jackson (ed.), *Cambodia*, pp. 8, 93–94, 105–7; and Quinn, 'The Pattern and Scope of Violence', pp. 197–207.

51 United Nations, *Report of the United Nations Fact-Finding Mission on Present Structures and Practices of Administration in Cambodia*, p. 135.

52 Ibid.

53 The Economic Institute of Cambodia estimated that 'the poverty rate was up from 39.4 in 2000 to 42.4 in 2004,' in Economic Institute of Cambodia, *Cambodia Economic Watch*, Phnom Penh: Economic Institute of Cambodia, October 2005, p. 3.

54 The World Bank seems to make a dubious claim when asserting that Cambodia has experienced 'relatively rapid poverty reduction'. See World Bank, *Cambodia: Halving poverty by 2015? Poverty Assessment 2006*, Phnom Penh: February 2006, p. i.

55 According to a report by the Economic Institute of Cambodia, 'job creation is lower than the increase in labor force . . . As a result, the unemployment rate has increased sharply since 2001.' See Economic Institute of Cambodia, *Cambodia Economic Watch*, p. 37.

56 World Economic Forum, *Global Competitiveness Report 2008–2009*, Palgrave Macmillan, 2008.

57 See for instance, Samuel P. Huntington, 'Social and Institutional Dynamics of One-Party System', in S. P. Huntington and Clement H. Moore (eds), *Authoritarian Politics in Modern Society: The Dynamics of Established One-Party Systems*, New York: Basic Books, 1970, p. 7.

58 Calavan, Briquets and O'Brien, 'Cambodian Corruption Assessment', p. 5.

59 Sorpong Peou, *Intervention and Change in Cambodia: Towards Democracy?* New York, NY: St. Martin's Press, 2000.

60 For more on theoretical issues, see David Marsh and Gerry Stoker (eds), *Theory and Methods in Political Science*, New York: Palgrave Macmillan, 2002, especially Chapter 3 on 'Rational Choice' and Chapter 4 on 'Institutionalism'. For more elaboration on complex realist institutionalism, see Peou, *International Democracy Assistance for Peacebuilding: Cambodia and Beyond.*

6 Political transition in Malaysia

The future of Malaysia's hybrid political regime

Lee Hock Guan and Helen E. S. Nesadurai

Introduction

Most casual observers would point to the leadership change of late 2003 as the most significant political transition experienced in Malaysia for more than 20 years. Dr Mahathir Mohamad, who served as Prime Minister of Malaysia for 22 years, finally retired on 31 October 2003, passing the reins of power to his deputy, Abdullah Badawi. This long-awaited, some would argue long overdue, leadership change is important because it took place in the context of major social and political changes in the country. First, Abdullah Badawi inherited a regime that Mahathir, by the time he retired, had transformed into a highly institutionalised party-state in which he personally dominated through 'packing', 'rigging' and 'circumventing' strategies.[1] Second, the 1997 financial crisis and 1998 political crisis seemed to have generated a profound shift in the traditional parameters of Malaysian politics; in particular, the emergence of the *Reformasi* movement[2] that eventually led to the formation of a multi-ethnic coalition opposition party, Barisan Alternatif (BA), and the realignment in the relations between the majority Malay community and the United Malays National Organisation (UMNO). The profound political changes, in fact, resulted in making the traditional hegemony of UMNO in the Malaysian political order less assured than it once was.

This chapter has two aims: first, to identify and describe the nature of the political transition experienced in Malaysia over the past decade; and second, to examine the degree to which that transition has led, or is leading, to the continuation (status quo), or further consolidation, of Malaysia's 'hybrid' regime – although with some degrees of liberalisation – or the real opening up of democratic space in the country.[3] We will also examine the implications of such a shift for the configuration of power associated with the Malaysian state, for the Malay-centric political regime and for broader state–society relations in Malaysia. While the major part of this chapter focuses on the transition from the Mahathir regime to the Abdullah Badawi leadership, our concluding section considers the results of, and developments since, the 8 March 2008 general elections when opposition parties, for the first time in Malaysian electoral history, denied the Barisan Nasional (BN, or National Front) incumbent coalition a two-thirds majority in parliament as well as formed the state government of five states in peninsular Malaysia. We ask whether the 'political tsunami' represented by these unprecedented happenings signal the (slow) withering of the Malaysian hybrid regime and the slow but steady consolidation of democracy in Malaysia. Alternatively, will authoritarian tendencies strengthen as UMNO attempts to restore its now-weakening dominance in Malaysian and especially Malay politics, thus consolidating further Malaysia's hybrid, 'competitive authoritarian' political regime?

The argument in brief and approach to the study

Steven Levitsky and Lucan A. Way[4] observed that while there is an extensive body of literature devoted to the study of the emergence of democratic regimes during the so-called 'third wave of democratization',[5] the emergence and persistence of mixed or hybrid regimes has received only lukewarm attention. This disproportionate scholarship is in part a consequence of the 'democratising bias' that Thomas Carothers[6] highlighted in his trenchant critique of the prevailing trend in the 'transition paradigm' literature. That the hybrid regimes continue to receive little attention in recent years is especially puzzling when about 80 out of the '100 countries [which] were considered as "transitional" in recent years' have failed to make the democratic grade.[7] It would indeed be naïve to assume that hybrid regimes are unstable such that they will eventually collapse and give way to democratic consolidation. On the contrary, many of these hybrid regimes are highly resilient and look like they will be around for a long time to come.

The regime in Malaysia, in power since independence in 1957, is one of the few hybrid regimes that have successfully thwarted many changes and challenges to its rule – *and* avoided catching the liberal democratic bug that seemed to spread like wildfire during the late 1980s and 1990s in much of the rest of the world. The Malaysia regime has variously being described as 'quasi-democratic',[8] 'semi-democratic',[9] 'statist democratic',[10] 'repressive-responsive',[11] 'illiberal democracy'[12] and so on. While there are differences in their emphasis, all the different descriptions concur that the Malaysian regime embodies both democratic and authoritarian features. Weiss describes it very well when she argues that the 'Malaysian polity has procedures and institutions characteristic of a democracy, but it is illiberal in its constraints on popular participation and civil liberties'.[13] Key features of the Malaysian political regime are adequately captured in what Levitsky and Way[14] called 'competitive authoritarian' regime. For them,

> competitive authoritarian regimes are civilian regimes in which formal democratic institutions are widely viewed as the primary means of gaining power, but in which fraud, civil liberties violations and abuse of state and media resources so skew the playing field that the regime cannot be labelled as democratic. Such regimes are competitive, in that democratic institutions are not merely a façade – opposition parties use them to seriously contest for power. They are, however, authoritarian in that opposition forces are handicapped by a highly uneven – and sometimes dangerous – playing field. Competition is thus real but unfair.[15]

In Levitsky and Way's structuralist explanation of regime outcomes, they assert that authoritarianism in Malaysia is stable because of the presence of strong incumbent capacity combined with low Western linkage and leverage.[16] And among the domestic factors that have largely shaped regime outcomes in Malaysia, strong incumbent capacity in the form of strong state and/or party organisations has generally ensured the continuity of competitive authoritarianism in Malaysia. Leadership, or agency, has had less 'causal weight' in determining regime outcomes because 'the coercive and party organizations that underlie incumbent capacity cannot easily be crafted or designed into existence by political leaders'.[17] In other words, state and party organisations built up over a long period of time would have more impact over regime outcomes than the leadership.

While there is little doubt that party organisations and the state helped to frame regime outcomes in Malaysia, one should not underestimate the role of agency, specifically the political elite. William Case argues that

> structures do not by themselves determine regime outcomes [and] . . . are better understood as generating pressures that leaders and elites then mediate. And this mediating activity, involving near-term calculations and behaviours, amounts to a voluntarism that can seriously distort the impact of structures.[18]

Schedler, in his article on the three basic approaches to the measurement of democratic consolidation – attitudinal, behavioural and structural – concludes that the

> three modes of measurement and explanation are hierarchically ordered. Behavioral evidence overshadows both attitudinal and structural factors. It seems that, whether political observers hold a democratic regime to be sustainable or not, depends primarily on whether actors behave democratically or not. Counterevidence at either the attitudinal or structural level may qualify conclusions drawn from behavioral evidence. But it will rarely override them.[19]

He thus concludes that democratic consolidation seems to 'take [. . .] empirical clues primarily from behavioural, rather than attitudinal or structural evidence'.[20] In other words, attitudes and structures invariably are indirect causal factors whose impact on regime outcome would depend on the behaviour of the mediators or human agency. Schedler's explanatory scheme to explain democratic consolidation is also applicable, we believe, to explaining the experience of authoritarian consolidation in Malaysia.

The role of agency in shaping the authoritarian form in Malaysia was perhaps most apparent during Mahathir's 22-year tenure as the prime minister of Malaysia and President of UMNO. A leader with strong personality, ideas and convictions, Mahathir successfully utilised the power and resources at his disposal to entrench his personal domination of the state and party institutions.[21] Mahathir 'packed' these institutions with his loyalists, 'rigged' their rules and procedures to deliver outcomes favourable to him, and sometimes 'circumvented' them by creating alternative policy channels and decision-making units.[22] Indeed, through 'packing', 'rigging' and 'circumventing', a capable leader like Mahathir could exert control over the 'highly institutionalised authoritarian organizations' to 'facilitate the personalization of power'.[23] As a result of his interventions, the authoritarian regime in Malaysia was transformed: from 1981 to 1987 it was an 'oligarchic collective', but, after the UMNO leadership crisis in 1987, it evolved, or rather degenerated into an 'autocratic individual' – Mahathir.

After 1987, many institutions were undermined by the Mahathir Administration, notably the police, the judiciary and political parties. During this period, the distinction between public and private became increasingly blurred, while state institutions increasingly became personalised under Mahathir, serving less as neutral regulatory regimes than as personal instruments through which the prime minister favoured corporate actors allied to key members of the political elite and weakened political opposition to him. The bureaucracy, while perhaps remaining fairly capable in terms of its technocratic expertise, was also marginalised during this period. Prime Minister Mahathir centralised decision making within the Prime Minister's Department.[24] Besides the personalisation of state institutions, Mahathir also reorganised UMNO in ways that entrenched his personal control over the party. Thus, it is not just UMNO hegemony that has been significant in the Malaysian political system; Mahathir's *personalised* hegemony was also salient in determining the course of Malaysian politics, the evolution in regime characteristics and in the choice of economic and other policies.[25]

Precisely because of Mahathir's successful personalisation of power and his consequent autocratic rule, Abdullah Badawi, on becoming prime minister in October 2003, inherited a system in which his decisions and actions would have disproportionate influence on the way in which political transition would unfold in the country. We will argue that since he assumed power Abdullah appears to have embarked on a process of de-personalising power and reforming core institutions of governance in Malaysia, notably the police, judiciary, civil service and the anti-corruption agency.

Importantly, Abdullah's assumption of power coincided with a number of developments in Malaysian society, including in the Malay community during the late 1990s, especially after the 1997 financial crisis and 1998 political crisis. By this time, the Malay community had emerged as an external check on the political elite due to its willingness to challenge political authority and abandon UMNO for the opposition, starkly displayed during the 1999 general elections when UMNO only garnered about 43 per cent of the votes in Malay-majority areas.[26] The broad Malay public began to demand a check on corruption and cronyism, and greater public accountability and transparency. Although opposition groups and non-governmental organisations (NGOs) had long championed such an agenda, the 1990s economic boom reduced its urgency for the public while good governance issues did not resonate fully with the broad Malay community that was preoccupied with advancing the 'Malay' cause.[27]

Although Prime Minister Abdullah had correctly read public signals and made good governance a central agenda item for his administration, the imperative of

Malay dominance in the Malaysian political regime and the continuing reality of powerful politics–business patronage networks associated especially with UMNO imposed constraints on how far and how fast a good governance agenda could be implemented *and* the degree of democratic openness and political equality that could be permitted. While curtailing the more egregious activities of Malay (and other) corporate actors could bring broad public approval, such moves had to be carefully calibrated if they were not to lead to the dismantling of Malay ownership of the economy. Abdullah had to balance his responses to a set of multiple, potentially conflicting demands from Malaysian society. Even *within* Malay society there were multiple demands – for good governance from Malay society at large, for preserving and realising Malay group goals, *and* to accommodate the interests of the Malay corporate sector and the powerful politics–business networks within UMNO. The task of governing becomes more complex once the political aspirations and demands of Malaysia's two major ethnic minority groups – the Chinese and Indians – are considered, as incumbent politicians discovered during the March 2008 general elections.

Indeed, the institutionalised presence of one key feature of democracy in Malaysia – regular general elections – enabled Malay society to register its grievances against UMNO in 1999 as highlighted earlier, which set in motion a number of the political changes we describe in the chapter. Increasing class differentiation of Malay society also meant differentiation of interests and expectations which, if not adequately regulated, would lead to fragmentation of Malay solidarity behind UMNO. In fact, signs of fragmentation of Malay support for UMNO had forced the delineation of constituencies to de-emphasise Malay majority seats.[28] Conversely, such acts could empower non-Malay voters, as witnessed in the 8 March 2008 general elections when non-Malay voters, deserting incumbent BN political parties, contributed significantly to opposition gains nationally as well as in key states like Selangor, Perak, Penang and Kedah. The 2008 elections thus paved the way for a greater role for the opposition at the federal level and in forming state governments in five states. Because one-third of Malay voters also deserted UMNO for Malay-based opposition parties like Parti Keadilan Rakyat (PKR, now led by Anwar Ibrahim) and Partai Islam Se-Malaysia (PAS) in 2008, the unprecedented opposition gains in these elections did not lead to inter-ethnic violence, unlike the situation in May 1969 when Chinese-based opposition parties secured significant wins, triggering Malay disaffection and ultimately Malay–Chinese ethnic riots. The significant Malay component within the opposition, in effect, 'stabilised' the transition and the political system.

Nevertheless, UMNO was weakened by the electoral debacle, which sparked the move for changes within the party by UMNO politicians looking also to replace Abdullah Badawi as party president. These internal changes within UMNO can either facilitate political transition towards greater democratisation in the country, or democratic consolidation can be hampered as UMNO seeks to regain its political hegemony by a mixture of change and stasis. To ensure its own survival as a Malay party *and* as the leader of a multi-ethnic BN coalition, UMNO will have to balance its traditional Malay agenda with a new non-ethnic or *Malaysian* agenda demanded by Malaysia's ethnic minorities fed-up with 40 years of ethnic politics and Malay dominance. Although UMNO will most likely review some aspects of the Malay agenda, we also argue that the fundamental principle of Malay dominance underpinning the Malaysian political regime – *ketuanan Melayu* – is set to remain as a key desideratum of Malay society and, consequently, of Malay-based political parties like UMNO and even PKR.

These contending dynamics of Malaysian politics make it more difficult to judge whether the political transition experienced thus far will lead to greater democratic space for Malaysian society and the consolidation of key political institutions and processes that underpin democracy, or whether we will witness a return to the political status quo in which democracy is limited or constrained by the presence of compromised state institutions (eg. judiciary, police, bureaucracy), repressive regulations that restrict open deliberations, and institutionally sanctioned ethnic inequalities. The rest of this chapter addresses this question.

The rise of autocratic authoritarianism, 1981–98

Levitsky and Way (2006) pointed out that effective state and party organisations are essential to an incumbent's survival and, more generally, an authoritarian regime's stability. In the 1980s, growing intra-party factionalism led to a major split in UMNO in 1987 such that it considerably undermined the party's capacity and resources. While a weakened UMNO unintentionally opened up the political system and made it more competitive, this interlude was short-lived when the factional struggle led certain contenders to manipulate the 'race card' that heightened ethnic tensions, thus providing Mahathir with the grounds to launch *Operation Lallang* in October 1987 – in which political opponents of Mahathir, opposition politicians and other vocal critics of the government were detained under the notorious Internal Security Act (ISA) without trial. The UMNO split in 1987, we will argue, enabled Mahathir to consolidate his power in ways that led to the emergence of an autocratic form of authoritarianism in Malaysia.[29]

When the Mahathir Government gained power in 1981, it inherited a political system where the institutions and electoral system were already democratically weak and the executive branch already dominated the parliament, judiciary and media.[30] The 'first-past-the-post' electoral system that had been modified by successive Alliance and then BN coalition governments to the advantage of the incumbent was maintained and refined in the 1980s and 1990s.[31] In terms of ethnic politics, a highly unequal apportionment of electoral constituencies deprived the ethnic minorities of fair representation while entrenching Malay dominance. In a nutshell, while opposition parties could win selected seats and even win control of selected state governments, the chances of their winning the electoral majority to form the federal government were almost impossible.[32]

Just like his predecessors, Mahathir could rely on an effective state machinery to maintain the authoritarian regime through a repressive-responsive approach.[33] The state has, to some extent, to be responsive to popular opinion and pressure since the regime's legitimation is partly derived from winning regularly held general elections. At the same time, challenges from opposition parties and civil society groups were efficiently curtailed through a variety of repressive instruments such as the ISA, Official Secrets Act (OSA), Sedition Act, Registrar of Societies Act, the Police Act, and the University and University Colleges Act (UUCA). The ISA, for instance, allows for detention without trial for up to two years, renewable by the Minister of Home Affairs.[34] Control of the media directly by the state or by private companies linked to the component parties of the BN ruling coalition hampered freedom of speech and open political debate in the country.[35] And any media outlet that dared to allow unpopular views to be aired or dissenting voices to speak risked losing its licence under the Printing Presses and Publications Act.

In Malaysia's federal system of government, inherited from the British Westminster system, separation of powers between executive, legislature and judiciary was constitutionally instituted to enable checks and balances in the system.[36] Although the devolution of power to the executive branch of government was already evident before Mahathir assumed office, it was during his rule that the power of the executive became even more entrenched.[37] In Malaysia's one-party dominant political system, the opposition parties were never able to win enough seats to prevent the UMNO-led government from amending the constitution, enacting new policies and so on.[38] Parliament was largely reduced to merely rubber-stamping the Cabinet's wishes and decisions. The BN's disproportionate control of parliament was also used over the years to enfeeble judicial independence, thereby compromising the judiciary's capacity to check and balance the other two branches, particularly the executive branch, of government.

When Mahathir first assumed the premiership, it was BN cohesion, in particular the inter-ethnic elite cohesion, and the capacity of the coalition that contributed to the consolidation of competitive authoritarianism in Malaysia.[39] However, UMNO domination of the BN had ballooned over the years to the extent that the other parties became essentially junior partners in the coalition.[40] The party's preeminent position had been buttressed by its capacity to rally the Malays behind it, which was most important given the heavily Malay-biased electoral system, and the appointment of Malays to key cabinet and civil service posts, especially the armed forces and police. Consequently, while leadership crises in the Malaysian Chinese Association (MCA) and the Malaysian Indian Congress (MIC) would only affect the respective parties, a UMNO leadership crisis would have significant impact on both UMNO and the ruling BN coalition, and could also potentially affect the authoritarian regime's foundations. In the 1980s, conditions and circumstances in UMNO did indeed quickly degenerate into a major leadership crisis.

In the early years of Mahathir's rule, elite cohesion in UMNO was rather fragile because of the presence of a few dynamic, powerful and equally ambitious leaders in the party – three in particular, namely Mahathir, his then-deputy Musa Hitam, and Tengku Razaleigh.[41] Because these three leaders could not reconcile their ambitions and interests, there was growing factionalism in the party, which culminated in a winner-take-all contest for the party leadership between the Mahathir–Ghafar Baba faction (Team A) and the Razaleigh–Musa faction (Team B) in April 1987.[42] After Mahathir won the 1987 party election by a slim majority, the two opposing factions, instead of seeking reconciliation, intensified their dispute. Both factions were unrelenting in their campaign to win the support of their fellow party members, and the general public was kept abreast of the crisis as the media gave it extensive coverage. A crucial turning point came when Team B supporters 'filed a suit challenging the legality of the elections' with the hope that the judiciary would order the holding of fresh party elections.[43]

An immediate outcome of the UMNO split was that it weakened and threatened certain foundations that buttressed the authoritarian regime's resilience. Specifically, the split considerably weakened the efficiency and capacity of UMNO, which could result in the party losing its grip over the Malay voters. The increasing challenge to Mahathir's government 'from within his own party' could, of course, make the political system potentially more 'competitive and accommodative'.[44] For Mahathir, the UMNO split would not only threaten his survival, it could also bring about instability and chaos in the country. Thus, when heightening ethnic tensions during that time quickly aroused fears of another ethnic riot reminiscent of the 1969 race riots,[45] Mahathir, then also the Minister of Home Affairs, could justify use of the state's coercive instruments to crack down on the opposition as well as seize the opportunity to deny Team B the resources and liberties to continue their campaign to unseat him.

In October 1987 around 150 people, including key opposition leaders and civil society activists, were detained under the ISA in 'Operation Lallang'[46] and the publishing licenses of two dailies, *The Star* and the *Sin Chew Jit Poh* and two weeklies, *The Sunday Star* and *Watan* were revoked. With major curbs on freedoms of association and speech, these repressive measures also generated a climate of fear in the country to the extent that people were afraid even to make critical remarks about the government in coffee shops.[47] In February 1988, the UMNO factional dispute worsened when the High Court judge, Justice Harun Hashim issued a ruling that took both Team A and B by surprise: UMNO was declared illegal based on a technicality.[48] Importantly, this presented Mahathir with a golden opportunity to use his incumbency to effectively neutralise Team B and their supporters, curtail their power and activities on the one hand and consolidate his personal control of UMNO and the state machinery on the other.

In the race to re-register UMNO, Mahathir used his incumbency to make certain that Team B's application was rejected and his team's application to form UMNO Baru (New UMNO) was accepted.[49] While excluding Team B's core leaders and many of their supporters from the party, Mahathir also successfully packed New UMNO's leadership with his loyalists and marginalised leaders who were identified as fence-sitters or sympathisers from Team B. When forced to choose, the majority of UMNO parliamentarians chose to support Mahathir, thus ensuring that he would continue to have complete control of parliament, which in turn permitted him to pass various Acts to consolidate his position and power. In the new UMNO itself, Mahathir also changed certain procedures and rules to make his position almost impregnable. Team B supporters had one last recourse to overturn Justice Harun's decision, and that was to appeal the decision. Mahathir swiftly eliminated this recourse, packing the judiciary with compliant judges while the more independent ones were sacked (this was the fate of the then-Lord President Salleh Abas), retired or marginalised.[50]

Clearly, Mahathir adroitly used his incumbency status to great effect; as prime minister he used the state's coercive instruments to repress the opposition, the parliament to pass new Acts to consolidate his premiership, and packed key government positions with compliant officials. As president of UMNO, he could handpick loyalists to key party positions, select preferred candidates to run in the election, change party procedures and rules, and, more generally, have the final say on the party's membership roll. The heightening ethnic tensions and Justice Harun's ruling that made UMNO an illegal party were quickly used by Mahathir to consolidate his position and power in the government and party. Consequently, in the aftermath of the UMNO split in 1987, the ways through which Mahathir consolidated his position and power resulted in an autocratic form of authoritarianism in Malaysia. Yet the limits of Mahathir's autocratic authoritarian rule were spectacularly exposed during the tussle with Anwar Ibrahim in 1998.

The limits of autocratic authoritarianism, 1998–2000

In contrast to the 1987 crisis that led to a major intra-UMNO elite split, the Mahathir–Anwar crisis of 1998 did not seriously jeopardise elite cohesion within UMNO – partly due to Mahathir's success in 'packing' the party's top leadership with his loyalists in his power struggle with Team B. It also helped that Mahathir was able to retain continued access to patronage resources despite the 1997 financial crisis, which considerably reduced the likelihood of elites breaking away from him.[51] Nevertheless, if Mahathir had successfully packed the top leadership in the 1987 UMNO crisis, Anwar had also taken advantage of that crisis to pack UMNO's second-rank leadership with his supporters and to recruit new party members from his pool of supporters, especially among Malay youths. Consequently, when Anwar was sacked, while cohesion among the top UMNO leadership was effectively maintained through a mix of 'packing', patronage and power, it was a different story as far as the wider party membership was concerned.

Mahathir employed a range of tactics in UMNO, including 'rigging' and 'packing', to isolate Anwar and his supporters and prevent them from challenging him. Failing to unseat Mahathir and his loyalists, Anwar's sacking subsequently led to a major rebellion of the UMNO second-rank leaders and its rank and file. For the first time, Malays began to abandon UMNO; membership of PAS jumped by 20 per cent in the 10 months after Anwar's sacking, and former UMNO members constituted a majority of the new party ADIL's (Movement for Social Justice) membership roll.[52] The dismantling of UMNO's second-rank leadership and rank and file severely weakened the party's capacity, which eventually also contributed to the party's dismal electoral performance in 1999.[53] Above all, the resiliency of Mahathir's autocratic regime was threatened by the party's deteriorating support among the wider Malay community.

Anwar was sacked from his government appointments on 2 September 1998, then a day later from his party posts. Before Mahathir placed Anwar under ISA detention, the latter had already initiated a series of nation-wide rallies calling for Mahathir's resignation and highlighting the abuse of power and corruption by his regime. This outright growing challenge to his regime led Mahathir to initially detain Anwar under the ISA, but then decided to charge Anwar in open court. At a preliminary hearing on 29 September 1998, the entire country and the world were shocked when Anwar arrived in court displaying signs of being brutally beaten while in custody.[54] There was no doubt that the sacking, arrest, beating and public humiliation of Anwar generated mass Malay disaffection with UMNO; above all, much of the anger was directed at Mahathir personally.

While the financial crisis did not directly *cause* the crisis between the two personalities, economics was, nevertheless, closely intertwined in the political struggle. Like Mahathir and former finance minister Daim Zainuddin, Anwar too had used access to UMNO and the government to build close ties to business, though on a lesser scale.[55] Although Anwar himself had used patronage to build up his business allies, he also acted against the corrupt practices of others when he was appointed Acting Prime Minister in mid-1997 when Mahathir went on leave abroad.[56] The financial crisis in actual fact allowed Anwar to burnish his credentials as a reformer, particularly in comparison with Mahathir. Anwar's initial resistance to the bailouts of key Mahathir corporate allies, including the prime minister's son Mirzan Mahathir, set the stage for his criticisms of Mahahtir's overbearing role in the patronage-based Malaysian political economy.[57]

Given Mahathir's autocratic control of the party-state machinery, it meant that the legitimacy of the latter was invariably linked to the credibility of the former. Thus, because Mahathir's credibility was badly tarnished by his mishandling of Anwar and by his alleged bailing out of his cronies and of his son Mirzan, public distrust of state institutions and the party reached a new low. For example, the mainstream news media suffered a major loss in credibility and thus its capacity to shape public opinion in favour of the regime was rendered ineffective. In particular, UMNO-owned newspapers suffered boycotts and consequently incurred huge financial losses as a result of falling readership. On the other hand, alternative sources for news experienced a significant spike in demand and circulation, and internet sites presenting alternative news of Malaysian politics increased in both numbers and hits.

While extensive inter-ethnic disputes characterised Malaysian politics during the 1970s and 1980s, reaching a high in the late 1980s, inter-ethnic conflicts have, since then, declined appreciably due to three key factors: the high growth rates that delivered material prosperity to citizens in general and the growth of a sizable middle class in particular, the scaling back of ethnic preferences in the economy, and the liberalisation of tertiary education and cultural/language policies that assuaged minority concerns. This is not to say that ethnicity was no longer deeply embedded in the fabric of Malaysian politics, economics and society, but rather that emerging class- and other non-ethnic-based issues have served to complicate the political culture in the 1990s.[58] Thus, the new politics – encapsulated by the *Reformasi*

movement – contributed to weakening the ethnicised polity and opened up opportunities for the opposition to challenge the UMNO-led ruling coalition's traditional
politics of ethnicity.

Initially born out of the people's anger at Mahathir's ruthless treatment and public humiliation of Anwar, *Reformasi* eventually turned into a more generalised
protest against corruption, cronyism, nepotism and government abuse of power. In
particular, the public humiliation of Anwar at the hands of the Mahathir-dominated
state machinery angered the Malay community as it violated Malay cultural norms
and the ancient Malay social contract between ruler and ruled that subjects were
never to be shamed and humiliated no matter how badly they behaved.[59] Street
protests in the capital city under the banner of *Reformasi* continued at least until the
middle of December 1998, where they attracted largely Malays, especially the
Malay middle class, and in numbers not seen in the country in the past 20 years.[60]
Although the protests quickly came to a halt after Mahathir placed a number of the
key organisers under ISA detention, *Reformasi* had by then put its message across,
emboldened the public to speak out and galvanised the opposition. The state
was thus facing a legitimation crisis and Mahathir's personal credibility was
irrevocably tarnished.

These developments reflect a significant element of political transition in
Malaysia along three key dimensions. First, and most importantly, they signified a
substantial erosion of UMNO's legitimacy in society, especially Malay society.
The Malay community's disenchantment with UMNO was unprecedented, especially given the party's traditional role as 'protector' of the Malay community, as
well as the previously pro-government attitudes of the Malay middle class. This
shift had potentially far-reaching implications for the Malaysian political regime,
since *Reformasi* broke the 'previous unquestioning loyalty' of Malays to their government and party leaders.[61] Second, *Reformasi* not only galvanised multi-ethnic
support, it also brought to the fore universal issues based on the need for broad-
based governance reform, especially for greater accountability, transparency and
the rejection of corruption and cronyism. Not only were ethnic tensions conspicu-
ously absent, but multi-ethnic networks were forming and articulating these universal issues.[62] Third, the Anwar crisis galvanised new forms of social mobilisation
in the country, particularly animating civil society and resulted in the formation of
at least two multi-ethnic coalitions to press for good governance and checks on government power. Between them, these two coalitions attracted both the urban, multi-
racial middle classes and lower-income citizens, especially in rural Malay
communities.[63] Later, Anwar's wife would form a reform organisation, ADIL,
which was the precursor to a multi-racial political party, Keadilan. Just before the
tenth general elections in 1999, the country's four main opposition parties (PAS,
Keadilan, the Democratic Action Party or DAP and the Socialist Party, PRM)
formed the Barisan Alternatif (BA, or Alternative Front) to contest the elections.[64]
In addition, a range of civil society activists also allied themselves to the BA
through their membership of its various component parties.

The formation of the BA coalition offered a new point of reference for
Malaysians wanting an alternative to BN-dominated rule. While similar opposition

coalitions had been formed in the past, most notably after the 1987 leadership contest in UMNO, these had been the outcome of elite splits with little resonance amongst the public. The formation of the BA was different in that it represented a response to growing *public* demand for an alternative political agenda based on universal good governance issues, as well as *public* anger over the brutal treatment and humiliation of Anwar Ibrahim. This meant that a multi-ethnic opposition coalition stood a better chance of garnering electoral support given the changed political mood in the country.

The 1999 general elections demonstrated quite clearly the loss of UMNO's legitimacy within the Malay community, its traditional power base. Despite alleged 'rigging' of these elections, the erosion of support for UMNO was spectacular, which undermined the long-standing single-party dominance that had been the basis of the post-1970s political order. Although the ruling BN coalition retained its two-thirds majority in parliament, securing 77 per cent of seats, its share of the popular vote fell from the high of 65 per cent in 1995 to 57 per cent in 1999.[65] It also lost a substantial proportion of the Malay vote, garnering only 43 per cent of votes in Malay-majority areas.[66] The big winner from UMNO's losses was PAS rather than the other opposition parties, garnering 27 parliamentary seats and taking its president to the position of opposition leader in the Malaysian Parliament for the first time in Malaysian electoral history.[67]

The Anwar crisis and its immediate aftermath evidently demonstrated the limits of Mahathir's autocratic regime. Nevertheless, the BA coalition was rather fragile, and it soon unravelled over three central issues – Malay dominance, ethnic quotas and Islam.[68] Combined with the return of good growth rates, UMNO's credibility among the Malays was gradually restored. This, coupled with the change in leadership from Mahathir to current Prime Minister Abdullah Badawi helped overturn, to a large extent, the losses suffered by UMNO and the BN in 1999, particularly in bringing Malay voters back to UMNO from the opposition.

Leadership change from Mahathir to Abdullah Badawi: reconsolidating competitive authoritarianism?

The change in leadership from Mahathir to Abdullah Badawi raised expectations among some quarters in Malaysian society that the leadership transition would herald a deeper shift in the underlying structures and institutions of politics in the country. Certainly there was a personal commitment to attacking corruption and enhancing transparency and accountability in government, while the new prime minister's personal traits – his thoughtfulness and preference for consensus – hinted at a more collaborative or deliberative approach to governing.[69] Abdullah also articulated his commitment to democracy in his first speech to parliament as prime minister in November 2003, noting that

> democracy is the best system of governance to ensure the participation of the people and for their voices to be heard ... We must be open and ready to accept criticism and contrary views to ensure that the culture of democracy thrives ...[70]

However, Abdullah went on to note in the same speech that

> Democracy does not mean absolute freedom. Issues that inflame religious, racial and cultural sentiments should not be sensationalised, while attempts to undermine national security and public order must be dealt with firmly ... We cannot compromise when dealing with the threats posed by extremism, terrorism and militancy. Therefore, the government's firmness in dealing with these threats must be fully supported to ensure the security and peace of our nation.[71]

Given these attitudes, it would be a mistake to view Abdullah as a political liberal. He has, no doubt, allowed greater political space for more open debate on previously sensitive issues, including those pertaining to Malay affirmative action, cultural and religious matters as compared to the Mahathir Administration. Abdullah, however, has not reviewed the coercive legislation that acts as a structural impediment to political opposition and open debate – key features of democracy. There is no indication that the most egregious of them, namely the ISA and the Printing Presses and Publications Act, would even be considered for review. In fact, Abdullah has defended the need for preventive detention laws such as the ISA.[72]

It might be argued that even liberals have come to accept the need for coercive legislation like the ISA in an age of terrorism, as seen in the growing turn to similar legislation even in established liberal democracies of the West. However, unlike in Western democracies, which have constitutional checks and balances on the use (and abuse) of such legislation and a relatively free and plural press that can freely report on such matters, the weak separation of powers between the executive, legislature and judiciary in Malaysia and the presence of other repressive legislation – notably the Printing Presses and Publications Act – undermines the potential role of these institutions as key checks on the misuse of preventive detention and other repressive laws. With Abdullah having inherited concentrated executive power from Mahathir, these authoritarian features of the Malaysian political system remain in place. Rather than a political liberal, Abdullah is better seen as a political conservative in terms of his political behaviour, intent on ensuring order and stability as the best safeguard of peace and prosperity in a multi-ethnic and multi-religious Malaysia. Notwithstanding the greater space for debate in Malaysia, there will always be limits to its practice, especially on matters deemed by the executive to be sensitive, which will be carefully mediated by the political leadership. To put it differently, the freedom to debate matters of importance to Malaysia will remain a privilege granted by the political leadership and not a right.

The controversy in 2006 over the Article 11 coalition illustrates our point that the freedom to debate remains a privilege rather than a fundamental political right. Article 11 was formed by 13 NGOs, including the Malaysian Bar Council, following a tussle over the burial rights of a Malaysian Indian man – Mr Moorthy – who the Islamic Religious Affairs Department claimed had converted from Hinduism, his original faith, to Islam despite protests to the contrary from Moorthy's widow. Under Islamic law, all Muslims must be given Muslim burial rights. More controversially, the division of property of Muslims is mandated by Syariah principles, which does not permit disposal of property belonging to a Muslim on his/her death to his/her non-Muslim family. Article 11 was formed to discuss the constitutional protection of religious freedoms for non-Muslims especially in the light of the Federal Court ruling (following a suit filed by Mr Moorthy's family) that civil courts had no jurisdiction over Islamic matters, which come under the purview of the Syariah courts.[73] This, it was feared, would bias judgements against non-Muslims in matters of dispute over religious conversions.

Although the government did not prevent Article 11's formation or its closed-door sessions in Penang and Johor Bahru, the latter were disrupted by pro-testors from various Muslim groups, including PAS and UMNO Youth, who saw the Article 11 coalition as a threat to Islam.[74] These groups also rejected the Inter-Faith Commission (IFC), an earlier proposal by the Malaysian Bar Council in 2005 to promote better understanding and respect among the country's religious groups. The IFC was rejected by several mainstream Islamic groups claiming that such a Commission would weaken Islam. As a result of the tensions created by the Article 11 forums, Abdullah called for an immediate cessation of further Article 11 events as well as activities related to the formation of the IFC. The media was also instructed to 'voluntarily' stop publishing and broadcasting on issues related to religious matters. Although Abdullah pledged not to invoke the ISA, he also cau-tioned the media not to 'force the government to take action when enough warning has been given'.[75] The Bar Council has since highlighted the double standards operating on this issue, as two Islamic groups reportedly held forums in 2006 to dis-cuss the challenges facing Islam despite the prime minister's instructions to the contrary.[76]

While there is greater freedom to publicly raise issues previously deemed sensi-tive, Abdullah has shown a preference for order/stability when it appears that the two sets of values are in collision. Whatever his personal convictions, he is com-pelled to act in ways that secure support from Malay Muslim voters – his and UMNO's primary constituency – while not alienating the non-Muslim/non-Malay public. This goes to the heart of political dynamics in Malaysia – the need to bal-ance a set of complex relationships between the political leadership and Malaysian society. How the UMNO-based political leadership manages its relationship with a Malaysian society divided along cultural, ethnic and religious lines will determine regime outcomes, a point we have already highlighted.

What Abdullah has done since taking office, as Case points out, is to 're-equilibrate the hybrid regime fully' in order to fulfil three potentially conflicting goals: (a) restore to UMNO the support of Malay society at large that had been lost during the late 1990s by Mahathir's harsh treatment of his then-deputy, Anwar Ibrahim and by revelations of corruption and cronyism in UMNO; (b) retain suffi-cient elite support for himself and his agenda in UMNO; and (c) strengthen the competitive characteristics of the hybrid regime so as to restore the Malaysian political regime's democratic credentials and thereby, its legitimacy among Malaysian civil society more broadly.[77] The last item has led to one of the most dis-tinguishing features of Abdullah's administration – the serious push towards reforming core Malaysian institutions such as the police, the judiciary and the bureaucracy. If successful, institutional changes such as these may have the effect of de-personalising key institutions of the regime once tightly controlled and manipulated by Mahathir. By increasing their accountability, capability and effectiveness, Abdullah may well restore a degree of independence to institutions that are at the centre of consolidated democracies while also serving to consolidate Abdullah's own authority amongst the wider Malaysian public.[78]

Thus, soon after assuming office in late 2003, Abdullah Badawi made public transparency and accountability of the civil service, as well as anti-corruption, a key agenda item for his administration. Under his anti-corruption drive and with a newly invigorated Anti-Corruption Agency (ACA), top corporate figures, government ministers and other senior government officials were charged with corruption, while investigations were launched on other cases.[79] On assuming the premiership, Abdullah adopted programmes for public disclosure of the assets of elected parliamentarians, withheld state contracts to the private sector, restrained corporate excesses, especially of the Malay corporate elite, and introduced strict rules to limit money politics during party election campaigning. A National Integrity Plan was launched in mid-2004, and four ministries were chosen to spearhead the government's anti-corruption drive.[80] These measures brought much public support for the new prime minister, UMNO and the incumbent government. The BN coalition registered a remarkable showing at the March 2004 general elections, its best-ever election victory and with UMNO trumping PAS in key constituencies. Abdullah's reform agenda had undermined a key platform of the opposition – corruption in the party and government. His Islamic credentials, moreover, attracted back Malay-Muslim voters who had deserted UMNO for PAS, the Islamic party at the 1999 general elections. In short, Abdullah had restored incumbent capacity to the BN, whose strength was further enhanced by the disarray of the opposition.

However, there were limits to how far Abdullah could proceed along this reform agenda without alienating powerful members of UMNO and the Malay corporate world.[81] Although Abdullah's initial moves against corruption won him many plaudits from the public, corporate Malaysia was reportedly unnerved, since corruption had long become entrenched in the corporate sector and within Malaysian political parties, UMNO in particular.[82] Measures that help UMNO regain *public* trust could, paradoxically, jeopardise Abdullah's political future within UMNO. This explains why, following the March 2004 general election win and before the September 2004 UMNO party elections, there was a marked slowdown in corruption arrests, the deadline for asset disclosure extended, and the freeze on awarding state contracts to businesses lifted.[83] In a similar move, the initial 'no campaigning' ban imposed to curtail money politics at the September 2004 UMNO General Assembly, which had generated much discontent among party candidates, was lifted a mere two weeks prior to party elections. Although Abdullah Badawi and his deputy, Najib Tun Razak, won their party posts unopposed, many of Abdullah's allies and incumbent cabinet members were defeated while party 'has-beens', including those tainted by past criminal accusations were voted in, allegedly due to money politics.[84] Given that he lacks an extensive supporting power base unlike other senior UMNO leaders better linked to corporate money, Abdullah's leadership of UMNO seemed to be tenuous at that time.[85]

The limits to reform were also revealed by the composition of Abdullah's Cabinet formed soon after the 2004 general election win. Many of its members not only served under Mahathir, they were also tainted by whispers of corruption. Abdullah had clearly not acted uniformly against all allegations of corruption made against ministers and politicians. Here, we need to keep in mind the point made by Case that Abdullah displayed considerable skill and pragmatism in recalibrating intra-elite and elite–mass relations so as to build up sufficient mass support for his own administration whilst not alienating elite support for his rule, especially within UMNO and the corporate world. Thus, Abdullah did not sack a number of ministers in his Cabinet inherited from Mahathir who were believed by the general public at that time to have engaged in corrupt practices. For instance, then-Entrepreneur Development Minister Nazri Aziz was expected to suffer the consequences of a much-publicised questioning by the ACA over the issuance of taxi permits.[86] Instead of facing dismissal as widely expected, Nazri was instead moved to the Prime Minister's Office.

While Abdullah has had to adopt a 'go-slow' on some reforms, it is important not to under-estimate the significance of some of his efforts at broader institutional change. The unprecedented establishment of the Special Commission to Enhance the Operations and Management of the Royal Malaysian Police promised to clean up a service that had gained an image of 'corruption, brutality and poor service'.[87] To chair the Commission, Abdullah appointed a former Federal Court judge 'widely regarded as at least mildly reformist'.[88] Its co-chair was Tun Haniff Omar, a former Inspector General of Police (IGP). The public release of its Report in May 2005 was unprecedented in Malaysia, especially since it openly criticised the police for corruption and abuse of power and provided details of such cases. Although the Report also noted the positive changes that had been made in the police force in the last year and identified the poor pay and service conditions for police personnel – a key factor undermining its professionalism and performance – the public release of the Report was noteworthy simply because public criticism of the police had been virtually impossible in the past given its key role in maintaining domestic regime security.

Abdullah's appointment of Bakri Omar, a well-respected police officer as the IGP in November 2003 was no doubt part of the process of rebuilding Malaysia's compromised institutions. Under him, the police had already begun an internal review of its personnel well before the release of the Commission's Report, with a growing number of internal suspensions of police officers on allegations of corruption and incompetence.[89] While Bakri had welcomed the Royal Commission's Report when it was first released for being fair and balanced in its findings and recommendations, there was, and remains, considerable resistance from within the police force to many of the recommendations.

In particular, there was much internal and even external opposition to one of the Royal Commission's 125 recommendations – to establish an Independent Police Complaints and Misconduct Commission (IPCMC) to restore the integrity of the police and public confidence in the institution. Many UMNO backbenchers in parliament concurred with internal police views that such a commission would lower morale in the force and undermine its ability to perform its duties, while a Muslim consumer group claimed it would 'soften' the police force.[90] In March 2006, IGP Bakri Omar publicly rejected the formation of the IPCMC, instead calling for complaints against the police to be addressed internally by a Police Commission.[91] Nevertheless, there was still considerable public support for the IPCMC, while cross-party support for the IPCMC came from the Parliamentary Caucus on Human Rights and Good Governance, which includes Members of Parliament from both the ruling coalition and the Opposition.[92] The resistance to the IPCMC has delayed its establishment, with another study, this time by the Attorney-General's chambers, undertaken in 2006 to garner fresh views on whether the IPCMC should be established.

Abdullah, however, revealed his personal preference for the IPCMC, but acknowledged that its establishment will take time given resistance to it, especially by the overwhelmingly Malay police force.[93] One could read the delays in the IPCMC's establishment as Abdullah's preference for consensus to be built up within the police for its own internal reforms – part of his agenda to empower institutions and rebuild them from the bottom-up. There were also pragmatic, instrumental reasons at work. As with his anti-corruption agenda, Abdullah has had to tread carefully when executing his agenda to reform Malaysia's key institutions, particularly one as crucial to domestic political order as the police which is also overwhelmingly Malay. We should, however, not ignore other progressive changes that were passed by parliament in July 2006 that will affect the way the police force conducts itself. Changes to the Penal Code and the Criminal Procedure Code (CPC) have been lauded by the Bar Council, the opposition and NGOs as much-needed reforms to improve the criminal justice system, in particular to secure the rights of individuals when arrested, detained and charged by the police.[94]

Abdullah's move to reform the police force was part of a broader and longer-term thrust that, if fully implemented, would have worked to re-establish the integrity of state institutions that had been undermined during the Mahathir era. The civil service too was slowly reintegrated into the policy-making process.[95] Most encouraging was Abdullah's effort to restore the integrity of the judiciary, long a respected institution until Mahathir began to undermine its independence from the late 1980s. Abdullah's appointment in 2004 of a highly respected reformist judge to the position of President of the Court of Appeal won praise from virtually all quarters of Malaysian public life. Lawyers, the Malaysian Bar Council, opposition politicians and rights activists fully endorsed Abdul Malek Ahmad's appointment to the second highest position in the judiciary, claiming the act marked the first step in the long journey to regain public confidence in this institution.[96] The overturning by the Malaysian courts in 2004 of a number of politically inspired cases, including the conviction under the OSA of Ezam Nor, then leader of the opposition Keadilan party's youth wing and most significantly Anwar Ibrahim's conviction on sexual misconduct charges, suggest that Abdullah had restored a degree of independence to the judiciary.[97] Despite these progressive shifts, civil liberties remain curtailed in Malaysia as virtually all illiberal legislation in the country remains in place, as already noted.

The outcome of these complex yet carefully calibrated shifts by Abdullah was the consolidation of competitive authoritarianism in Malaysia. While he has restored the hybrid regime's competitive or democratic elements to some degree, he has nevertheless retained core authoritarian features associated with it. It would be difficult, given these trends, to argue that political transition in Malaysia under Abdullah Badawi was clearly heading towards democratic consolidation. At most, we can argue that competitive/democratic elements were restored, especially by setting in motion a process of de-personalising power in Malaysia through his attempts at rebuilding and empowering core institutions. Although greater space was allowed for more open debate on matters once deemed too sensitive, this remains a privilege granted by the political executive rather than a fundamental right. The preservation of repressive legislation works to ensure that these privileges can be revoked at any time.

To the extent that leadership, or agency, matters, then Abdullah's tenure was important for restoring the competitive authoritarian political regime, and in moving away from the autocratic features entrenched during the Mahathir years. However, Abdullah's hold on power has been rather fragile, even before the 8 March 2008 general elections. Three factors were salient in this regard. The adverse sentiments of the local business elite – particularly the Malay corporate elite – towards Abdullah's leadership style and reform agenda, public criticism of Abdullah's leadership style and policies by former Prime Minister Mahathir and the 'Khairy' factor weakened Abdullah's hold on power. These issues are interlinked; they are fundamentally related to who has control over money (patronage) and power.

Interestingly, Mahathir's strident criticisms during 2005–2006 were directed less at Abdullah's broader governance agenda and the broad strategic direction he had set for the country than at other issues. Instead, the former prime minister focused on three policy shifts adopted by Abdullah that had the potential to undermine key mega-projects initiated during Mahathir's administration, including Proton (the national car company), the 'crooked' bridge to Singapore, and MV Augusta, an unviable, debt-ridden European motorcycle company purchased under questionable circumstances by Proton. At the heart of the drama was the simple fact that Abdullah chose not to protect Mahathir's legacy 'in the widest sense of the word',[98] including a Mahathir-aligned corporate elite that had previously enjoyed unprecedented access to a leader presiding over concentrated power and willing to make quick decisions without due consultation. Abdullah's controversial son-in-law Khairy Jamaluddin, who at the time of writing is also UMNO Youth Deputy Chief,[99] has proved to be a liability. Khairy has been accused of controlling access to the prime minister, monopolising policy advice to him on crucial matters of state and economy, and amassing wealth through exploiting his personal relationship with Abdullah. The thrashing received by the BN at the 8 March 2008 general elections not only undermined the political power of UMNO and the BN, it also set in motion a tussle for the UMNO leadership and the ouster of an already weakened Abdullah Badawi.

Impact of the 8 March 2008 'political tsunami'

We began this chapter by asking whether the political transition experienced as a result of the leadership shift from Mahathir to Abdullah Badawi will lead to greater democratic space for Malaysian society and the consolidation of key political institutions and processes that underpin democracy, or whether we will witness a return to the political status quo in which democracy is limited or constrained by the presence of compromised state institutions (eg. judiciary, police, bureaucracy), repressive regulations that restrict open deliberations, and institutionally sanctioned ethnic inequalities.

Our analysis suggests that under Abdullah, we witnessed a consolidation of the competitive authoritarian hybrid regime, with its competitive/democratic elements restored to some degree while core authoritarian features were retained. Although Abdullah had set an agenda of reforming core state institutions (and in the process, de-personalising power), coercive legislation remains firmly in place. As a result of the latter, the opening of space under the Abdullah Administration for political debate on matters once deemed sensitive remains a privilege granted by the executive and not a fundamental right. It would be difficult, given these trends, to argue that political transition in Malaysia is clearly heading towards democratic consolidation, especially since Abdullah had stepped down as UMNO President in March 2009, and thus, as Malaysian Prime Minister, as a result of internal pressure from within UMNO following the 8 March 2008 election debacle. Abdullah has been conveniently blamed for the defection of a considerable number of BN and UMNO supporters to opposition parties in the 8 March 2008 election. We suggest that these unprecedented electoral developments do not signal democratic consolidation following the 'political tsunami' so much as a period of flux in the Malaysian polity as UMNO attempts to regain its hegemony within the Malay community, whilst having to work within the shifting structural realities of a new Malaysian electorate and civil society.

The 8 March 2008 General Elections – Malaysia's twelfth – saw a number of unexpected events: (a) the win by opposition parties, principally the DAP, PAS and PKR, of 82 seats in the 222-seat Malaysian Parliament, thereby denying the government the two-thirds majority that would have allowed it to amend the Federal Constitution without needing opposition support; (b) the loss of five state governments in Selangor, Penang, Perak, Kedah and Kelantan to the opposition, up from one state government (Kelantan) in the previous 2004 elections; (c) the routing of key BN coalition parties – the Gerakan, MCA and the MIC – that have traditionally represented the Chinese and Indian constituencies within the ruling government; and (d) the desertion of the BN by non-Malay voters incensed by the continued insistence on the non-negotiability of *Ketuanan Melayu* (Malay dominance) by UMNO, the implied threat by UMNO Youth leaders and members that violence would be the answer to a non-Malay (i.e. Indian and especially Chinese) challenge to Malay dominance, and the religious anxieties of non-Muslims over Islamic encroachment into their personal religious space. In addition to the defection of non-Malay voters from the BN, which these communities had traditionally supported, a significant one-third of Malay voters now support the opposition Pakatan Rakyat coalition (PR, or Citizens' Coalition) between the PKR, DAP, and PAS formed after the 2008 general election.[100] The PR coalition was engineered by Anwar Ibrahim, and has thus far managed to put together a working government in the four newly captured opposition states. Thus there is sizable support from the Malay community for the opposition in general, and PKR and its leader Anwar Ibrahim in particular. UMNO has now to contend with two opposition parties able to garner Malay votes, namely, PKR and PAS, which gives the PR coalition considerable legitimacy and capacity to act as the contender to the BN in a two-party political system.[101] Anwar's agency played a significant role in the way politics unfolded in the country up to and following the 8 March general elections.

Given the threat to UMNO's continued dominance in Malaysian politics, and in particular to its identification as the champion of the Malays, UMNO politicians have responded by trying to incite racial and religious sentiment especially among the Malays and by recourse to the available coercive legislation.[102] Initially, Abdullah, emboldened by the electoral losses suffered by UMNO and BN which were also attributed to his now-moribund reform agenda, pushed ahead with further governance reforms. He reinvigorated the anti-corruption agency and set in motion further moves to reform the judiciary. Most significantly, he appointed an UMNO member dropped from the party's electoral list in 2008 as the new Minister for Law and tasked him with overseeing judicial reform. One could argue that Abdullah's 2003 reform agenda had petered out due to the overwhelming support given to the BN in the 2004 elections, which bred complacency within the ruling coalition's main parties, especially UMNO. The shock losses in 2008 provided the prime minister with the political space to revive the reform process in response to what were clear demands from the electorate to stem what they perceived as worsening corruption at all levels of the government and to reform key institutions of governance. In time, however, a weakened Abdullah became the primary scapegoat for the BN's losses in 2008, and had been manoeuvred to relinquish his post as UMNO President in March 2009 in favour of his deputy, Najib Tun Razak. Interestingly, contest for internal party posts has become liberalised within the BN component parties of MCA, Gerakan and UMNO. However, this has not translated into democratic consolidation at the wider, national level.

Significantly, the threat to UMNO has sparked the use of racial sentiments amongst a number of UMNO politicians to reassert their claim to represent the Malays. In September 2008, the head of a key UMNO Division in Penang, Ahmad Ismail, openly called Malaysia's ethnic Chinese citizens *pendatang* or outsider (or migrant) in Malaysia (in contradistinction to the Malays as the land's 'original' inhabitants, a claim that does not go unchallenged). Ahmad Ismail refused to apologise, although Deputy Prime Minister Najib Tun Razak clarified that UMNO did not regard the Chinese as *pendatang* but instead saw them as partners in nation-building.[103] UMNO, in a disciplinary hearing, also suspended Ahmad Ismail, a clear move to assuage non-Malay sentiments on the position of the Chinese and Indians in Malaysia. Encouragingly, these attempts at racial incitement have not resulted in any form of violence.

Unfortunately, the BN Government has not refrained from using coercion against its political opponents and anyone else perceived as threatening to UMNO. The ISA was used against an opposition politician, a news reporter and an activist blogger in September 2008 over a variety of charges. However, widespread public outrage greeted the detentions without trial of Teresa Kok, a DAP MP and State Assemblywoman who had garnered the highest majority in the recent elections; an award-winning news reporter from a Chinese-language daily who first reported the *pendatang* remark of the UMNO politician; and activist blogger Raja Petra who manages the alternative news website, *Malaysia Today* that has published some controversial and allegedly defamatory articles on UMNO politicians, including Deputy Prime Minister Najib Tun Razak. This time, even senior BN politicians criticised the use of the ISA with at least nine Cabinet Ministers from all the major BN parties speaking out against the use of the ISA while one UMNO minister – the newly appointed Law Minister – resigned his post. The reporter was released within 24 hours of her detention, Teresa Kok a week following her arrest and blogger Raja Petra was only released in early November 2008.

The double standards practised by the BN Government in these arrests stand out clearly. Teresa Kok had been detained for allegedly handing over a petition from residents in her constituency to the local mosque to tone down the volume of its religious sermons. This particular allegation was made by the former UMNO Chief Minister of Selangor state, Mohamad Khir Toyo and repeated in the Malay-language daily, *Utusan Malaysia*. Although two officials from the said mosque denied that Teresa Kok had been involved in the residents' petition, the Home Minister and the police went ahead and detained Kok for posing a threat to 'national security'. Importantly, Dr Siti Mariah, a Malay-Muslim MP from the Islamic Party PAS lodged a police report defending Teresa Kok against Mohamad Khir Toyo, while the PAS Chief also condemned the detention.[104] It appears that the members of the opposition PR coalition in 2008 are more aware of the need to appeal to a broader multi-ethnic and multi-religious constituency than their traditional support base, a change from their stance in the BA coalition during 1999–2000. As for the reporter from the Chinese-language daily, the Home Minister clarified that she had been detained 'for her own safety' after publishing Ahmad Ismail's *pendatang* statement, a claim that was met with ridicule from the public and opposition politicians.[105] Neither Khir Toyo, *Utusan Malaysia* nor Ahmad Ismail were even questioned despite the police reports lodged against them and despite their utterances and writings being clearly seditious with the potential to incite racial unrest, an offence under Malaysia's Sedition Act.

Earlier, even before the March 2008 elections, five key figures of Hindraf, the Hindu Rights Action Force social movement that had staged a massive demonstration in Kuala Lumpur on 25 November 2007, were detained under the ISA. They remained in detention even though one of them was elected to a state assembly seat in the state of Selangor on an opposition DAP ticket in the March elections. In fact, many ethnic Indian citizens contested the general elections on opposition tickets rather than under the MIC/BN banner. The Hindraf movement galvanised an unusually large following of Malaysians of Indian origin to protest the community's continued marginalisation in the country, especially as a result of preferential treatment accorded to the Malays in employment and education, whilst it also protested against Islamic encroachment on the rights of the Hindu family members of apparent Hindu converts to Islam. Some of these conversions only came to light following claims from the religious authorities after the death of these 'converts'. The conversions issue also struck a chord in the wider non-Muslim public as it resonated with their own fears over the religious rights of non-Muslims. The resultant large swing in Indian votes against the MIC, the traditional party of choice for Malaysians of Indian origin towards opposition parties like the DAP, PKR and even PAS in the March 2008 elections shocked MIC politicians and the BN who remained sadly out of touch with grassroots sentiments right up to polling day. Although not constituted as a formal organisation, Hindraf was officially banned in October 2008 for 'promoting extremism' and thus, posing a security threat to Malaysia.[106]

Conclusion

Despite the unprecedented opposition gains in the 2008 general elections, and a reinvigorated civil society that continues to challenge the more egregious practices of UMNO and the government, we remain convinced that Malaysia is not yet clearly on the road towards democratic consolidation. Instead, competitive authoritarianism continues to be consolidated. There is now greater space for opposition parties to win political office. Moreover, opposition parties like the DAP and PAS that had traditionally been strongholds of the ethnic Chinese and Malay-Muslim communities respectively have begun speaking to, and speaking for, other constituencies, possibly paving the way for a genuine two-party political system to emerge rather than a one-party, UMNO-dominated system.

On the other hand, ethno-religious politics remains entrenched in Malaysia.[107] To the extent that policies and rules favouring or entrenching Malay dominance are reviewed, they will be done pragmatically and most likely in response to competitive economic pressures as in the past, rather than representing a shift towards liberal norms stressing the equality of all citizens. Even some PKR representatives, despite the party's multicultural image and official platform, continue to champion the Malay cause and the rights of Islam. The worry is that such sentiments will not only tip over into a suppression of minority rights, it will end up dividing again the Malaysian electorate that had hitherto risen above ethno-religious sentiment in the March 2008 elections to vote across ethnic and religious lines.

With UMNO having begun the process of leadership change, it remains to be seen whether the post-Abdullah era will see internal reform within the party and a more genuine partnership with the other component parties of the BN, rather than the hegemonic relationship UMNO has enjoyed from the 1970s. It also remains to be seen whether Abdullah's revived agenda to reform the police, judiciary and the ACA will continue after he steps down as prime minister and as UMNO President. While the strengthening of Malaysian opposition parties and Malaysian civil society is likely to continue, the presence of Malaysia's suite of coercive legislation acts as a key constraint to democratic consolidation. Given the contending structural and agency dynamics in Malaysian politics, Malaysia's hybrid political regime will likely remain in place for the next few years, although changes will take place at the margins.

Notes

1 Dan C. Slater, 'Iron Cage in an Iron Fist: Authoritarian Institutions and the Personalization of Power in Malaysia', *Comparative Politics*, vol. 36, no. 1, 2003, pp. 81–101.
2 Both civil society groups and opposition political parties participated in the *Reformasi* movement. See Meredith Weiss, *Protest and Possibilities: Civil Society and Coalitions for Political Change in Malaysia*, Stanford, California: Stanford University Press, 2006.
3 Liberalisation is, of course, not tantamount to democratisation. See Guillermo O'Donnell and Philippe C. Schmitter, *Transitions from Authoritarian Rule: Tentative Conclusions about Uncertain Democracies*, Baltimore: The Johns Hopkins University Press, 1986, Chapter 2.
4 Steven Levitsky and Lucan A. Way, 'Autocracy by Democratic Rules: The Dynamics of Competitive Authoritarianism in the Post-Cold War Era', paper prepared for the 'Conference on Mapping the Great Zone: Clientalism and the Boundary between Democratic and Democratising', Columbia University, 4–5 April, 2003.
5 The idea of the 'third wave of democratization' was famously coined by Samuel Huntington, *The Third Wave: Democratization in the Late Twentieth Century*, Norman: University of Oklahoma Press, 1991.
6 Thomas Carothers, 'The End of the Transition Paradigm', *Journal of Democracy*, vol. 13, no. 1, January 2002, pp. 5–21.
7 Ibid., p. 9.
8 Zakaria Ahmad, 'Malaysia: Quasi-Democracy in a Divided Society', in Larry Diamond, Juan J. Linz and Seymour Martin Lipset (eds), *Democracy in Developing Countries*, Vol. 3, Boulder, Co: Lynne Rienner, 1989.
9 William Case, *Semi-democracy in Malaysia: Pressures and Prospects for Change*, Canberra, ACT, Australia: Political and Social Change, Research School of Pacific Studies, Australian National University, 1992.
10 James V. Jesudason, 'Statist Democracy and the Limits to Civil Society in Malaysia', *The Journal of Commonwealth & Comparative Politics*, vol. 33, no. 3, 1995, pp. 335–57.
11 Harold Crouch, *Government and Society in Malaysia*, St. Leonard's: Allen & Unwin, 1996.
12 Meredith Weiss, *Protest and Possibilities*.
13 Ibid., p. 35.
14 Steven Levitsky and Lucan A. Way, *Competitive Authoritarianism: The Origins and Dynamics of Hybrid Regimes in the Post-Cold War Era* (mimeo), 2006.
15 Ibid., p. 4.
16 Levitsky and Way, 'Autocracy by Democratic Rules'. By low Western linkage and leverage, the authors mean that external democratising pressure has had minimal impact on regime outcomes in Malaysia.
17 Levitsky and Way, *Competitive Authoritarianism*, p. 83.
18 William Case, *Politics in Southeast Asia: Democracy or Less*, Richmond, Surrey: Curzon Press, 2002, p. 12.
19 Andreas Schedler, 'Measuring Democratic Consolidation', *Studies in Comparative International Development*, vol. 36, no. 1, Spring 2001, pp. 66–92 at 85.

20 Ibid., p. 84.
21 See Khoo's excellent political biography of Mahathir. Khoo Boo Teik, *Paradoxes of Mahathirism: An Intellectual Biography of Mahathir Mohamad*, Kuala Lumpur: Oxford University Press, 1995.
22 Slater, 'Iron Cage in an Iron Fist', pp. 87–91.
23 Ibid., p. 96.
24 Edmund Gomez and K. S. Jomo, 'Malaysia' in Ian Marsh, Jean Blondel and Takashi Inoguchi (eds), *Democracy, Governance and Economic Performance: East and Southeast Asia*, Tokyo, New York, Paris: United Nations University Press, 2001, pp. 230–60 at 252.
25 Khoo Boo Teik, *Beyond Mahathir: Malaysian Politics and its Discontents*, London and New York: Zed Books, 2003, pp. 169–74. In addition to coercive measures and positive incentives or accommodative measures, including patronage, Mahathir also built his hegemony using a set of ideas based on developmentalism to cultivate consent amongst Malaysian society for the regime, more broadly, and for his leadership, more specifically. See also John Hilley, *Malaysia: Mahathirism, Hegemony and the New Opposition*, London and New York: Zed Books, 2001.
26 Yang Razali Kassim, 'Enter the Badawi Era: Implications of Malaysia's General Election 2004', *IDSS Commentaries*, Institute of Defence and Strategic Studies, Singapore, 5 April 2004.
27 The official slogan of a 'clean, efficient and trustworthy' government during the 1980s and early 1990s did not translate into concrete good governance practices.
28 In past elections, when the majority of Malays overwhelmingly voted for UMNO, the formula was to create as many seats as possible with an over 70 per cent Malay majority. After the 1997 financial crisis and 1998 political crisis, because UMNO could no longer rely on receiving overwhelming Malay support but still could win more non-Malay support over PAS, the formula was to reduce the Malay majority to around 60 per cent to 65 per cent.
29 Others have also labelled it as 'personalised hegemony'. See Hwang In-Won, *Personalised Politics: The Malaysian State Under Mahathir*, Thailand: Silkworm Books; Singapore: Institute of Southeast Asian Studies, 2003.
30 S. Barraclough, 'The Dynamics of Coercion in the Malaysian Political Process', *Modern Asian Studies*, vol. 19, no. 4, 1985, 797–822; Chandra Muzaffar, *Freedom in Fetters: An Analysis of the State of Democracy in Malaysia*, Penang: Aliran Kesedaran Negara, 1986.
31 S. S. Rachagan, *Law and the Electoral Process in Malaysia*, Kuala Lumpur: University of Malaya Press, 1993.
32 The gerrymandering of the electoral system started with the first Prime Minister Tunku Abdul Rahman in the aftermath of the 1959 general election. Since then the opposition parties have only managed to wrest, at different times, Kelantan, Trengganu and Sabah from the ruling coalition.
33 Harold Crouch, *Government and Society in Malaysia*, St. Leonards: Allen & Unwin, 1996.
34 The ISA was created by the British in the war against the communists, but since independence the Malaysian state has also use it to intimidate and silence its opponents, both communist and non-communist, as well as to detain criminal elements.
35 Nain Zaharom, 'The Structure of the Media Industry: Implications for Democracy', and Mustafa K. Annuar, 'Defining Democratic Discourses: The Mainstream Press', in Francis Loh Kok Wah and Khoo Boo Teik (eds), *Democracy in Malaysia: Discourses and Practices*, Richmond, Surrey: Curzon Press, 2002.
36 The separate functions of the three entities are defined and protected in the Malaysian Constitution. In some ways, the hereditary rulers (Sultans) can be regarded as another source of power, albeit limited.
37 A series of constitutional amendments has essentially reduced the Malaysian *Agung*

(King) into a titular symbolic (Malay) figure with no powers. See Andrew James Harding, *Law, Government and the Constitution in Malaysia*, Kuala Lumpur: Malaysian Law Journal; and The Hague: Kluwer Law International, 1996, Chapter 5.

38 The government needs a two-thirds majority in Parliament to be able to amend the Federal Constitution. It was only at the recent 8 March 2008 general election that the government lost this majority, garnering 63 per cent of the 222 seats in the Parliament.

39 William Case, *Elites and Regimes in Malaysia: Revisiting a Consociational Democracy*, Clayton, VIC: Monash Asia Institute, 1996.

40 Arguably, the Alliance Party could be described as a consociation in that even though UMNO was the dominant partner, the Malaysian Chinese Association (MCA) and the Malaysian Indian Congress (MIC) did have some sort of veto power in decision mak-ing. However, in the aftermath of the 1969 ethnic riots, UMNO-Malay dominance became institutionalised.

41 The conflict between Mahathir and Tengku Razaleigh began when Mahathir was cho-sen over the more senior-ranked Razaleigh as the deputy Prime Minister in 1976. And when Mahathir became Prime Minister in 1981, Razaleigh was again snubbed when Musa was appointed deputy Prime Minister.

42 See A. B. Shamsul, 'The "Battle Royal": The UMNO Elections of 1987', *Southeast Asian Affairs 1988*, Singapore: Institute of Southeast Asian Studies, 1988, 170–88; Stephen Chee, 'Malaysia 1988: A Fractured Polity', *Southeast Asian Affairs 1989*, Singapore: Institute of Southeast Asian Studies, 1989, 211–35; Khoo Kay Jin, 'The Grand Vision: Mahathir and Modernisation', in Joel S. Kahn and Francis Loh Kok Wah (eds), *Fragmented Vision: Culture and Politics in Contemporary Malaysia*, North Sydney, Australia: Allen & Unwin Pty Ltd., 1992. Musa Hitam, because of differences with Mahathir, resigned as deputy Prime Minister in 1986 and was replaced by Ghafar Baba.

43 Harding, *Law, Government and the Constitution in Malaysia*, p.144.

44 Hwang, *Personalised Politics: The Malaysian State Under Mahathir*, p. 11. However, it could have destabilised and fractured Malay political dominance if the two camps were to fail to reconcile their differences and divisions.

45 In part, the heightening ethnic tensions were generated by a series of actions taken by senior UMNO politicians such as the then-Minister of Education Anwar Ibrahim's decision to appoint and promote non-Mandarin speakers to administrative posts in Chinese schools, and the racially provocative demonstration in Stadium Negara organ-ised and led by the then-UMNO Youth Chief and Minister of Culture, Youth and Sports Najib Tun Razak.

46 Eventually, the detention of 106 persons was extended.

47 The deteriorating situation was further aggravated by an incident in September 1987 when a soldier ran amok with his M16, which invoked ethnic fears of another May 1969. In hindsight, this incident was totally unrelated to the state of ethnic relations.

48 Harding, *Law, Government and the Constitution in Malaysia*, pp. 142–48.

49 Even with the support of Tunku Abdul Rahman, the first Prime Minister of Malaysia, and a few other prominent old party stalwarts, Team B's application was rejected by the Registrar of Societies.

50 See Tun Mohamed Salleh Abas for his account. Mohamed Salleh Abas, *May Day for Justice: The Lord President's Version*, Kuala Lumpur: Magnus Books, 1989. In a series of articles in *Malaysiakini* in September–October 2006, George Seah, one of the judges forced to resign, gave his version of the 1988 judicial crisis.

51 Case, *Politics in Southeast Asia*, p. 136.

52 Weiss, *Protest and Possibilities*.

53 See John Funston, 'Malaysia's Tenth Elections: Status Quo, Reformasi or Islamization?' *Contemporary Southeast Asia*, vol. 22, no. 1, 2000, for a detailed analysis of the 1999 election.

54 A photograph of Anwar with a black eye was quickly picked up by the mass media and circulated throughout Malaysia, especially via the Internet, and as well as throughout the world by the international media.

55 Edmund Gomez and K. S. Jomo, *Malaysia's Political Economy: Politics, Patronage and Profits*, Cambridge: Cambridge University Press 1997, p. 99.

56 Case, *Politics in Southeast Asia*, p. 132.

57 Helen E. S. Nesadurai, 'In Defence of National Economic Autonomy? Malaysia's Response to the Financial Crisis', *The Pacific Review*, vol. 13, no. 1, 2001, pp. 73–113 at 97–98. It was, however, Anwar's ally and UMNO Youth leader, Ahmad Zahid Hamidi's denouncement of 'corruption, collusion and nepotism' at the June 1998 UMNO General Assembly that eventually precipitated Anwar's sacking in September. By using the rallying cry of the anti-Suharto demonstrators who brought down the Suharto regime in May 1998, Zahid's speech not only portrayed the Malaysian Prime Minister in the same light as Suharto, it also raised the spectre of a similar fate for Mahathir.

58 Francis Loh Kok Wah and Khoo Boo Teik (eds), *Democracy in Malaysia: Discourses and Practices*.

59 Khoo, *Beyond Mahathir*, p. 103.

60 Ibid., p. 104.

61 Francis Loh, 'A Nation on Trial', *Aliran Monthly*, vol. 18, no. 9, 1998.

62 Hwang, *Personalised Politics: The Malaysian State Under Mahathir*, p. 317.

63 Ibid., pp. 314–15.

64 Lee Hock Guan, 'Malay Dominance and Opposition Politics in Malaysia', *Southeast Asian Affairs 2002*, Singapore: Institute of Southeast Asian Studies, 2002, pp. 177–95.

65 More significantly, UMNO suffered serious losses in most of the Malay-dominated states of the Northern Malay heartland (Kedah, Perlis and Pahang) while losing control of the state governments of Kelantan once again as well as Terengganu. Moreover, UMNO suffered double-digit declines in its share of the popular vote in the more multi-ethnic states like Malacca, Negeri Sembilan, Selangor and Penang, although UMNO did not lose any seats (Francis Loh, 'Post-NEP Politics in Malaysia: Ferment and Fragmentation', paper presented at the Second Australia-Malaysia Conference, Australian National University, Canberra, 24–26 May 2000; Hwang, *Personalised Politics: The Malaysian State Under Mahathir*, p. 326). Of the BN's loss of 58 state assembly seats, UMNO accounted for 55 seats lost (Khoo, *Beyond Mahathir*, p. 119). UMNO also 'lost' four ministers, six deputy ministers, one chief minister, and several state executive councillors and parliamentary secretaries (Hwang, pp. 325–26).

66 Kassim, 'Enter the Badawi Era'.

67 Funston, 'Malaysia's Tenth Elections', p. 50.

68 Lee, 'Malay Dominance and Opposition Politics in Malaysia'.

69 Bridget Welsh, 'Malaysia's Transition: Elite Contestation, Political Dilemmas and Incremental Change', *Asia Program Special Report* 116, New Jersey: Woodrow Wilson International Center for Scholars, 2003, p. 4.

70 Speech by Abdullah Badawi to the Malaysian Parliament, 3 November 2003. Online. Available HTTP: http://www.pmo.gov.my.Accessed on 17 October 2006.

71 Ibid.

72 William Case, 'How's My Driving?' *The Pacific Review*, vol. 18, no. 2, 2005, p. 153.

73 While Article 11 of the Federal Constitution guarantees non-Muslims religious freedoms, Article 121 stipulates that the civil courts, to which non-Muslims are bound, have no jurisdiction over matters pertaining to Islam, including disputes over conversions.

74 In both cases, police advised the Article 11 organisers to call off the debate as they could not guarantee the safety of the proceedings. *New Sunday Times*, 'Article 11 forum disrupted again', 23 July 2006.

75 *New Straits Times (NST)*, 'Media advised against raising religious issues', 28 July 2006.

76 *The Sun*, 'Bar Council: Allow forums to be held', 18 August 2006.

77 Case, 'How's My Driving?'.

78 Welsh, 'Malaysia's Transition', p. 7; Case, 'How's My Driving?', pp. 151–53.

79 Leslie Lopez, 'Abdullah gains in corruption fight', *Far Eastern Economic Review*, 4 March 2004. Transparency International ranked Malaysia 37th out of 133 countries in its 2003 corruption-perception index, a fall from 33rd position the previous year.

80 *The Star*, 'Four ministries to lead fight on graft', 28 June 2004.

81 Case, 'How's My Driving?', p. 146.

82 Leslie Lopez, 'Abdullah gains in corruption fight'.

83 Case, 'How's My Driving?'.

84 *NST*, 'UMNO elections 2004: Shock results', 24 September 2004.

85 Kassim, 'Enter the Badawi Era', p. 3.

86 Case, 'How's My Driving?', p. 146.

87 *Malaysiakini*, 'Ex-CJ Dzaiddin to head Royal Police Commission', 4 February 2004. Online. Available HTTP: http://www.malaysiakini.com/news/2000420400113898. php. Accessed on 17 October 2006.

88 Case, 'How's My Driving?', p. 145.

89 *NST*, 'Leading by example', 20 February 2006.

90 *Malay Mail*, 'Muslim consumer group against setting up of police commission', 8 February 2006.

91 *New Sunday Times*, 'No to police watchdog', 26 March 2006.

92 The vote on this matter was taken without the involvement of the Chair of the Caucus who is also a Cabinet Member. The Deputy Chair of the Caucus is the Opposition Leader of Parliament. *Malay Mail*, 'Caucus wants IGP to resign', 31 March 2006.

93 *NST*, 'AG to advise on formation', 27 June 2006.

94 *NST*, 'Changes for better criminal justice system, police image', 29 July 2006.

95 Author's (Nesadurai) interview with Malaysian political scientist, Edmund Terence Gomez, June 2004.

96 *South China Morning Post*, 'Abdullah elevates reformist judge', 8 June 2004.

97 Ezam rejoined UMNO in May 2008.

98 In the words of a prominent Malaysian human rights lawyer, R. Sivarasa, as reported by *BBC News*, 'Mahathir fights to protect legacy', 15 August 2006.

99 In November 2008, Khairy had received enough nominations to run against Muhkriz Mahathir, Mahathir's youngest son, for the UMNO Youth's Chief post at the March 2009 UMNO General Assembly.

100 Wong Chin Huat, 'Divided We Stand: How Electoral Systems Make Ethnic Politics Viable', *Off the Edge*, vol. 46, October 2008, pp. 52–55 at 54.

101 Ibid.

102 The second sodomy charge brought against Anwar Ibrahim by his former aide in mid-2008 is widely seen as being orchestrated by UMNO although the latter has vehemently denied this charge. Sodomy is a criminal offence in Malaysia, and a conviction would take Anwar Ibrahim permanently out of politics given his age and health.

103 *The Star*, 'Najib: Chinese are always regarded as partners, not *pendatang*', 7 September 2008.

104 Zainah Anwar, 'In step with the *Rakyat*', *The Star*, 5 October 2008.

105 Ibid.

106 *Indo-Asian News Service*, 'Hindraf banned for "promoting extremism": Malaysian Home Minister', 23 October 2008.

107 Wong, 'Divided We Stand'.

7 Networked autocracy

Consolidating Singapore's political system

Cherian George

Introduction

In any survey of political change in Southeast Asia, or indeed the world, Singapore stands out as an anomaly. It has witnessed regime continuity to an extent matched only by totalitarian states such as Cuba, but combined with a First World standard of living comparable to Western Europe or North America. In the 2006 general elections, the People's Action Party (PAP) was returned to power yet again, winning two-thirds of the popular vote and 82 out of 84 parliamentary seats. Prime Minister Lee Hsien Loong's new Cabinet included both his predecessors, with a total of 45 years of prime ministerial experience between them, as well as several ministers in their forties, positioned to govern Singapore for another decade or two. The continued presence of Singapore's first Prime Minister Lee Kuan Yew at the heart of government – he holds the title of Minister Mentor in the Prime Minister's Office – is one of the main enigmas surrounding the political system. It is both a key dimension of Singapore's current stability, as well as a possible source of future disruption. A continued dependence on Lee could be a symptom and a cause of a lack of institutional development, prompting Samuel Huntington, among others, to ask if the Singapore system can outlive Lee.

This chapter reviews developments in recent years and offers a framework for understanding political change in Singapore. Singapore's political system has been variously described as a semi-democracy[1] a would-be communitarian democracy,[2] a hegemonic electoral authoritarian regime[3] and a dictatorship.[4] Each of these terms helps illuminate aspects of Singapore politics. For heuristic value, rather than scientific classification, this chapter suggests that much can be gained from viewing Singapore as a *networked autocracy*. The system is autocratic in its centralisation of power in the hands of a small number of individual leaders within the executive branch, with few of the institutionalised checks and balances associated with full-fledged democracies. This autocratic quality, euphemistically described by the country's leaders as a dominant party model, accounts for certain positive features of the Singapore success story: the absence of administrative gridlock or military coups, and immunity to populist pressures for short-term palliatives in policy formulation. The strong Singaporean state has been able to respond decisively to threats such as epidemics and terrorism, providing security to its citizens and businesses.

Authoritarian regimes are, of course, traditionally associated with other kinds of risk: they tend to become increasingly unresponsive to citizens' needs and preferences. For example, Amartya Sen has pointed out that famines – distributional tragedies that manifest extreme neglect of large numbers of people by a country's elites – only occur in non-democracies.[5] It is also obvious that authoritarian regimes are more prone to violent overthrow than consolidated democracies, though *un*consolidated democracies can be even less stable than some authoritarian states.

In assessing the level and quality of political stability, therefore, a country's position on any democracy index may be less consequential than its capacity to manage the multiple pulls and pressures to which it is subject. It is the *networked* quality of Singapore's authoritarian model that may account for its exceptional resilience. Unlike most highly centralised states, Singapore's regime has kept itself open and connected – to its mass base to which it remains highly responsive, to elites whom it works hard to co-opt, and to global economic forces with which its policies are kept in tune. Such openness does not amount to democracy as it is generally understood. Control over the state is jealously protected, even as increasingly elaborate systems are developed to ensure responsiveness to the nation's needs. While barriers to mobilisation and organisation by potential competitors remain high, individual participation in public affairs has been encouraged. Thus far, these painstakingly built connections appear to have compensated for the lack of genuine democracy, at least in a utilitarian sense. By becoming increasingly networked, the autocratic core of the Singapore state has been spared the fate of many others – corruption, ossification and poor governance. Whether this strategy will continue to work is uncertain, but the longevity of the PAP in Singapore recommends caution in predicting its imminent demise.

Electoral competition and contentious politics

Before exploring the networked quality of the Singapore system, it is necessary to account for the absence of serious electoral competition for the ruling PAP. Good governance may be part of the answer, but it is also the case that competition is systematically dampened. Andreas Schedler's 'chain of democratic choice' lists the links that must be intact if citizens are to enjoy genuine choice – and that a regime can systematically try to break, if it wants to 'reap the fruits of electoral legitimacy without running the risks of democratic uncertainty' (see Table 7.1).[6] In Singapore, many of these links remain reasonably intact, and the country is free of the more flagrant abuses associated especially with larger and less-developed countries. Despite publicly stated misgivings about democracy and rotating governments, the PAP Government has never blocked the formation of opposition parties and has continued to call elections at least every five years as required by the Constitution. This is not entirely surprising, given that elections have been kind to the PAP. Early in its history, the PAP successfully used the ballot box to trump the extra-parliamentary struggle of its radical leftist opponents. Indeed, the wonder is that PAP leaders are not more trusting about a system – and a citizenry – that put it in power and kept it there.

Table 7.1 The chain of democratic choice (adapted from Schedler)

Dimension of choice and its normative premise	Authoritarian states' strategies of norm violation	Singapore situation
Object of choice: Decision-making authority must be delegated to those elected.	Reserved positions: Key offices are not subject to election. Reserved domains: Elected offices have limited jurisdiction.	No significant violation.
Range of choice: Citizens must be free to form, join and support parties, candidates and policies.	Exclusion: Opposition forces disallowed access to electoral arena. Fragmentation: Opposition forces prevented from developing through informal or institutional means.	Participation in Opposition politics discouraged by long history of harassment and lawsuits against Opposition politicians.
Formation of preferences: Citizens must be able to learn about alternatives through ready access to information.	Repression: Restricting political and civil liberties. Discretionary licensing Unfairness: Restricting access to media and money.	Restrictions on public speaking and events. Restrictive system for newspapers and broadcasters. Ban on political films.
Agents of choice: Adult citizens must have equal rights of participation in an election.	Disenfranchisement: Formal and practical restrictions on suffrage.	No significant violation.
Expression of preferences: Citizens must be free to express their electoral preferences.	Coercion: Voter intimidation. Corruption: Vote buying.	Constituencies offered faster upgrading of public housing estates in return for votes.
Aggregation of preferences: Votes must be weighed equally.	Redistribution of votes: Electoral fraud or institutional bias.	No significant violation.
Consequences of choice: Elections must be irreversible and have consequences.	Tutelage: Preventing elected officers from exercising power. Reversals: Preventing victors from taking office or completing their terms.	No significant violation.

There is, at least, a clear if grudging recognition of the reality that elections are ultimately the only means by which legitimacy is bestowed on leaders. Elections are therefore treated seriously enough to benefit from the government's legendary efficiency. There have been no credible allegations of electoral fraud, even from the serially unsuccessful opposition.

There have, however, been several other complaints concerning the PAP's management of the democratic process. Using Schedler's list as a touchstone, three sets of problems are apparent. The first concerns the freedom to participate in electoral politics. The PAP considers joining politics as the highest calling in the land, but only if it is on its side. It has been common for one or more opposition politicians to be facing either a police investigation or a civil suit at any one time, thwarting their ability to function while at the same time discouraging others from taking part in opposition politics. Historically, the 1963 round-up of some 150 opposition politicians, activists and journalists in Operation Coldstore was the most decisive of these moves, removing in one fell swoop some of the brightest political stars from what had been and could have continued to be a vibrant political stage.[7] Actions against the opposition have not been – and have not needed to be – as repressive since then. However, Singapore continues to be inhospitable to opposition politics. Of particular concern is PAP politicians' use of libel law. While there is a well-established legal principle that people, including politicians, must be able to defend their reputations against unfounded attacks, the PAP has successfully sought from the courts an uncommonly low threshold, such that statements that would be considered part of the cut and thrust of heated political debate elsewhere are judged deserving of legal redress in Singapore. The size of the awards has been sufficient to bankrupt two prominent opposition leaders, disqualifying them from contesting in elections.

Second, the opposition's ability to spread its messages is severely constrained. Mainstream mass media, which operate under annually renewed permits, are generally unsympathetic to the opposition. Since PAP candidates are much more likely to hold office and affect Singaporeans' lives, editors' news judgement – in addition to any political pressure – tells them to devote the lion's share of time and space to PAP positions and policies, further disadvantaging the opposition. Media formats that are not subject to discretionary licensing – and thus might be tapped by the opposition to compensate for the mainstream media's pro-PAP bias – have been restricted through other regulations. In the 2006 elections, political parties were not allowed to use the Internet as a video platform or for viral campaigning, through e-mail chain letters, for example. There is also an outright ban on political films, thus precluding the possibility of harnessing an increasingly accessible medium. Outdoor talks, marches and other common tools for communication and mobilisation are also subject to discretionary licensing. While these regulations theoretically apply to the ruling party as well, it is the opposition that is more disadvantaged, as it needs these avenues more to challenge the PAP's dominance over the mass media.

Third, since the 1990s, the PAP Government has taken advantage of its incumbency to link votes to benefits. The large carrot takes the form of the long-term 'upgrading' programme, through which major improvements are made to the public housing estates where around eight in 10 Singaporeans live, mostly as owner-occupiers. Although residents pay a portion of the cost, upgrading generally results in significant appreciation in the value of one's apartment. In the past few elections, it has been the stated policy of the government to treat constituencies' electoral preferences as an indicator of support for upgrading: all things being equal, constituencies that vote PAP will be ahead in the upgrading queue. In the 2006 elections, the two sole opposition wards were also offered multi-million dollar development plans on top of upgrading if they switched allegiances. Although the effectiveness of this strategy is unclear – neither opposition ward took the bait – many Singaporeans view it as compromising the fairness of the election. While it falls short of more blatant forms of vote buying, which would be illegal under Singapore law, the votes-for-upgrading policy has been criticised as unethical inducement.

The PAP's electoral success cannot, however, be explained away by unfair elections. The party has also systematically covered the ground, leaving little space for opposition parties to cultivate in their search for support. The official explanation for PAP dominance is its good governance. However, social theory and comparative politics tell us that, no matter how good a government, there is always the potential for antagonisms and divisions – potential that can be exploited by opponents. Therefore, the relevant question to ask of the Singapore case is how the PAP has limited such opportunities for would-be challengers. Singapore's history as well as a cursory look at its population profile suggest that there are two main sociopolitical constituencies whose activation and capture could sweep a political party into power: the working class and the ethnic Chinese majority. With its socialist roots, the PAP has never risked taking the support of labour for granted. While its policies have been among the world's most hospitable to international capital, it has also rolled out aggressive redistributive programmes to ensure that the overwhelming majority of Singaporeans benefit from improvements in standards of living. These have not erased concerns over the rising cost of living and job insecurity due to competition from emerging Asian economies. However, grievances at the household level are not allowed to coalesce into any organised opposition against the government – an approach that will be explored later. Trade unions come under the umbrella of the National Trades Union Congress, formed in 1961 and headed by a secretary general who is also a Cabinet minister.

In numerical terms, the only other readymade bloc large enough to pose a theoretical challenge to PAP dominance is the majority within the ethnic Chinese population – in particular the Chinese-speaking 'heartlanders' (as they are referred to in Singaporean discourse), who are economically and culturally distinct from the English-educated cosmopolitans such as Lee Kuan Yew and most of the PAP leadership. At one time, these citizens could have provided a mass base for politicians harbouring two historical grievances: pro-English language policies that marginalised Chinese-educated intellectuals and professionals, and economic policies that favoured government-linked companies and multi-national corporations over the mainly Chinese local business and merchant class. The PAP has tried to avoid completely alienating the Chinese cultural lobby, particularly by retaining the 'mother tongue' as a compulsory examination subject in schools. More importantly, the government devised a Constitutional fix in the 1980s to guarantee that no Chinese chauvinist party could oust the multi-ethnic PAP (in the way that the Hindu nationalist BJP in India would later do at the expense of the Congress Party in the late 1990s). Most electoral divisions have been grouped into so-called Group Representation Constituencies or GRCs. Each GRC must be contested by a team that includes an ethnic minority. This system not only guarantees minority representation in parliament, but also reduces the likelihood of an ethnic-based party gaining a foothold.

The GRC system has helped consolidate PAP rule in another way. This has to do with their sheer size. GRCs have been enlarged from three and four seats each to five and six seats each. Thus, in 2006, the fate of 84 parliamentary seats was decided by just 23 constituencies – nine single-member wards and 14 GRCs. While each single-member constituency had an average of 24,310 voters, each GRC comprised 138,566 voters on average. For small opposition parties with few potential candidates and limited resources, GRCs are practically impossible to contest meaningfully, particularly as door-to-door campaigning remains an important method of raising candidates' visibility. Furthermore, large GRCs are unlikely to be affected by the local and municipal factors that have been known to tilt single-seat battles in the opposition's favour. Distinctive demographic pockets with concentrations of a particular ethnic group or class – which could be exploited by opposition candidates – are in the first place rare because of a deliberately integrative public housing programme. Any vestigial pockets are then swamped by the GRCs, which are very much microcosms of the national profile and unlikely to deviate significantly from the overall voting pattern. Thus in 2006, there was a 40-point spread in the PAP vote in single-seat constituencies, but only a 20-point spread in GRCs. None of this is to say that opposition victories are inconceivable. There are significant barriers to entry for small and narrowly focused opposition parties, but a large broad-based party could make major inroads via GRCs. The GRC system can also benefit mid-sized opposition parties by raising the visibility of a few large contests, instead of spreading public attention thinly over more than 80 separate electoral battles.

It is not just opposition party challenges that are conspicuous in their absence. Equally remarkable is the virtual non-existence of organised contentious politics of any kind. While this has been ascribed to harmonious Asian-style social consensus, the more credible explanation lies in the PAP's systematic quashing of civil society through strategies of coercion, co-optation and corporatist reconfiguration of potentially contentious groups and institutions. The first to receive the PAP's attention was the trade union movement in the 1960s, followed by the press and the universities in the 1970s, and religious institutions and professional groups in the 1980s. In every case, the initial rupture was dealt with by using the government's powers of arrest without warrant and detention without trial, under colonial regulations that evolved into the Internal Security Act (ISA). (In the case of the press, the May 1971 crackdown included the closure of two newspapers under equally draconian press licensing laws.) In every case, the government's victory appeared total, but that was not the end of the story. The use of the security laws would be followed within a few years by the introduction of new legislation specifically designed to prevent the rupture happening again. Thus, for example, the 1987 ISA arrest of Catholic church workers allegedly influenced by liberation theology was followed in 1990 by the passage of the Maintenance of Religious Harmony Bill, which prohibited the mixing of religion and politics and provided for gagging orders to silence preachers suspected of sowing discord. Similarly, the regulatory frameworks for trade unions, university and student organisations, newspapers and the legal profession were restructured not long after errant individuals from those institutions were detained.

The new frameworks typically left the institutions concerned in the hands of relevant professionals and allowed them to continue operating with some autonomy – but precluded the possibility of challenging the government's overriding authority ever again. This was achieved either through specific legislation prohibiting such insurgent action – as in the case of religious groups and the legal profession – or by restructuring the institution into a corporatist framework, as in the labour movement. While in the last resort the ISA could guarantee victory in a fight with a challenger, the government evidently preferred not to have to fight in the first place. Indeed, there have been no ISA arrests of non-violent political opponents since 1987 – an indication of how effective newer legislation has been in discouraging contentious politics. This pattern of law-making reveals another, relatively understudied, pillar of PAP dominance: its use of calibrated coercion – using enough force to suppress dissent but not enough to produce a political backlash.[8] Social theorists Antonio Gramsci, Hannah Arendt and Michel Foucault have all posited an inverse relationship between coercion and power.[9] Many states, failing to appreciate this, engage in political overkill (too often, literally) playing into the hands of opponents who are then able to tap on the public's moral outrage to mobilise protest and launch revolutions. While an inventory of Singapore legislation would reveal an armoury full of draconian laws common to authoritarian regimes, it is equally important to recognise the relative restraint with which these laws are actually used. Coercion is less salient when it is calibrated, encouraging citizens to believe the political stability is entirely the result of strong normative consent.

Growing networks

Singapore's autocratic system, with some features that are almost totalitarian, would seem to invite creeping corruption and growing unresponsiveness to the needs of the people. However, it is argued here that the absence of electoral competition and contentious politics has been moderated by the embedding of the state in networks of information and influence. Some of these links, such as the government's various feedback mechanisms, have been deliberately developed to compensate for one-party dominance. Others have their origins outside of politics, but may have the same effect.

The more self-conscious exercises to keep the ruling elite connected with the ground date from the early 1980s. At a by-election in late 1981, opposition leader J. B. Jeyaretnam broke the PAP's absolute monopoly of parliament. A second seat was lost to the opposition in the 1984 general elections. The defeats, though miniscule by international standards, shocked Lee Kuan Yew and the PAP because they were convinced they deserved better. Appreciating that opposition support came largely from protest votes, the PAP realised that it would have to build more feedback channels for public grievances, rather than letting these erupt at the polls. The 1980s also saw party renewal in earnest, with a second generation of PAP leaders – Goh Chok Tong, Tony Tan, Ong Teng Cheong and S. Dhanabalan – taking over key Cabinet positions from the mid-1980s. Recalling the first generation's entry during more tumultuous times, Lee Kuan Yew was worried that the new leaders had been denied the opportunity to develop close bonds with the public, who saw them as distant technocrats. What fate denied, institutions would have to provide: the government engineered a public consultation exercise to bring new leaders closer to the people. Wider consultation and participation was also increasingly seen as necessary for nation-building. Alarming emigration statistics provoked a bout of national soul-searching, which pointed to the need to give Singaporeans a greater sense of ownership of their country – and not merely by enabling them to be home owners.

Citizen consultation is institutionalised in the government's Feedback Unit. Renamed Reach in 2006, it organises closed-door discussions on controversial policy issues. The traditional Meet the People Sessions continue to be run weekly, receiving constituents wishing to ask their Members of Parliament (MPs) to intercede in solving problems ranging from unemployment to school placement. These grassroots clinics, often underrated by analysts, are seen by the PAP as a vital source of intelligence on how policies are working on the ground. More high-brow is the series of ad-hoc national consultation exercises designed to help new MPs destined for higher office to come up with new ideas and to help build consensus on future directions. Starting with the action committees of the 1980s, the process continued with the 'Next Lap' document in the early 1990s, followed by Singapore 21 and Remaking Singapore. Committee chairpersons have tried hard to make these processes as inclusive as possible, although final reports and actual policy outcomes may not adequately reflect more radical positions expressed.

In addition to these more explicitly political feedback processes, there has also been a trend towards more technocratic forms of networking, designed to make governance more efficient and effective. Underlying this is a growing recognition of the public sector's inherent limitations in policy formulation and execution. While in no doubt that it must continue to monopolise power in the public sector, the PAP has become more accustomed to the idea of plugging itself into both the private and public sectors. This is related to the government's growing faith in market forces, which had already been quite firm when it entered government in 1959. In the 1980s, an emerging global consensus – expressed in Thatcherism and Reaganomics – shunned state control of production. When Singapore suffered an economic recession in the mid-1980s, the government's Economic Committee, chaired by future Prime Minister Lee Hsien Loong, stated that the private sector would have to be the main engine of economic growth, and recommended the privatisation of various government agencies. Meanwhile, the state was facing the prospect of overstretch. With basic needs addressed, people were turning to the state to take care of increasingly diverse and complex tasks, ranging from care of the aged sick to raising the school performance of minority children. Highly allergic to the whiff of welfarism, the state would need to boost volunteerism and philanthropy from its low levels to share its burden.

By the late 1990s, the so-called knowledge economy, the dot-com boom and the rise of creative industries in global business discourse all gave Singapore's economic planners new respect for the entrepreneurial and innovative potential of individuals and small firms on the margins of 'Singapore Inc' as previously understood. From a political economy perspective, the entrenching of what could be termed neoliberal values has probably been the most consequential development of recent decades, dwarfing in significance any revitalisation of civil society. Singapore has embraced market forces as the most efficient mechanism for organising the production and delivery of goods and services, as a result of which a large number of activities have been transferred from government departments to commercial (including government-owned) firms. A few of these, notably Singapore Telecom, have added substantially to the country's economic strength. An increasingly plural system of moderately autonomous institutions, while not explicitly political, could reduce the discretionary power of the executive and hence its capacity to do harm. In a sense, this is already emerging through the privatisation and corporatisation of a large number of government organisations, making their chief executives answer as much to the market as to ministers.

The new reliance on private and public sectors has been institutionalised in a variety of networks. In specific policy domains, the new norm has been to consult all relevant civil society and private sector groups. This is practised most seriously in areas such as financial and economic policy making, for which business leaders – foreign and local – are invited to sit on high-level boards and advisory committees. The highly influential Economic Development Board, for example, includes the regional chiefs of Microsoft, Exxon Mobil and Toyota as board members. That degree of high-level and institutionalised access is less common in other domains. On the National Arts Council board, for example, business sector representatives outnumber those from arts groups. Artists, who have had a difficult relationship with the government, tend to be consulted through ad-hoc dialogues. In certain domains, new civil society organisations have been allowed or even encouraged, with a view to harnessing their energy and resources in dealing with social problems. For example, the government also encouraged the setting up of the Singapore Environment Council to lead private and public sector green initiatives. When a group of Muslim professionals challenged the government's existing structures for dealing with Malay and Muslim issues, the government deftly embraced it, promising matching grants for any social and educational programmes that it wanted to run. The resulting Association of Muslim Professionals remained independent but was successfully co-opted into the existing framework for managing Singapore's largest minority group.

Holding the centre

While the creation of new institutions and practices has been driven by various impulses, many of them non-political in origin, the net result has been a proliferation of connectivity between the state and non-state actors. A dense network has emerged, with information and influence flowing both ways, even if asymmetrically. In describing Singapore as a networked autocracy, two central claims are being made. First, the connections in the network appear to be functioning well enough to have spared Singapore the political risks associated with autocracy – namely a widening gulf between rulers and ruled resulting in bad policy, instability and collapse. Second, however, the network is not so open as to threaten the autocratic hub or to permit competing nodes to emerge and challenge the centre. There is obviously an inherent tension in this system, which translates into a practical governance challenge for the PAP. Overprotecting the centre would cut off the flow of information and incentives for sound policy making and hasten its own demise. Yet, empowering the network can have the same effect, by allowing challengers to emerge.

It may be erroneous, however, to see this as an impossible conundrum. The PAP has proven adept at applying its controls strategically at points that are politically threatening, while loosening its hold in other areas. In particular, the government has been increasingly liberal towards individual self-expression, but continues to police organised dissent much more rigorously. As Przeworski notes, 'as long as no collective alternatives are available, individual attitudes toward the regime matter little for its stability'. He explains: 'What is threatening to authoritarian regimes is not the breakdown of legitimacy but the organization of counterhegemony: collective projects for an alternative future. Only when collective alternatives are available does political choice become available to isolated individuals'.[10] Thus, the Singapore government has allowed, and even encouraged, individual Singaporeans to express their grievances through newspapers' letters pages, government feedback channels, personal blogs and discussion boards, and public fora. Each of these channels is regulated differently based on its controllability, status, reach and its ability to influence the jealously guarded public agenda. For example, public intellectuals speak freely at academic forums but may earn stern rebukes when they make the same arguments in *The Straits Times*' op-ed pages. Bloggers, similarly, are given more leeway online than in opinion columns in the mainstream newspapers. The government is especially vigilant at the border between individual expression and more organised dissent – a line policed through laws regulating societies and public gatherings. In the arena of sexual politics, for example, there is a vibrant underground gay culture. Singapore hosts some of the region's most sophisticated gay websites as well as lively gay parties. However, attempts to register a gay rights lobby group, People Like Us, have been blocked by the Registrar of Societies, limiting the scope of its work.

Allowing citizens to vent their grievances at the individual level and to pursue private lifestyle choices is not an insignificant concession, given the diversity within what has always been a cosmopolitan meeting point of cultures. Conflict is part of politics even in Singapore, the government's vision of a harmonious 'Asian' democracy notwithstanding. While *electoral* conflict may be unusually muted in Singapore, there remain other divisions and debates that cut across party lines and have therefore not surfaced as election issues as such. The strategy of managing dissent and disaffection by separating the private from public, and the individual from the organised, extends to non-political controls. Even Singapore's world-famous chewing gum ban applies only to the import and sale, not to the individual consumer – contrary to many reports, it is not against the law to chew gum that one may have brought into the country for personal consumption or given by a visitor. More broadly, anti-smuggling customs operations depend largely on the use of intelligence to crack down on large shipments by syndicates. Checks on individuals passing through airport are rare, helping to preserve Changi Airport's reputation for speedy clearances that enable visitors to reach their downtown hotels within an hour of touching down.

The customs example is instructive, because it suggests that a key reason for the relatively liberal or light-touch approach to the regulation of individual conduct is not any ideological commitment to personal freedoms, but the premium placed on efficiency. Governance principles in Singapore include a commitment to trim the size of government. Lee Kuan Yew himself appears to subscribe to a view of human nature that says that vices cannot be eradicated – only channelled into spaces where they cause less offence and damage to social norms. These principles have, despite Lee's seemingly totalitarian impulses, spared Singapore from the police state intrusions of, say, Honnecker's East Germany or Saddam's Iraq, or the year zero nightmares of Khmer Rouge's Cambodia or Khomeini's Iran. Such experiments – which grossly overestimate the capacity of the state to transform society – inevitably collapse, while the PAP's more modest autocracy persists. The PAP has understood, with Przeworski and others, that individual opinion, even in large numbers, still needs to be organised before it is politically potent. Control and disruption of organisation can therefore preserve the centre's power without the need for extensive individual-level control.

Neoliberal ideology has also helped the PAP strike a balance in its seemingly contradictory priorities. Neoliberalism has reframed the relationship between elite and mass, activating Singaporeans as consumers and market at the expense of their nascent identity as citizens and public. A major exercise in civil service reform, for example, encouraged officials to see themselves as 'managers' catering to 'customers', in order to inject into the bureaucracy the best practices of private sector 'service delivery'. (The trend has been accentuated by the devolution of an increasing number of government functions to privatised agencies.) Similarly, in activating Singaporeans as 'stakeholders', the PAP has focused on people's responsibilities to their community, and the self-actualisation they can enjoy through earning and spending in a vibrant economy. What is left out is any emphasis on Singaporeans' rights as citizens, such as the Constitutional protections they enjoy. Thus, if the 1970s Singaporean could be characterised as cowering, voiceless, in the shadow of an impenetrable state, the Singaporean of 30 years later seems far better able to communicate to the government his wants and needs, and even to engage in entrepreneurial activity that would add to the country's social capital and economic wealth. What is neglected, though, is any notion of a public with civic duties and rights. In this framework, customers are assured efficient handling of their specific requests, but citizens have limited ability to probe the workings of the system. There is no question of introducing freedom of information legislation, for example.

If the PAP is not in danger of eroding its own power, the opposite risk may be harder to mitigate. The party remains so convinced of its indispensability that it is resolutely anti-competitive. Can an organisation with such a glorified self-image stay focused on governing for the people, no matter how networked it tries to be? An autocratic system such as Singapore's, no matter how well clued-in to its society and its external environment, still carries the risk of massive government failure and collapse – and without the safety net of an alternative government to take over, as would be the case in a competitive democracy. Singapore's all-eggs-in-one-basket approach to governance has therefore been criticised as fundamentally unstable, regardless of its record to date. In particular, there seems to be no guarantee that the autocratic system will remain as benign as it has been. Power has been exercised largely in the public interest, albeit in illiberal ways. This PAP benevolence – as well as PAP intolerance – has been attributed to the seemingly incorruptible and all-powerful father figure of Lee Kuan Yew. The question arises, therefore, whether the PAP and Singapore will degenerate, post Lee.

The PAP counter-argument is that the dystopian scenario simply underlines the need to stick with a party with the most ingrained culture of incorruptibility. Its doctrine also argues that, in the Singapore case, political competition is overrated because policy options are extraordinarily narrow, dictated by global forces that a small island state has no ability to affect. This argument deserves some scrutiny. It is indeed the case that Singapore has been embedded in the highly unforgiving and penetrating network that is global capitalism. Indeed, with more and more policy areas opened up to market forces, there is a real sense in which economics forces the kind of self-correction ordinarily provided only by competitive politics. This is certainly not to claim that the free market empowers citizens and renders civil liberties redundant. However, without necessarily changing the balance of power between state and society, global economic forces may provide some check and balance against the whimsical, idiosyncratic and idiotic policies sometimes associated with autocracy.

On the other hand, it is precisely such porosity to the global economy that constitutes one of the most fundamental policy dilemmas for Singapore today. It is associated with a growing income gap, the emergence of a permanent underclass, and a massive inflow of immigrants – all contentious political issues whose resolution has been fast-tracked by the PAP. In the government's eyes, this demonstrates the strength of the Singapore system: the ability to implement 'unpopular but correct' policies. From a democratic perspective, of course, there is a dangerously thin line between this and an elitism that dismisses legitimate grievances for the sake of self-preservation.

While Singapore lacks institutionalised checks and balances against such abuse, the young republic's political culture may provide some protection. The very success of the Singapore system at delivering the goods appears to have engendered extremely low public tolerance for corruption and non-performance. Anecdotal evidence suggests that a slip in the PAP's high governance standards would be met with massive moral outrage. In 2005, revelations that Singapore's largest charity had duped the public with exaggerated claims provoked a huge outcry and a government apology for its lax supervision. Furthermore, while not seeming to value civil liberties highly, Singaporeans are nevertheless sensitive to other human rights of their fellow citizens. Freedom to protest may not be high on their agenda, but freedom from want is. This is reflected in the national press. Stories about down-and-out families, which would not be news in most cities, are splashed across the covers of tabloid newspapers, indicating their status as severe norm violations in a society that prides itself as offering everyone a decent standard of living. A new PAP Member of Parliament, writing about his first 100 days, provided an insight into the level of responsiveness that Singaporeans have grown to expect:

> I was in a business meeting overseas. My mobile phone buzzed: It was a phonecall that I hoped I'd never receive. A resident, his spouse and four children were stranded outside their flat. Their HDB flat had been repossessed by a commercial bank. They were now homeless, with only five hours left to nightfall. The family was in distress. Immediate calls were made to my parliamentary colleagues . . . from the Ministry of National Development and Ministry of Community Development, Youth and Sports respectively, to inform them that we needed immediate attention from their agencies. Coordinated out of our People's Action Party branch, we had the residents' committee on the ground within the hour, together with government officials, to work out various options. By nightfall, we had a resolution: The family had a place to stay and a long-term housing solution was in the works.[11]

Citizens' high expectations could compensate for the high barriers faced by Singapore's opposition parties. The PAP may not need to slacken by much for voters to protest loudly in the only way the can – by hoisting more opposition members into parliament. It is perhaps because they know this – and not just because of Lee Kuan Yew's presence – that PAP has confounded its critics and remained a disciplined and responsive political force. The Singapore case thus raises a question that is profoundly unsettling for democrats: is it conceivable that Singapore's networked autocracy will be as resilient as any consolidated democracy?

The functional or instrumental case for democracy hinges mainly on its ability to self-correct. Governments operating within properly functioning democratic systems have strong political incentives to be responsive to their people and correct mistakes of policy; those that fail to do so can be replaced. Undemocratic governance is usually unresponsive, sometimes dangerously so. If Singapore continues to avoid the pitfalls associated with autocracy, part of the explanation may lie in the aforementioned account. By systematically creating networks around its autocratic centre, the PAP seems to have been able to avail itself of the information and ideas needed for sound policy making. In place of the civil liberties associated with liberal democracies – such as freedom of the press and of protest – the PAP has constructed multiple channels for individual citizens and special interest groups to express grievances and contribute ideas. While these channels cannot substitute for the intrinsic value of democratic freedoms, they may serve quite adequately as functional equivalents in an instrumental sense, and Singapore may continue to confound its critics.

Notes

1 William Case, *Politics in Southeast Asia: Democracy or Less*, Richmond, Surrey: Curzon Press, 2002.
2 Chua Beng-Huat, *Communitarian Ideology and Democracy in Singapore*, London; New York: Routledge, 1995.
3 Larry Diamond, 'Thinking about Hybrid Regimes', *Journal of Democracy*, vol. 13, no. 2, April 2002, pp. 21–35.
4 Carl A. Trocki, *Singapore: Wealth, Power, and the Culture of Control* (Asia's Transformations Series), New York: Routledge, 2005.
5 Amartya Sen, 'Democracy as a Universal Value', *Journal of Democracy*, vol. 10, no. 3, July 1999, pp. 3–17.
6 Andreas Schedler, 'Elections Without Democracy: The Menu of Manipulation', *Journal of Democracy*, vol. 13, no. 2, April 2002, p. 37.
7 Trocki, *Singapore*.
8 Cherian George, 'Calibrated Coercion and the Maintenance of Hegemony in Singapore', *Asia Research Institute Working Papers Series* 48, 2005.
9 See for example, Perry Anderson, 'The Antinomies of Antonio Gramsci', *New Left Review*, no. 100, 1976; Hannah Arendt, *On Violence*, Orlando, Florida: Harcourt Brace Jovanovich, 1970; Michel Foucault, *Power/Knowledge: Selected Interviews and Other Writings 1972–77*, Colin Gordon (ed.), New York: Pantheon Books, 1980.
10 Adam Przeworski, *Democracy and the Market: Political and Economic Reforms in Eastern Europe and Latin America*, Cambridge: Cambridge University Press, 1991.
11 Zaqy Mohamad, 'What I've Learnt in My First 100 Days as MP', *The Straits Times*, 11 August 2006.

8 Conclusion

Reflections on political change, democratic transitions, and regional security in Southeast Asia

Mely Caballero-Anthony

Among the main objectives of this study on Political Transitions in Southeast Asia is to examine whether these transitions will re-define the political landscape in the region and make it more open and democratic. And if so, another key question that this book aims to examine is – do democratic transitions enhance the prospects of regional security in Southeast Asia? As stated in the introduction, there is the assumption that democratic change, though without risk, would benefit the region in the long run as the democratic transition taking place in one or two states will extend to other states, thus facilitating the complementary of the region's institutional architecture. Given such a scenario, regionalism in Southeast Asia will deepen and thus enhance regional peace and stability.

Why is this an important issue to include in this volume? I argue that this has indeed become very important given the changing face of regionalism in Southeast Asia. One would observe that in tandem with the ongoing political transitions that were taking place in some states in the region were significant developments taking place at the level of regional institutions. Since 2003, the Association of Southeast Asian Nations (ASEAN), which comprises all ten member countries in Southeast Asia, has embarked on changing the nature of regional interaction by proposing the establishment of a number of new regional mechanisms. These were reflected in the 2003 adoption of ASEAN's Bali Concord II which set out to establish the ASEAN Community constituting the three pillars: the ASEAN Economic Community (AEC), the ASEAN Security Community (ASC) and the ASEAN Socio-Cultural Community (ASCC). The Bali Concord II has certainly added a new dimension to regionalism in Southeast Asia which primarily aims to move ASEAN beyond its informal modalities – often known as the 'ASEAN Way' – and improve regional institutional capacity in order to respond to emerging transnational security challenges. These include threats from environmental degradation, irregular migration, transnational crimes, infectious diseases and many others.

Given the rapidly changing global environment, the 'ASEAN Way' – which in many ways is essentially a process-oriented approach in inter-state conduct, defined by norms and principles of non-interference, peaceful settlement of disputes, non-confrontational attitudes to conflicts, and emphases on musyarah (consensus) and muafakat (consultation) – has been deemed to be inadequate to address a host of new threats.[1]

Among the three pillars set out in the Bali Concord, the ASC has been particularly interesting insofar as the measures and mechanisms under the ASC blueprint have salient implications for the normative modalities of the grouping. It is also important to mention that the idea of creating an ASC was initiated by Indonesia, just prior to assuming the chairmanship of the ASEAN Standing Community in 2003.[2] As outlined in the blueprint, the ASC is intended to provide a regional framework – rather than the bilateral or international forums – to handle security matters and disputes within ASEAN. Following the adoption of the ASEAN Security Community, a number of regional initiatives geared to enhance political cooperation and deepen regional integration in ASEAN were laid out in the Vientiane Action Programme (VAP). They included not merely preventing conflict but also resolving it and rebuilding the peace afterwards. The intention was both to shape and share general norms, and to help member states achieve, in particular, political development – including, by implication, democratisation.[3] In the language of the VAP, the ASC is aimed at building 'a democratic, tolerant, participatory and open community in Southeast Asia.'[4]

With the formal adoption of the ASEAN Charter in 2007 and its ratification by ASEAN members in December 2008, one could therefore argue that any analyses of the prospects of implementing the provisions of the charter, particularly pertaining to political development and regional security would make for a deeper, more compelling, understanding of the experiences of political transitions. Despite the prevailing reservations on the prospects of democratic transitions in the region, the new political actors who have emerged from these transitions and the new domestic agendas on political reforms and governance that have dominated the discourses in many ASEAN capitals are significant forces in moving ASEAN beyond the confines of its (restrictive) normative institutional framework. Thus, the challenges facing ASEAN now include finding ways to navigate the forces of change against the tide of conservatism that is still prevalent in the region, as well as protecting the region against the destabilising forces of political transition that endanger peace and security.

The ASEAN Security Community: Protecting the peace in Southeast Asia

There is a school of thought that posits that the process of transition from authoritarian rule to democratisation engenders instability and disorder. To quote Edward D. Mansfield and Jack Snyder:

> Countries do not become mature democracies overnight. More typically, they go through a rocky transitional period, where democratic control over foreign policy is partial, where mass politics mixes in a volatile way with authoritarian elite politics, and where democratisation suffers reversals. In this transitional phase of democratisation, countries become more aggressive and war-prone, not less, and they do fight wars with democratic states.[5]

Why this negative correlation? A good part of their explanation has to do with the structural consequences of democratic transitions, especially the widening of the political spectrum, with spaces being pried open by a number of political forces with irreconcilable goals, resulting therefore in a political impasse and the weakening of the central authority of democratising states. Democratising states also have a tendency towards what Huntington called 'Praetorianism', where pressures for participation are strong but institutions for effective participation are weak.

Looking back a decade since the onset of the round of transitions that has occurred in the region, one is tempted to share some of the pessimism expressed earlier. Why? Although one could say that most of the transitions that took place in this region were generally peaceful in some cases, they were nevertheless quite dramatic. Indonesia, for instance, remains very much at the cusp of political transition after 33 years of being under the Suharto New Order regime. As pointed out in Rizal Sukma's chapter in this book, building resilient political institutions is still very much a critical challenge facing the country if it is to successfully pave the way for democratic consolidation. What happens along Indonesia's road to democratic consolidation will therefore have salient implications on regional stability.

It has always been argued that a stable Indonesia is important for peace and security in Southeast Asia. Indonesia had carried the mantle of leadership in ASEAN since the organisation was established in 1967 and the long-serving Suharto was a constant feature in the region. The unexpected downfall of Suharto has inadvertently resulted in a leadership vacuum in ASEAN that has yet to be filled despite the number of changes in political leadership that have taken place in other states in the region. Over the last ten years, Malaysia and Singapore had seen the changing of the guard of long-serving political leaders who had been part of the old circle of political elites that had shepherded the direction of regional relations in Southeast Asia. Malaysia's Mahathir Mohamed stepped down after 22 years in power while Singapore's Goh Chok Tong had made way for Lee Hsien Loong after 14 years at the helm of the People's Action Party-led government. How the new generation of ASEAN leaders will set the tone for maintaining and even strengthening bilateral and intra-regional relations is significant in ASEAN's quest to build an ASEAN Community that shares the common values of peace, stability, prosperity, and a common identity.[6]

However, there is always the concern that the rise of weak leaders in transitioning states can be destabilising given their temptation to shore up their prestige and legitimacy by whipping up nationalism, which in turn results in competitive mass mobilisations vis-à-vis their domestic rivals and pursuit of victories abroad. The conflict that broke out in July 2008 between Thailand and Cambodia over the Preah Vihear Temple is a case in point. Located between a district of northeastern Thailand and a province of northern Cambodia, the temple has been the subject of renewed tensions over ownership claims by the two countries. Despite the 1962 ruling by the International Court of Justice (ICJ) in The Hague that awarded ownership of the eleventh-century temple to Cambodia, Thailand refused to respect the ICJ decision. When Cambodia submitted an application to UNESCO in 2008 to have the 900-year-old temple designated as a World Heritage site, Thailand argued that the application included land surrounding the temple which is part of Thai territory. The decision by UNESCO to agree to the Cambodian request sparked protest from Thailand led by the People's Alliance for Democracy (PAD) which used it as a focal point of protest against the People's Power Party Government of Prime Minister Samak Sundaravej in an attempt to unseat the cabinet. Tensions were eventually defused after both countries agreed to form the Thai–Cambodian Joint Border Committee that would look at demarcation of borders in the disputed areas.[7] Meanwhile, Samak's weak regime lasted less than six months and he was soon replaced by two other prime ministers.

There had also been a number of troubling events that had raised concerns about the ability of new regional leaders to manage bilateral tensions as compared to how the previous ASEAN leaders had dealt with them before. The ongoing insurgency in the three Thailand southern provinces of Yala, Narathiwat and Pattani has contributed to the recent bilateral tensions between Thailand and Malaysia, although the latter plays an important role in efforts to improve security in Thailand's south, as the three violence-wracked provinces share the same border with the four Malaysian states of Kelantan, Perak, Perlis and Kedah. The majority of the population of Thailand's three southern provinces is Malay-Muslim, and shares strong ethnic, religious, linguistic and cultural bonds with the people across the border. Over the years, Malaysia has repeatedly proclaimed its disapproval over what it perceived as heavy-handed attempts by the Thai authorities at managing the insurgency. Meanwhile, while the Thai government alleged that the Muslim militants were using Malaysian territories for refuge. Between 2004 and 2006, bilateral relations were severely affected due to an incident where 131 Thai Muslims asylum seekers fled across the Southern Thai border to seek refuge in Malaysia. Instead of returning the 'asylum seekers', Malaysia responded by internationalising the situation when it called on the United Nations High Commission on Refugees.[8] On the other hand, in early 2005, Bangkok had also accused Kuala Lumpur of supporting southern Thai separatists – charges the Malaysians had strongly denied. This had led to an exchange of words between the officials of the two countries.[9]

Besides these bilateral tensions were worrying concerns about the territorial dispute between Indonesia and Malaysia over the Ambalat block. The diplomatic tension began on 16 February 2005 when Petronas, Malaysia's national oil company, awarded production sharing contracts to Anglo-Dutch giant Royal Dutch/Shell and Petronas Carigali Sdn Bhd – Petronas' exploration and production arm for the ultra-deepwater blocks off the east coast of Malaysia's Sabah state. The disputed area is partially situated in Indonesia's claimed area which is referred to by Jakarta as Ambalat and East Ambalat, off East Kalimantan's coast. The 15,235-square-kilometre region is believed to be rich in oil and gas reserves which could be exploited for 30 years.

The diplomatic row reached its peak when Indonesia and Malaysia sent warships to the disputed area, consequently leading towards nationalistic fervour on both states. The magnitude of the conflict could perhaps be measured by the Indonesian public and officials called for the 'use of military force' and 'revival of konfrontasi' against Malaysia. Furthermore, in the following weeks of heightened political and military tension, government and state agencies websites belonging to both countries were attacked and defaced by hackers believed to be acting on nationalist sentiment. Scholars and political observers believe that the Ambalat border dispute was actually a by-product of other issues such as Malaysia's treatment of Indonesian migrant workers, and also due to Indonesia's loss of the islands of Sipadan and Lingitan to Malaysia at the International Court of Justice in 2002.[10]

But despite these events and warnings from security analysts and political pundits, war has yet to break out in Southeast Asia. And, while these tensions may have occurred during periods of political transitions, it was during these periods when we saw ASEAN members introduce significant policy initiatives that promoted closer regional relations and democratisation. As mentioned earlier, Indonesia's call for an ASEAN Security Community was introduced at the time when the country was preparing to hold the first ever direct presidential elections.[11] It has also been during these troubled periods of political transitions in Thailand that the ASEAN Charter was officially endorsed and ratified by all member states.[12]

In this regard, one could argue that the experiences of democratic transitions have not been as bad for Southeast Asia as the critics of democratic peace would hold, and that the dangers of democratisation creating risks of war could in fact be overstated. Nonetheless, the question of whether these newly adopted regional mechanisms indicate that ASEAN is well on its path to democracy persists.

The ASEAN Charter: Plotting the course of democratisation in Southeast Asia

From the time the idea was announced at the 13th ASEAN Summit in Kuala Lumpur, Malaysia in 2005, it took ASEAN two years to formally adopt a Charter and another year to ratify it. But prior to this, there had already been much rhetoric in the region about the need for ASEAN to promote community building, regional identity, inclusiveness, and become more people-centred. Interesting also have been the discourses on the 'shared vision and common values to achieve peace, stability, democracy and prosperity in the region'.[13] The latter has significantly raised expectations that ASEAN was at the cusp of a normative transformation. The sense that emerged was that after 40 years, ASEAN would finally have a Charter that would spell out clearly its institutional norms and values, which in turn would commit member states to the promotion of democracy, protection of human rights and human security.

Arguably, such optimism at that time was warranted given that the 10-member Eminent Persons Group (EPG),[14] which was appointed by ASEAN with the mission of providing the ASEAN leaders 'bold and visionary' recommendations for the charter, had released a Report that called for 'the active strengthening of democratic values', as well as official declarations that urged adherence to 'the promotion of democracy, human rights and obligations'.[15] In sum, these developments, if pushed through to their logical conclusion, could indeed have been a milestone in ASEAN, as it signalled that democracy and human rights were its next policy frontiers.[16]

But the optimism was short-lived and quickly turned to pessimism. Following a series of events – from the brutal crackdown on demonstrators in Myanmar two months prior to the scheduled ASEAN Summit in Singapore in November 2007; the *volte-face* of inviting and then later 'dis-inviting' the Special Envoy of the UN Secretary General to Myanmar, Ibrahim Gambari, to brief the Summit about events in the country in the face of strong objections from Myanmar; to the unveiling of what then came to be regarded as the watered-down version of the charter which did not go far enough to operationalise how the regional human rights body was going to be constituted and how it was going to function, plus the absence of any provision for sanctions or punitive mechanism on violations of norms of democracy – it soon became clear to many that the hopes that the charter had raised were not quite realistic.[17]

To be sure, chartering ASEAN's many transitions to democracy faces huge challenges. Among these are the political transitions that are yet to take place in countries like Laos and Vietnam which have remained under a communist political system, and the seemingly unchanging feature of the military regime in Myanmar. But against these hurdles, one must not lose sight of the special significance of the ASC and the ASEAN Charter. What should not be missed in the plethora of criticisms about ASEAN is that with the emphasis on political development within the ASC and provision for a regional human rights in the ASEAN Charter, human rights, democracy and human security have reached a critical threshold where elites and civil society groups are pressing for these issues to be addressed and no longer swept under the carpet. Thus, regardless of its perceived shortcomings and the criticisms that the ASEAN Charter has received from a range of political actors in the region coming from the track-two policy communities and civil society organisations, democratisation and human rights are now part of the official regional discourse – issues that were tacitly considered taboo in a pre-political transition ASEAN.[18] Thus, despite what appeared to be a lost opportunity in pushing for a more credible charter, one still could argue that the momentum in pressing ahead with change is already gaining ground in the region.

Whether by force of circumstances or as a part of a globalised international environment, the black box of the states in ASEAN has been pried open despite efforts by certain political leaders to keep it closed. The Indonesian proposal for an ASC was not accidental. It came at a time when the region was and still is in the throes of rapid significant changes. The ASC and other initiatives were also compelled by the urgent need to address emerging transnational security challenges. Hence, if one works on the premise that structures and practices are dynamic, and that actors change the rules and norms which are constitutive of their interaction, then the study of political transitions, democracy and security regionalism in Southeast Asia must take into account the emerging processes that are leading to some – albeit incremental – changes.

Notes

1 For more discussion on the changing dynamics of the 'ASEAN Way', see Mely Caballero-Anthony, *Regional Security in Southeast Asia: Beyond the ASEAN Way*, 2nd edition, Singapore: Institute of Southeast Asian Studies, 2008.

2   'Indonesia Proposing ASEAN Security Community Concept', *Jakarta Post*, 16 June 2003, and 'ASEAN Plans Security Forum', *The Nation*, 17 June 2003.
3   See *ASEAN Vientiane Action Programme*, 2004. Online. Available HTTP: http://www.aseansec.org./VAP-10thASEANSummit.pdf. Accessed on 1 October 2006.
4   *ASEAN Vientiane Action Programme*, section 1.2.
5   Edward D. Mansfield and Jack Snyder, 'Democratisation and the Danger of War', *International Security*, vol. 20, no.1, Summer 1995, 5.
6   See *The ASEAN Vision 2020*. Online. Available HTTP: http://www.aseansec.org.
7   'Thailand Protests Against Cambodian Intrusion', *AseanAffairs.Com*, 5 October 2008. Online. Available HTTP: http://www.aseanaffairs.com/thailand_cambodia_border_dispute_thailand_protests_against_cambodian_intrusion (accessed on 3 February 2009).
8   See for example, Peter Hourdequin, 'Malaysia's 2005–6 Refugee Stand-off with Thailand: A Security Culture Analysis', *International Relations of the Asia-Pacific*, vol. 8, 2008, pp. 175–90.
9   Yang Razali Kassim, 'ASEAN Cohesion: Making Sense of Indonesian Reactions to Bilateral Disputes', *IDSS Commentaries* 15/2005, 6 April 2005.
10 See for example, Joo Nam Mak, 'Sovereignty in ASEAN and the Problem of Maritime Cooperation in the South China Sea', *IDSS Working Paper Series*, No. 156, S. Rajaratnam School of International Studies, Nanyang Technological University, 23 April 2008, and Mokhzani Zubir, *Exchange of 'cyber-fire' during the Malaysia-Indonesia Ambalat Dispute: A Lesson for the Future*, Kuala Lumpur: Centre for Maritime Security and Diplomacy, Maritime Institute of Malaysia, March 2005.
11 The ASC initiative was announced in November 2003, just a few months before Indonesia was to hold its first direct presidential election in April 2006 where the incumbent President Megawati Sukanoputri had to face a number of presidential contenders including former military generals, Susilo Bambang Yudhoyono (SBY) and Wiranto. SBY eventually won after two rounds of presidential elections that lasted six months.
12 Despite concerns that the political turbulence in Thailand that had already seen months of sustained street demonstrations and again the installation of a new government headed by Democrat Party leader, Abhisit Vejjajiva, the ASEAN Charter was nonetheless ratified on schedule. Thailand successfully hosted the first part of the 15th ASEAN Summit in February 2009.
13 See the ASEAN Security Community Plan of Action, Viantiane, 29 November 2004.
14 The EPG is composed of 10 representatives, one from each of the ASEAN member countries and chaired by Musa Hitam, the former Deputy Prime of Malaysia and Chairman of Malaysia's Human Rights Commission, Suaram. Apart from its official mandate, the EPG was also encouraged by the ASEAN leaders to conduct a series of consultations with civil society groups and business networks in keeping with the new thrust of the grouping to become a more inclusive organisation. The initiative for a bottom-up consultative process was announced by Malaysia's Prime Minister Abdullah Badawi, speaking in his capacity as the 2005 ASEAN Chair. According to him, ASEAN had to be 'transformed' to become a more people-centred community.
15 Kuala Lumpur Declaration of the Establishment of the ASEAN Charter, Kuala Lumpur, 12 December 2005.
16 See Mely Caballero-Anthony, 'Non-Traditional Security, Democracy, and Regionalism in Southeast Asia' in Donald K. Emmerson (ed.), *Hard Choices: Security, Regionalism and Democracy in Southeast Asia*, Stanford: The Walter H. Shorensten Asia-Pacific Center, 2008, pp. 191–218.
17 Mely Caballero-Anthony, 'The ASEAN Charter: An Opportunity Missed or One that *Cannot* be Missed?' *Southeast Asian Affairs 2008*, Singapore: Institute of Southeast Asian Studies, pp. 71–85.
18 After the adoption of the charter in the 2007 ASEAN Summit in Singapore, a number of civil society groups who had earlier taken part in the consultative process of drafting the

charter openly criticised the 'watered-down version' of the charter since it failed to incorporate issues of sanctions on ASEAN member states who were seen to be in violation of the ASEAN principles, including democracy. Similarly, a prominent Indonesian figure in ASEAN-ISIS (a Track-2 organisation in the region) urged his country's parliament not to ratify the charter and called on ASEAN to 'go back to the drawing board' and come up with a document more in tune with actual Southeast Asian conditions and outlooks.

Bibliography

Abas, M. Salleh, *May Day for Justice: The Lord President's Version*, Kuala Lumpur: Magnus Books, 1989.

Ahmad, Zakaria, 'Malaysia: Quasi-Democracy in a Divided Society', in Larry Diamond, Juan J. Linz and Seymour Martin Lipset (eds), *Democracy in Developing Countries, Vol. 3*. Boulder, Co: Lynne Rienner, 1989.

Albritton, Robert B., 'Cambodia in 2003: On the Road to Democratic Consolidation', *Asian Survey*, vol. 44, no. 1, January/February 2004, pp. 102–9.

Amer, Ramses, 'The Ethnic Vietnamese in Cambodia: A Minority at Risk?' in Sorpong Peou (ed.), *Cambodia: Change and Continuity in Contemporary Politics*, Aldershot; Burlington USA, Singapore and Sydney: Ashgate, 2001.

Anderson, Perry, 'The Antinomies of Antonio Gramsci', *New Left Review*, no. 100, 1976, pp. 5–80.

Annuar, Mustafa K., 'Defining Democratic Discourses: The Mainstream Press', in Francis Loh Kok Wah and Khoo Boo Teik (eds), *Democracy in Malaysia: Discourses and Practices*, Richmond, Surrey: Curzon Press, 2002.

Arendt, Hannah, *On Violence*, Orlando Florida: Harcourt Brace Jovanovich, 1970.

Arugay, Aries A., 'The Accountability Deficit in the Philippines: Implications and Prospects for Democratic Consolidation', *Philippine Political Science Journal*, vol. 26, no. 9, 2005.

ASEAN Statistical Yearbook 2001, Jakarta: ASEAN Secretariat, 2001.

Aspinall, Edward, *Opposing Suharto: Compromise, Resistance, and Regime Change in Indonesia*, Stanford: Stanford University Press, 2005.

—— 'Politics: Indonesia's Year of Elections and the End of the Political Transition', in Budy P. Resosudarmo (ed.) *The Politics and Economics of Indonesia's Natural Resources*, Singapore: Institute of Southeast Asian Studies, 2005.

Barraclough, S., 'The Dynamics of Coercion in the Malaysian Political Process', *Modern Asian Studies*, vol. 19, no. 4, 1985, pp. 797–822.

Barron, Patrick, Melina Nathan and Bridget Welsh, 'Consolidating Indonesia's Democracy: Conflicts, Institutions, and the "Local" in the 2004 Legislative Elections', *Conflict Prevention and Reconstruction Working Paper* No. 31, December 2005, Washington DC: World Bank.

Becker, David G., 'Latin America: Beyond "Democratic Consolidation"', *Journal of Democracy*, vol. 10, no. 2, 1999, pp. 138–51.

Berger, Mark T., 'Old State and New Empire in Indonesia: Debating the Rise and Decline of Suharto's New Order', *Third World Quarterly*, vol. 18, no. 2, June 1997, pp. 321–62.

Bertrand, Jacques, *Nationalism and Ethnic Conflict in Indonesia*, Cambridge: Cambridge University Press, 2004.

Brzezinski, Zbigniew, 'The Primacy of History and Culture', *Journal of Democracy*, vol. 12, no. 4, October 2001, pp. 20–6.

Bunbongkarn, Suchit, 'Democracy Under Siege', in James W. Morley (ed.), *Driven by Growth: Political Change in the Asia-Pacific Region*, New York: M.E. Sharpe, 1999, pp. 161–75.

Bunce, Valerie, 'Rethinking Recent Democratization: Lessons from the Postcommunist Experience', *World Politics*, vol. 55, no. 2, January 2003, pp. 167–92.

—— 'Comparative Democratization: Big and Bounded Conclusions', *Comparative Political Studies*, vol. 33, nos. 6–7, August–September 2000, pp. 703–34.

Caballero-Anthony, Mely, 'Non-Traditional Security, Democracy, and Regionalism in Southeast Asia' in Donald K. Emmerson (ed.), *Hard Choices: Security, Regionalism and Democracy in Southeast Asia*, Stanford: The Walter H. Shorensten Asia-Pacific Center, 2008, pp. 191–218.

—— *Regional Security in Southeast Asia: Beyond the ASEAN Way*, 2nd edition, Singapore: Institute of Southeast Asian Studies, 2008.

—— 'The ASEAN Charter: An Opportunity Missed or One that *Cannot* be Missed?' *Southeast Asian Affairs 2008*, Singapore: Institute of Southeast Asian Studies, pp. 71–85.

Calavan, Machiel, Sergio Diaz Briquets and Jerald O'Brien, 'Cambodian Corruption Assessment', Washington: Report prepared for USAID/ Cambodia, 2004.

Carney, Timothy, 'Organization of Power', in Karl Jackson (ed.) *Cambodia, 1975–78: Rendezvous with Death*, Princeton, NJ: Princeton University Press, 1989.

Carothers, Thomas, 'The Rule of Law Revival', *Foreign Affairs*, vol. 77, no. 2, March–April 1998.

—— 'The End of the Transition Paradigm', *Journal of Democracy*, vol. 13, no. 1, January 2002, pp. 5–21.

Case, William, *Semi-democracy in Malaysia: Pressures and Prospects for Change*, Canberra, ACT, Australia: Political and Social Change, Research School of Pacific Studies, Australian National University, 1992.

—— *Elites and Regimes in Malaysia: Revisiting a Consociational Democracy*, Clayton, VIC: Monash Asia Institute, 1996.

—— *Politics in Southeast Asia: Democracy or Less*, Richmond, Surrey: Curzon Press, 2002.

—— 'How's My Driving?' *The Pacific Review*, vol. 18, no. 2, 2005, pp. 137–57.

—— 'Thailand: An Unconsolidated Democracy', in *Politics in Southeast Asia: Democracy or Less*, Richmond, Surrey: Curzon Press, 2002.

Chaibong, Hahm, 'The Ironies of Confucianism', *Journal of Democracy*, vol. 15, no. 3, July 2004, pp. 93–107.

Chee, Stephen, 'Malaysia 1988: A Fractured Polity', *Southeast Asian Affairs 1989*, Singapore: Institute of Southeast Asian Studies, 1989, pp. 211–35.

Chua Beng-Huat, *Communitarian Ideology and Democracy in Singapore*, London; New York: Routledge, 1995.

Clark, Cal, 'Modernization, Democracy and the Developmental State in Asia: A Virtuous Cycle or Unraveling Strands', in James F. Hollifield and Calvin Jillson (eds), *Pathways to Democracy*, New York: Routledge, pp. 160–77.

Co, Edna E. A., Jorge V. Tigno, Maria Elissa Jayme Lao and Margarita A. Sayo, *Philippine Democracy Assessment: Free and Fair Elections and the Democratic Role of Political Parties*, Diliman, Quezon City: Friedrich Ebert-Stiftung and the National College of Public Administration and Governance, 2005, pp. 75–110.

Coronel, Sheila S., Yvonne T. Chua, Luz Rimban and Rooma B. Cruz, *The Rulemakers: How the Wealthy and Well-born Dominate Congress*, Quezon City, Metro Manila: Philippine Center for Investigative Journalism, 2004.

Crouch, Harold, *Government and Society in Malaysia*, St. Leonards: Allen & Unwin, 1996.

Crouch, Harold and James Morley, 'The Dynamics of Political Change', in James W. Morley (ed.), *Driven by Growth: Political Change in Asia-Pacific Region*, New York: M.E. Sharpe, 1999.

De Dios, Emmanuel S. and Paul D. Hutchcroft, 'Political Economy', in Arsenio M. Balisacan and Hal Hill (eds), *The Philippine Economy: Development, Politics, and Challenges*, Diliman, Quezon City: University of the Philippines Press, 2003.

Diamond, Larry, 'The Globalisation of Democracy: Trends, Types, Causes, and Prospects', in Robert O. Slater, Barry M. Schutz and Steven R. Dorr (eds), *Global Transformation and the Third World*, Boulder: Lynne Reinner, 1992.

—— 'Thinking about Hybrid Regimes', *Journal of Democracy*, vol. 13, no. 2, April 2002, pp. 21–35.

Diamond, Larry, Juan J. Linz and Seymour Martin Lipset (eds), *Democracy in Developing Countries, Vol. 3*. Boulder, Co: Lynne Rienner, 1989.

Doronilla, Amando, *The Fall of Joseph Estrada: The Inside Story*, Pasig and Makati: Anvil Publishing, Inc. and Philippine Daily Inquirer, Inc., 2001.

Doyle, Michael, *UN Peacekeeping in Cambodia: UNTAC's Civil Mandate*, Boulder and London: Lynne Rienner Publishers, 1995.

Economic Institute of Cambodia, *Cambodia Economic Watch*, Phnom Penh: Economic Institute of Cambodia, April 2005.

—— *Cambodia Economic Watch*, Phnom Penh: Economic Institute of Cambodia, October 2005.

Englehart, Neil A., 'Democracy and the Thai Middle Class: Globalisation, Modernisation and Constitutional Change', *Asian Survey*, vol. 43, no. 2, March–April, 2003, pp. 253–79.

EU Election Observation Mission, *Members of the National Assembly Elections*, 27 July 2003.

Evans, Kevin, 'Hasil Pemilihan Umum 2004' [The Results of 2004 Elections], *The Indonesian Quarterly*, vol. 33, no. 2, June 2004.

Foucault, Michel, *Power/Knowledge: Selected Interviews and Other Writings 1972–1977*, Colin Gordon (ed.), New York: Pantheon Books, 1980.

Freedman, Amy L., *Political Change and Consolidation: Democracy's Rocky Road in Thailand, Indonesia, South Korea and Malaysia*, New York: Palgrave Macmillan, 2006.

Frye, Timothy, 'The Perils of Polarization: Economic Performance in the Postcommunist World', *World Politics*, vol. 54, no. 3, April 2002, pp. 308–37.

Fukuyama, Francis, *The End of History and the Last Man*, New York: The Free Press, 1992.

Funston, John, 'Malaysia's Tenth Elections: Status Quo, Reformasi or Islamisation?' *Contemporary Southeast Asia*, vol. 22, no. 1, 2000.

Galaydh, Warsame, 'Thailand and the Region of Southeast Asia: Transitioning to Liberal Democracies', unpublished thesis, Carleton College, USA, 2008.

George, Cherian, 'Calibrated Coercion and the Maintenance of Hegemony in Singapore', *Asia Research Institute Working Papers Series* 48, 2005.

Gill, Graeme, *The Dynamics of Democratization: Elites, Civil Society and Transition Process*, London: Macmillan Press, 2000.

Girling, John, 'Thailand in Gramscian Perspective', *Pacific Affairs*, vol. 57, no. 3, Autumn 1984, pp. 385–403.

Gomez, Edmund and K. S. Jomo, *Malaysia's Political Economy: Politics, Patronage and Profits*, Cambridge: Cambridge University Press, 1997.

—— 'Malaysia' in Ian Marsh, Jean Blondel and Takashi Inoguchi (eds), *Democracy, Governance and Economic Performance: East and Southeast Asia*, Tokyo, New York, Paris: United Nations University Press, 2001, pp. 230–60.

Harding, Andrew James, *Law, Government and the Constitution in Malaysia*, Kuala Lumpur: Malaysian Law Journal; and The Hague: Kluwer Law International, 1996.

Haynes, Jeff (ed.), *Democracy and Political Change in the 'Third World'*, London; New York: Routledge, 2001, pp. 1–20.

Heder, Steve, 'Cambodia's democratic transition to neoauthoritarianism', *Current History* 94, 1995, pp. 425–9.

Heder, Steve and Judy Ledgerwood (eds), *Propaganda, Politics, and Violence in Cambodia: Democratic Transition under United Nations Peace-keeping*, Armonk, New York, and London, England: M. E. Sharpe, 1996.

Higley, John and Richard Gunther (eds), Elites and Democratic Consolidation in Latin America and Southern Europe, Baltimore: The Johns Hopkins University Press, 1992.

Hilley, John, *Malaysia: Mahathirism, Hegemony and the New Opposition*, London and New York: Zed Books, 2001.

Hollifield, James and Calvin Jillson (eds), *Pathways to Democracy: The Political Economy of Democratic Transitions*, New York: Routledge, 2000.

Hourdequin, Peter, 'Malaysia's 2005–6 Refugee Stand-off with Thailand: A Security Culture Analysis', *International Relations of the Asia-Pacific*, vol. 8, 2008, pp. 175–90.

Hughes, Caroline, 'Cambodia: Democracy or Dictatorship?' *Southeast Asian Affairs 2001*, Singapore: Institute of Southeast Asian Studies, 2001, pp. 113–28.

—— *The Political Economy of Cambodia's Transition, 1991–2001*, London: RoutledgeCurzon, 2003.

Huntington, Samuel P., *Political Order in Changing Societies*, New Haven, Conn.: Yale University Press, 1968.

—— 'Social and Institutional Dynamics of One-Party System', in S. P. Huntington and Clement H. Moore (eds), *Authoritarian Politics in Modern Society: The Dynamics of Established One-Party Systems*, New York: Basic Books, 1970.

—— *The Third Wave: Democratization in the Late Twentieth Century*, Norman: University of Oklahoma Press, 1991.

—— 'Democracy for the Long Haul', *Journal of Democracy*, vol. 7, no. 2, 1996, pp. 3–13.

—— *The Clash of Civilizations and the Remaking of World Order*, New York: Simon & Schuster, 1996.

Huxley, Tim, *Disintegrating Indonesia: Implications for Regional Security*, Adelphi Paper No. 349, London: IISS, 2002.

Hwang In-Won, *Personalised Politics: The Malaysian State Under Mahathir*, Thailand: Silkworm Books; Singapore: Institute of Southeast Asian Studies, 2003.

International IDEA, *Democratization in Indonesia: An Assessment*, Stockholm: IDEA, 2000.

International Republican Institute, *Cambodia 2003: National Assembly Elections*, Washington DC: International Republican Institute, 26 September 2003.

Jackson, Karl, 'The Ideology of Total Revolution', in Karl Jackson (ed.) *Cambodia, 1975–1978: Rendezvous with Death*, Princeton, NJ: Princeton University Press, 1989.

Jeldres, Julio, 'Cambodia's Fading Hopes', in Sorpong Peou (ed.) *Cambodia: Change and Continuity in Contemporary Politics*, Aldershot; Burlington USA; Singapore and Sydney: Ashgate, 2001.

Jesudason, James V., 'Statist Democracy and the Limits to Civil Society in Malaysia', *The Journal of Commonwealth & Comparative Politics*, vol. 33, no. 3, 1995, pp. 335–57.

Kachatan, Sirivalaya, *Democracy and the Military Coup in Thailand*, paper presented at the Annual Meeting of the Southern Political Science Association, Hotel Intercontinental, New Orleans, LA, 9 January 2008.

Kassim, Yang Razali, 'Enter the Badawi Era: Implications of Malaysia's General Election 2004', *IDSS Commentaries*, Institute of Defence and Strategic Studies, Singapore, 5 April 2004.

—— 'ASEAN Cohesion: Making Sense of Indonesian Reactions to Bilateral Disputes', *IDSS Commentaries* 15/2005, Institute of Defence and Strategic Studies, Singapore, 6 April 2005.

Kausikan, Bilahari, 'Asia's Different Standard', *Foreign Policy* 42, Fall 1993, pp. 24–51.

—— 'Governance That Works', *Journal of Democracy*, vol. 8, no. 2, April 1997, pp. 24–34.

Kawamura, Koichi, 'Political reform in the Post-Suharto Era', in Yuri Sato (ed.), *Indonesia Entering a New Era: Abdurrahman Wahid Government and its Challenge*, Tokyo: IDE-JETRO, March 2000.

Khoo Boo Teik, *Paradoxes of Mahathirism: An Intellectual Biography of Mahathir Mohamad*, Kuala Lumpur: Oxford University Press, 1995.

—— 'Economic Nationalism and its Discontents', in Richard Robison, Mark Beeson, Kanishka Jayasuriya, and Hyuk-Rae Kim (eds), *Politics and Markets in the Wake of the Asian Crisis*, London: Routledge, 2000, pp. 212–37.

—— *Beyond Mahathir: Malaysian Politics and its Discontents*, London and New York: Zed Books, 2003.

Khoo, Kay Jin, 'The Grand Vision: Mahathir and Modernisation', in Joel S. Kahn and Francis Loh Kok Wah (eds), *Fragmented Vision: Culture and Politics in Contemporary Malaysia*, North Sydney, Australia: Allen & Unwin Pty Ltd., 1992.

Kim, Dae Jung, 'Is Culture Destiny? The Myth of Asia's Anti-Democratic Value', *Foreign Affairs* 73, November–December 1994, pp. 189–94.

Kim, Dong-Yeob, 'The Politics of Market Liberalization: A Comparative Study of the South Korean and Philippine Telecommunications Service Industries', *Contemporary Southeast Asia*, vol. 24, no. 2, August 2002.

King, Charles, 'Post-Postcommunism: Transition, Comparison, and the End of "Eastern Europe"', *World Politics*, vol. 53, no. 1, October 2000, pp. 143–72.

Lande, Carl, 'The Return of "People Power" in the Philippines', *Journal of Democracy*, vol. 12, no. 2, April 2001, pp. 88–102.

Laquian, Aprodicio A. and Eleanor R. Laquian, *The ERAP Tragedy: Tales From the Snakepit*, Manila: Anvil Publishing, Inc., 2002.

Lee Hock Guan, 'Malay Dominance and Opposition Politics in Malaysia', *Southeast Asian Affairs 2002*, Singapore: Institute of Southeast Asian Studies, 2002, pp. 177–95.

Levitsky, Steven and Lucan A. Way, 'Autocracy by Democratic Rules: The Dynamics of Competitive Authoritarianism in the Post-Cold War Era', paper prepared for the 'Conference on Mapping the Great Zone: Clientalism and the Boundary between Democratic and Democratising', Columbia University, 4–5 April, 2003.

—— *Competitive Authoritarianism: The Origins and Dynamics of Hybrid Regimes in the Post-Cold War Era* (mimeo), 2006.

Liddle, William, 'Indonesia's Unexpected Failure of Leadership', in Adam Schwarz and Jonathan Paris (eds), *The Politics of Post-Suharto Indonesia*, New York: Council on Foreign Relations, 1999.

Linz, Juan. J. and Alfred Stepan, *Problems of Democratic Consolidation*, Baltimore: The Johns Hopkins University Press, 1996.

Loh, Francis, 'A Nation on Trial', *Aliran Monthly*, vol. 18, no. 9, 1998.

—— 'Post-NEP Politics in Malaysia: Ferment and Fragmentation', paper presented at the Second Australia-Malaysia Conference, Australian National University, Canberra, 24–26 May 2000.

McCargo, Duncan (ed.) *Reforming Thai Politics*, Amsterdam: Nordic Institute of Asian Studies, 2002.

—— 'Toxic Thaksin', *Foreign Affairs*, 27 September 2006. Available online at http://www.foreignaffairs.org/20060927facomment85575/duncan-mccargo/toxic-thaksin.html.

McCargo, Duncan and Ukrist Pathmanand, *The Thaksinisation of Thailand*, Copenhagen: Nordic Institute of Asian Studies, 2005.

McFaul, Michael, 'The Fourth Wave of Democracy and Dictatorship: Noncooperative Transitions in the Postcommunist World', *World Politics*, vol. 54, no. 2, January 2002, pp. 212–44.

Mahbubani, Kishore, 'The Pacific Way', *Foreign Affairs* 74, January–February 1995, pp. 100–111.

Mak, Joo Nam, 'Sovereignty in ASEAN and the Problem of Maritime Cooperation in the South China Sea', *IDSS Working Paper Series*, No. 156, S. Rajaratnam School of International Studies, Nanyang Technological University, 23 April 2008.

Mainwaring, Scott, 'Democratic Survivability in Latin America', in Howard Handelman and Mark A. Tessler (eds), *Democracy and its Limits: Lessons from Asia, Latin America, and the Middle East*, Notre Dame: University of Notre Dame Press, 2000.

Mainwaring, Scott and Timothy R. Scully, 'Introduction: Party Systems in Latin America', in Scott Mainwaring and Timothy R. Scully (eds), *Building Democratic Institutions: Party Systems in Latin America*, Stanford, CA: Stanford University Press, 1995.

Manent, Pierre, 'Modern Democracy as a System of Separations', *Journal of Democracy*, vol. 14, no. 1, January 2003, pp. 114–24.

Mansfield, Edward D. and Jack Snyder, 'Democratization and the Danger of War', *International Security*, vol. 20, no.1, Summer 1995.

Marks, Stephen P., 'The New Cambodian Constitution: From Civil War to a Fragile Democracy', in Sorpong Peou (ed.) *Cambodia: Change and Continuity in Contemporary Politics*, Aldershot; Burlington USA; Singapore and Sydney: Ashgate, 2001.

Marsh, David and Gerry Stoker (eds), *Theory and Methods in Political Science*, New York: Palgrave Macmillan, 2002.

Mietzner, Marcus, 'The Politics of Military Reform in Post-Suharto Indonesia: Elite Conflict, Nationalism, and Institutional Resistance', *Policy Studies* 23, Washington DC: East-West Center, 2006.

Melo Commission, *Report of The Independent Commission to Address Media and Activist Killings. Created under Administrative Order No. 157* (s. 2006), Melo Commission, 2007.

Montes, Manuel F., 'The Philippines as an Unwitting Participant in the Asian Economic Crisis', in Karl D. Jackson (ed.), *Asian Contagion: The Causes and Consequences of a Financial Crisis*, Boulder, Colorado: Westview Press, 1999.

Morley, James W. (ed.), *Driven by Growth: Political Change in Asia-Pacific Region*, New York: M. E. Sharpe, 1999.

Morlino, Leonardo, '"Good" and "Bad" Democracies: How to Conduct Research into the Quality of Democracy', *Journal of Communist Studies and Transition Politics*, vol. 20, no. 1, March 2004, pp. 5–27.

Muzaffar, Chandra, *Freedom in Fetters: An Analysis of the State of Democracy in Malaysia*, Penang: Aliran Kesedaran Negara, 1986.

Nain, Zaharom, 'The Structure of the Media Industry: Implications for Democracy', in Francis Loh Kok Wah and Khoo Boo Teik (eds), *Democracy in Malaysia: Discourses and Practices*, Richmond, Surrey: Curzon Press, 2002.

National Democratic Institute, *The 2002 Cambodian Commune Elections*, Washington DC: National Democratic Institute for International Affairs, 2002.

Neher, Clark and Ross Marlay, *Democracy and Development in Southeast Asia: The Winds of Change*, Boulder, Colorado: Westview Press, 1992.

Nelson, Michael H., 'Thaksin Overthrown, Thailand's Well Intentioned Coup of September 19, 2006', in *Eastasia.at*, vol. 6, no.1, June 2007, p. 9. Available online at http://www.eastasia.at/vol6_1/article01.pdf.

Nesadurai, Helen E. S., 'In Defence of National Economic Autonomy? Malaysia's Response to the Financial Crisis', *The Pacific Review*, vol. 13, no. 1, 2001, pp. 73–113.

Nissen, Christine J., *Corruption and Cambodian Households*, Phnom Penh: Center for Social Development, March 2005.

—— *Living Under the Rule of Corruption*, Phnom Penh: Center for Social Development, March 2005.

O'Donnell, Guillermo and Philippe C. Schmitter, *Transitions from Authoritarian Rule: Tentative Conclusions about Uncertain Democracies*, Baltimore: The Johns Hopkins University Press, 1986.

Osborne, Milton, 'Cambodia: Hun Sen Consolidates Power', *Southeast Asian Affairs 2000*, Singapore: Institute of Southeast Asian Studies, 2000, pp. 101–11.

Peang-Meth, Abdulgaffar, 'Understanding Cambodia's Political Development', in Sorpong Peou (ed.) *Cambodia: Change and Continuity in Contemporary Politics*, Aldershot, Burlington USA, Singapore and Sydney: Ashgate, 2001.

Peou, Sorpong, *Conflict Neutralization in the Cambodia War: From Battlefield to Ballot-Box*, Kuala Lumpur, New York and Singapore: Oxford University Press, 1997.

—— *Intervention and Change in Cambodia: Towards Democracy?* New York, NY: St. Martin's Press, 2000.

—— (ed.) *Cambodia: Change and Continuity in Contemporary Politics*, Aldershot; Burlington USA, Singapore and Sydney: Ashgate, 2001.

—— *International Democracy Assistance for Peacebuilding: Cambodia and Beyond*, Hampshire and New York: Palgrave Macmillan, 2007.

Pongsudhirak, Thitinan, 'What happened to Thai Democracy?' Paper presented at the Workshop on Political Transitions and Democratic Consolidation in Southeast Asia, Jakarta, Indonesia, 30–31 July, 2007.

Proceedings: Policy Dialogue Series 2004: Academe Meets the Party-List Representatives, *Kasarinalan: Philippine Journal of Third World Studies*, vol. 19, no. 2, 2004, pp. 119–48.

Przeworski, Adam, *Democracy and the Market: Political and Economic Reforms in Eastern Europe and Latin America*, Cambridge: Cambridge University Press, 1991.

Quinn, Kenneth, 'The Pattern and Scope of Violence', in Karl Jackson (ed.) *Cambodia, 1975–1978: Rendezvous with Death*, Princeton, NJ: Princeton University Press, 1989.

Rachagan, S. S., *Law and the Electoral Process in Malaysia*, Kuala Lumpur: University of Malaya Press, 1993.

Rakhmat, Jalaludin, 'Islam di Indonesia: Masalah Definisi' [Islam in Indonesia: The Problem of Definition], in M. Amien Rais (ed.) *Islam di Indonesia: Suatu Ikhtiar Mengaca Diri* [Islam in Indonesia: An Attempt at Self Reflection], Jakarta: Rajawali, 1986.

Ratner, Steven R., 'The Cambodia Settlement Agreements', in Sorpong Peou (ed.) *Cambodia: Change and Continuity in Contemporary Politics*, Aldershot; Burlington USA; Singapore and Sydney: Ashgate, 2001.

Rice, Susan and Stewart Patrick, *Index of State Weakness in the Developing World*, Washington DC: Brookings Institution, 2008.

Ringuet, Daniel Joseph and Elsa Estrada, 'Understanding the Philippines' Economy and Politics since the Return of Democracy in 1986', *Contemporary Southeast Asia*, vol. 25, no. 2, August 2003.

Rivera, Temario C., *Landlords and Capitalists: Class, Family, and State in Philippine Manufacturing*, Diliman, Quezon City: University of the Philippines Press, 1994.

Roberts, David, *Political Transition in Cambodia 1991–99: Power, Elitism and Democracy*, Richmond, Surrey: Curzon Press, 2001.

Robison, Richard and Vedi R. Hadiz, *Reorganising Power in Indonesia: The Politics of Oligarchy in an Age of Markets*, London: RoutledgeCurzon, 2004.

Rustow, Dankwart, 'Transitions to Democracy: Toward a Dynamic Model', *Comparative Politics* 2, April 1970, pp. 337–63.

Samudavanija, Chai-Anan, 'The Military, Bureaucracy and Globalisation', in Kevin Hewison (ed.) *Political Change in Thailand: Democracy and Participation*, London and New York: Routledge, 1997.

Sartori, Giovanni, *Parties and Party Systems: A Framework for Analysis*, New York: Cambridge University Press, 1976.

Schedler, Andreas, 'What is Democratic Consolidation?' *Journal of Democracy*, vol. 9, no. 2, 1998, pp. 91–107.

—— 'Measuring Democratic Consolidation', *Studies in Comparative International Development*, vol. 36, no. 1, Spring 2001, pp. 66–92.

—— 'Elections Without Democracy: The Menu of Manipulation', *Journal of Democracy*, vol. 13, no. 2, April 2002, pp. 36–50.

Shamsul, A. B., 'The "Battle Royal": The UMNO Elections of 1987', *Southeast Asian Affairs 1988*, Singapore: Institute of Southeast Asian Studies, 1988, pp. 170–88.

Sida Advisory Team on Democratic Governance, *Civil Society and Democracy in Cambodia*, Stockholm and Phnom Penh: Sida Advisory Team on Democratic, March 2003.

Slater, Dan C., 'Iron Cage in an Iron Fist: Authoritarian Institutions and the Personalization of Power in Malaysia', *Comparative Politics*, vol. 36, no. 1, October 2003, pp. 81–101.

Sebastian, Leonard C., 'The Paradox of Indonesian Democracy', *Contemporary Southeast Asia*, vol. 26, no. 2, August 2004, p. 261.

Sen, Amartya, 'Democracy as a Universal Value', *Journal of Democracy*, vol. 10, no. 3, July 1999, pp. 3–17.

Shin, Doh Chull, 'On the Third Wave of Democratisation: A Synthesis and Evaluation of Recent Theory and Research', *World Politics* 47, October 1994.

Smith, Benyamin, '"If I Do These Things, They Will Throw Me Out": Economic Reform and the Collapse of Indonesia's New Order', *Journal of International Affairs*, vol. 57, no. 1, Fall 2003.

Smith, Hugh (ed.) *International Peacekeeping: Building on the Cambodian Experience*, Canberra, Australia: Australian Defence Studies Centre and Australian Defence Force Academy, 1994.

Special Representative of the Secretary-General for Human Rights in Cambodia, *The 2003 National Assembly Elections*, New York: United Nations Cambodia Office of the High Commissioner for Human Rights, December 2003.

Sukma, Rizal, 'The Security Problematique of Globalisation and Development: The Case of Indonesia', in David Dewitt and Carolina Hernandez (eds), *Development and Security*, London: Ashgate, 2003.

—— 'Security Operations in Aceh: Goals, Consequences, and Lessons', *Policy Studies* 3, Washington DC: East-West Center, 2004.

—— 'Ethnic Conflict in Indonesia: Causes and the Quest for Solution', in Kusuma Snitwongse and W. Scott Thompson (eds), *Ethnic Conflict in Southeast Asia*, Singapore: Institute of Southeast Asian Studies, 2005.

Tadjoeddin, M. Zulfan and Mansoob Murshed, 'Socioeconomic Determinants of Everyday Violence in Indonesia: An Empirical Investigation of Javanese Districts, 1994–2003', online paper for the International Peace Research Institute, Oslo, 2006. Available online at http://www.prio.no/files/manual-import/neps/tindbergen2006papers/Murshed_amsterdam_2006.pdf.

Tarr, Chou Meng, 'The Vietnamese Minority in Cambodia', in Sorpong Peou (ed.) *Cambodia: Change and Continuity in Contemporary Politics*, Aldershot; Burlington, USA; Singapore and Sydney: Ashgate, 2001.

Thompson, Mark R., 'Whatever Happened to "Asian Values"?' *Journal of Democracy*, vol. 12, no. 4, October 2001, pp. 154–65.

Torres, Crisline, 'The Philippine Pro-Parliamentary Position and the Comparative Constitutional Design Literature', *Philippines Political Science Journal*, vol. 25, no. 48, 2004, pp. 59–63.

Transparency International, *Transparency International Corruption Index 2005*, Berlin, Germany: Transparency International Secretariat, 18 October 2005.

Trocki, Carl A., *Singapore: Wealth, Power, and the Culture of Control* (Asia's Transformations Series), New York: Routledge, 2005.

United Nations, *Report of the United Nations Fact-Finding Mission on Present Structures and Practices of Administration in Cambodia*, New York: United Nations, 24 April–9 May 1990.

UNDP, *Report on the Elections of the Commune Councils*, Phnom Penh: UNDP, March 2002.

Valenzuela, Samuel J, 'Democratic Consolidation in Post-Transitional Setting: Notion, Process, and Facilitating Conditions', in S. Mainwaring, G. O'Donnell and S. Valenzuela (eds), *Issues in Democratic Consolidation: The New South American Democracies in Comparative Perspective*, Notre Dame: University of Notre Dame Press, 1992, pp. 57–104.

Verzola, Roberto, 'The True Results of the 2004 Philippine Presidential Election Based on the NAMFREL Tally', *Kasarinlan: Philippine Journal of Third World Studies*, vol. 19, no. 2, 2004, pp. 92–118.

Vijghen, John L., *Cambodian Human Rights & Democracy Organizations*, Phnom Penh: Experts for Community Research, April 2001.

Wanandi, Jusuf, 'Indonesia: A Failed State?' *The Washington Quarterly*, vol. 25, no. 3, Summer 2002.

Weiss, Meredith, *Protest and Possibilities: Civil Society and Coalitions for Political Change in Malaysia*, Stanford, California: Stanford University Press, 2006.

Welsh, Bridget, 'Malaysia's Transition: Elite Contestation, Political Dilemmas and Incremental Change', *Asia Program Special Report* 116, New Jersey: Woodrow Wilson International Center for Scholars, 2003.

Wong Chin Huat, 'Divided We Stand: How Electoral Systems Make Ethnic Politics Viable', *Off the Edge*, vol. 46, October 2008, pp. 52–55.

World Bank, *Cambodia: Having Poverty by 2015? Poverty Assessment 2006*, Phnom Penh: World Bank, February 2006.

World Economic Forum, *Global Competitiveness Report 2005–2006*, Palgrave Macmillan, 2006.

World Economic Forum, *Global Competitiveness Report 2008–2009*, Palgrave Macmillan, 2008.

Zakaria, Fareed, 'Culture is Destiny: A Conversation with Lee Kuan Yew', *Foreign Affairs* 73, March–April 1994, pp. 109–26.

—— 'The Rise of Illiberal Democracy', *Foreign Affairs*, vol. 76, no. 6, November 1997.

Index

For Product Safety Concerns and Information please contact our EU
representative GPSR@taylorandfrancis.com
Taylor & Francis Verlag GmbH, Kaufingerstraße 24, 80331 München, Germany

www.ingramcontent.com/pod-product-compliance
Lightning Source LLC
Chambersburg PA
CBHW072240270326
41930CB00010B/2212

9 781138 995000